BUILDING SOCIETY LAW IN IRELAND

— A Guide —

A

Also by Henry Murdoch:

Invention and the Irish Patent System (1971) — published by the Administrative Research Bureau, Dublin University.

Working Women, An International Survey (1984) — Chapter on Ireland — published by John Wiley & Sons, London.

A Dictionary of Irish Law (1988) — published by Topaz Publications, Dublin.

BUILDING SOCIETY LAW IN IRELAND

— A Guide —

by

Henry Murdoch

BE, CEng, FIEI, MBA
Barrister

Topaz Publications, Dublin 1989

Published in 1989 by Topaz Publications, 64 Upper Georges Street, Dun Laoghaire, Co Dublin.

Computer typeset and printed in Ireland by Dublin University Press Limited, 17 Gilford Road, Sandymount, Dublin 4.

British Library Cataloguing in Publication Data.
Murdoch, Henry
Building society law in Ireland: a guide.
1. Ireland, (Republic). Building sociéties. Law
I. Title
344.1706'73

ISBN 0 9514032 2 2 (paperback)

Cover: Design Council, 22 Crofton Road,
Dun Laoghaire,
Co. Dublin

To my father and to my wife Davida
and my children Maeve and Breffni.

CONTENTS

PREFACE

There is currently no book which deals with the important area of building society law in Ireland; hence this modest attempt to state the law in a manner which is designed to be convenient, useful and practicable.

I am hopeful that the book will serve the information needs of the wide group of persons who are involved with or have an interest in building societies eg barristers and solicitors, accountants, auctioneers, auditors, bankers, insurance personnel, surveyors, students of business and of law, directors and staff of building societies themselves, the public regulatory authorities, and of course, the members of societies who, as shareholders and often borrowers, are the lifeblood of the societies.

While the law dealing with building societies is primarily contained in the reforming and consolidating Building Societies Act 1989 (No 17 of 1989, enacted on 12th July 1989), there are many areas of law not contained in that Act which impact on building societies and the services they offer or may offer in the future eg the law in relation to mortgages, housing, land, landlord and tenant, banking, insurance and negotiable instruments. Consequently, while dealing extensively with the 1989 Act, I have endeavoured to include brief references to those other areas of law which are specifically mentioned in the 1989 Act or which, I believe, will be of particular concern or interest to persons involved with building societies.

In this Guide, I have followed the general style and format in my previous book "A Dictionary of Irish Law". There is a set of instructions on how to use the Guide on page xi, followed by an Introduction to building society law. The Guide itself is in an alphabetical format and hence provides its own index. Also, there is extensive cross- referencing between entries in the Guide and the appendices, which hopefully will assist the reader to get quickly to the point of particular interest.

Also included is a typical building society mortgage instrument (in Appendix 5) with cross-referencing between it and the Guide.

The commencement date for all sections of the Building Societies Act 1989, except Part IX (which deals with savings protection), has been fixed by the Minister for the Environment as the 1st September 1989 (SI No 182 of 1989). However, some sections of the 1989 Act require regulations to be made to make a section effective, and also some sections may be amended by regulation. No regulation has been made at the time of writing; however, a Table has been set out in Appendix 2 to enable the user of the Guide to enter the regulations as they are made, and thereby keep the Guide right up to date.

In addition, the offences under the 1989 Act are collected together in Appendix 1, with cross-references to the main Guide.

I wish to thank the very many persons who were helpful to me in writing this book, particularly: Nuala Smith who converted the data from "writing" to "floppy discs"; Peter Allman and his staff at Dublin University Press who were ever helpful in translating the discs into a book; the staff of Trinity College Library and of the Registry of Building Societies (particularly Brendan Shanahan) who were most helpful in locating reports and research material for me; the staff of the Department of the Environment, and the Central Bank of Ireland for all their assistance; Eric Beck of the First National, who as Chairman of the Republic of Ireland Centre of the Chartered Building Societies Institute, supplied me with valuable information concerning that professional body; the individual building societies for their annual reports, historical information about their societies, and for providing me with their standard mortgage deeds, and particularly Michael Fingleton of the Irish Nationwide for providing the accounts of his society for 1873.

I am also grateful to the staff of the Bills Office in Leinster House, particularly Marie Kennedy, who could not have been more helpful. I appreciate all the help I have obtained from my friend Michael Burke of Topaz Publications and I wish also to acknowledge with thanks the permission given to me by the Controller of the Stationery Office to quote extracts from the Explanatory Memorandum to the Building Societies Bill 1988 and from the Reports of the Registrar of Building Societies.

Despite all the assistance given to me, responsibility for any errors or omissions in this book rests squarely with me; I would appreciate any being pointed out to me.

It is my earnest hope that this book will contribute to a greater knowledge and understanding of how building societies operate in Ireland and how they are controlled and regulated.

I have endeavoured to state the law as accurately as possible on the sources available to me on 22nd July 1989.

10 Haddington Lawn
Glenageary
Co. Dublin

22nd July 1989

HOW TO USE THE GUIDE

Consider this typical entry in conjunction with the notes below:

> **director.**[1] A member of the board of directors of a corporate body with powers and duties to manage the business of the body. In a building society, it includes any person occupying the position of director, by whatever name called: BS Act 1989 s.2(1).[2] A society must have at least 3 directors (ibid s.48(1)).[3] The board of directors must appoint a chairman (qv)[4], a chief executive (qv)[4] and a secretary (qv)[4] (ibid ss.48(3) and 49(1)). The board must take reasonable steps to ensure that the chief executive and secretary appointed are persons who have the knowledge and experience to discharge the functions of those offices (ibid s.49(3)). .... See Farrell v Irish Permanent Building Society (1989) HC.[5] .... See BODY CORPORATE; CO-OPTION; DIRECTOR'S BANK ACCOUNT; DISQUALIFICATION.[6]

1. The entries are in alphabetical order in bold print. There may be further entries based on the key word eg in this example there are further entries under: **director, election of; director, nomination of; director, removal of; director, retirement of** etc.

2. A reference is usually given to the statutory basis for an entry, with the section (s.) or sections (ss.) of the relevant Act identified. The Building Societies Act 1989 is identified as BS Act 1989. A list of Abbreviations is listed below. A Table of Statutes commences at page xiii.

3. Any further references to the last mentioned source are identified by "ibid"; eg in the example, s.48(1) refers to the BS Act 1989.

4. "(qv)" or "(qqv)" after a word or series of words indicates that there is a separate entry or entries in the Guide for that word or for the series of words. In the example, there are separate entries under "**chairman**", "**chief executive**" and "**secretary**".

5. Reference is made to the more significant or interesting case law, both Irish and UK, which could be usefully consulted. A Table of Cases commences at page xxvii and the list of law reports and abbreviations is in Appendix 3.

6. The final reference in capital letters directs the reader to another relevant or associated entry in the Guide eg in the example, there are separate entries under "**body corporate**", "**co-option**", "**director's bank account**", and "**disqualification**".

7. Throughout the Guide, the male includes the female unless the context suggests otherwise.

ABBREVIATIONS

app	= appendix
art	= article
BS	= Building Societies
DCR	= District Court Rules 1948 (as amended)
DPP	= Director of Public Prosecutions
ibid	= referring to the same source
LG(P&D)	= Local Government (Planning and Development)
LRC	= Law Reform Commission
No	= Number
O	= Order Number
p	= page
para	= paragraph
qv	= (see HOW TO USE THE GUIDE para 4)
r	= rule
rr	= rules
RCC	= Circuit Court Rules 1950 (as amended)
RSC	= Rules of the Superior Courts 1986
regs	= regulations
s	= section
sch	= schedule
SGSS	= Sale of Goods and Supply of Services
SI	= Statutory Instrument
SR & O	= Statutory Rules and Orders
ss	= sections
1937 Constitution	= The Constitution of Ireland enacted by the People on 1st July 1937 and which came into operation on 29th December 1937.

See Appendix 3, page 181, for abbreviations of Law Reports.

TABLE OF STATUTES

TABLE OF CASES

Pages

Pages

Pages

Pages

Pages

Pages

Pages

INTRODUCTION

Building societies in Ireland are tremendously important financial institutions with combined assets amounting to some IR£3,800 million. The vast majority of the loan assets of the 10 societies operating in the State are in the form of loans secured on residential property (approximately 165,000 mortgages) while about 97% of the funding of societies is currently in the form of shares held by the public. They are strong mutual institutions with some 900,000 members.

Historical perspective

Building societies began in the late 18th century, initially as "terminating societies". Typically ten or more persons would save together by regular contributions until they had enough money to buy land and start building. These members would draw lots to decide who would be housed first; the members however would continue to contribute until all were housed and then the society would terminate.

In the early 19th century, societies started to pay interest to members who had savings to invest but who did not need housing. These societies did not cease to exist when their members were housed, but continued to borrow money from savers to lend onwards to others in need of housing. The "permanent" building society was born.

Building societies were first given statutory recognition in 1836 by the Benefit Building Society Act which applied to Ireland. The Royal Commission on Friendly Societies reported in 1871 and there followed the Building Societies Act 1874, which although subsequently amended, continued as the basic legal framework for building societies in the Republic of Ireland for the next 102 years, until consolidated and updated in the Building Societies Act 1976. The 1874 Act had earlier been updated and consolidated in the UK by their Building Societies Act 1962. The 1976 Act was subsequently amended in 1980, 1983 and 1986, and then repealed in 1989.

Growth of building societies in Ireland

Of the 10 building societies operating in the State in 1989, four were established over a century ago, viz the Irish Permanent, First National, Irish Nationwide and the ICS. The First National (then the Workingman's Benefit Building Society) was the first to be established (in 1861); it was incorporated in 1875 under the 1874 Act. There followed the ICS (then named the Irish Civil Service Permanent Building Society) in 1864, which was incorporated in 1874.

The Irish Nationwide (then named the Irish Industrial Benefit Building Society) was the third to be established (in 1873); it was incorporated in 1878. Its assets in 1873 stood at £1044-3s-3d and it paid its secretary the princely salary of £6-17s-6d. The fourth society, the Irish Permanent (then the Irish Temperance Permanent Benefit Building Society) was incorporated in 1884.

By 1922 when the Irish Free State had been established, there were 23 building societies operating in the State, with combined assets of £0.6 million and some 5,000 shareholders. The 1930's then saw the establishment of the Educational (1935) and the Metropolitan (1939) societies. The total number of societies declined to 16 by 1950; the Midland & Western was incorporated in 1956. The number of societies rose again to 20 by 1970, when there were some 71,000 shareholders and combined assets of £87m.

The 1970's and 1980's saw the explosive growth of the assets of societies and the incorporation of the relative newcomers, viz Irish Mutual (then named the Allied Irish in 1970), Norwich Irish (1974) and Irish Life (1979). It also saw the winding up by order of the court of one society, the Irish Savings Building Society in 1984, and the cancellation of the registration of nine other societies. (See Appendix 4, Table 5).

While the overall number of societies declined in this period by a combination of these closures and other mergers to 11 by 1984, assets expanded to £2,570m and shareholders increased to almost 900,000.

By the end of 1988, the combined assets of building societies had further increased to £3,805m and the number of societies had declined to their present ten:

Assets £m @ Dec 31, 1988

Irish Permanent	1,374.9
First National	811.0
Educational	766.3
Irish Nationwide	306.7
ICS	301.4
Irish Life	86.4
Irish Mutual	73.9
Norwich Irish	53.0
Midland & Western	24.4
Metropolitan	6.8
TOTAL	£3,805.0

(figures are rounded to nearest single decimal)
Source: 1988 Annual Reports of individual Societies
(See Appendix 4 for statistics).

Nature of a building society
A building society is constituted by the agreement of several persons who take shares of a certain fixed value and on which interest is paid. Advances are made from time to time to members, on security of land or house property, the money advanced most traditionally being repayable by instalments, comprised of principal and interest and spread over a period

of years. Societies also borrow money by taking deposits from the public and on the wholesale money markets.

An investing member of a building society may withdraw his shares but he seldom transfers his shares. A company shareholder on the other hand may transfer his shares but he cannot withdraw them. The share capital of a building society is consequently fluid, whereas that of a limited company by comparison is fixed.

The balance sheets of building societies have consequently been quite simple historically. The main assets have been loans to members secured on mortgage (typically 76% of the total), liquid assets (about 21%), and fixed assets, such as land, buildings and equipment (usually about 2 to 3% of the total). The liability side of the balance sheet has consisted largely of shares and deposits from individual members. The excess of assets over liabilities is the general reserve, representing accumulated surpluses over the years and typically being about 5% of total assets. (See Appendix 4 for statistics).

Building societies traditionally borrow short and lend long; they consequently require to have a significant proportion of their assets in readily realisable form in order to meet the inevitable fluctuations in cash flow. This liquidity is typically about 19% of liabilities.

Because of the fluid nature of shares in a building society, the capital base of a society is really its reserves; unlike a company it cannot expand its capital base rapidly eg by say a rights issue of shares. Consequently, its ability to undertake new activities with possibly higher risks than its traditional business, has to be judged by different criteria than in say a company or a bank.

Need for reform in the law

In April 1986, the Government published a "Discussion Document on Legislative and Regulatory Arrangements in relation to Building Societies" which recognised the revolution which was taking place in the financial markets and proposed significant changes in the law relating to the powers of building societies and their prudential supervision and control. There followed the Building Societies Act 1986, and the regulations made under it, which introduced the first real reforming measures in over 100 years eg (a) by allowing certain societies to engage, to a limited extent, in unsecured lending for bridging finance and house improvement works; (b) by eliminating redemption fees, prohibiting new tiered interest loans, allowing access by members to property valuation reports, liberalising requirements in relation to insurance, reducing legal charges and providing for mortgage protection insurance; and (c) by making the director elections of societies more democratic. These reforms were very limited however.

Historically, as has been stated, building societies existed for one purpose ie to raise funds directly from the public and to lend funds on the security of a mortgage on land. Increasingly in recent times, other financial institutions, notably banks, have entered the traditional market of the societies, while societies have been inhibited by legislation from offering a wider range of services to match those of their competitors.

The proposed liberalisation of banking and capital movements across the frontiers of the European Community by 1992, will further increase the pressures on Irish building societies, from competitors who can offer a wider range of services and who have access to a wider range of funds than Irish societies have been permitted to have in the past. This was recognised in the UK where in 1986, their building societies had their powers considerably widened under the UK Building Societies Act 1986.

It was against this background that the Building Societies Act 1989 was enacted in Ireland in July 1989, replacing in one comprehensive and consolidating Act, all previous building society legislation.

Objectives of the 1989 Act

The objectives of the 1989 Act have been stated to be:

" (i) to strengthen the competitive position of building societies by extending their powers so that they can provide a much wider range of services;

(ii) to transfer statutory responsibility for the regulation and supervision of building societies from the Registrar of Building Societies to the Central Bank of Ireland and to strengthen the powers available to the Bank as supervisory authority;

(iii) to improve and update the statutory provisions relating to the running and management of societies, their accounts and audit;

(iv) to enable the provisions of the deposit protection scheme as contained in the Central Bank Act 1989, to be applied to building societies;

(v) to give building societies the option of investing directly in residential and other development;

(vi) to help keep down the transaction costs associated with house purchase;

(vii) to allow societies to operate abroad; and

(viii) to provide a statutory framework and mechanism whereby societies can, on certain conditions, convert from mutual to public limited company status."

(*Source:* Explanatory Memorandum to the Building Societies Bill 1988)

The 1989 Act retains the appropriate provisions of earlier legislation and applies to building societies, with appropriate modifications, legislative provisions regarding companies and banks, with the objective that there be a desireable degree of consistency in the law relating to all these corporate bodies.

Main provisions of the 1989 Act

A building society is redefined under the 1989 Act. It is no longer restricted, as it was formerly, to being a society established for the purpose of raising funds (by the subscription of the members, and the acceptance of deposits and loans) for making loans to members. It is now a society incorporated or deemed to be incorporated under the 1989 Act, with all the powers given by that Act, which are considerable. It continues to be a body corporate with perpetual succession and the power to hold land.

There are provisions in the Act dealing with the formation of a society. It must have a memorandum stating its objects and powers; and it must have as one of its objects the provision of mortgage funds for housing. It may have other objects consistent with its powers under the Act. It also must have rules for the regulation of the society.

Societies are empowered under the Act to engage in providing a whole range of new services (auctioneering, conveyancing, financial, and services relating to land) as well as to invest in residential and commercial property, provided the society "adopts" the power by means of a special resolution and obtains the approval of the Central Bank. Societies are similarly empowered to operate abroad.

The Central Bank is given wide powers to control and supervise societies eg it has power to control the involvement of societies in the provision of these new services and to impose whatever conditions and requirements it considers appropriate. It also has similar powers over societies as it has over banks eg it may (a) impose prudential ratios to be maintained by societies, (b) impose requirements relating to the structure and composition of liabilities and assets (including liquid assets), (c) impose conditions on or revoke a society's authorisation, or (d) give a direction to a society to suspend the raising of funds or the making of payments. The Bank may also cancel the registration of a society.

The mutual status of societies is maintained by a requirement that at least half of a society's funds must be in the form of shares issued to members. Any person holding shares of any description in a society is a member and his liability is limited to the amount of his shareholding. Weighted voting is allowed in respect of ordinary resolutions but each member has only one vote on special resolutions and conversion resolutions irrespective of the size of his shareholding. However, a society may de-mutualise by converting to a public limited company, where its shareholders and "borrowing members" vote to do so by a conversion resolution, and the Central Bank confirms the conversion scheme.

Every society must have a board of directors of at least three persons. There are detailed provisions in the Act dealing with the election, co-option, retirement and removal of directors, their remuneration and the disclosure of large volume business between a society and any company or firm of which a director is also a director or partner. There is a requirement for an independent supervisor to oversee all stages of the election of directors and to report to the Central Bank whether the election has been properly and fairly conducted. There is a prohibition on canvassing by employees of a society at their workplace or a meeting of the society on behalf of any particular candidate.

Societies are given the option under the Act of having resolutions and elections decided by postal ballot rather than by voting at a meeting. A member is entitled to appoint a proxy to attend, vote and speak for him at a meeting of the society; however, generally, only one proxy instrument may be issued to a member and there is a prohibition on canvassing by employees in relation to proxies.

There are provisions in the Act for the settlement of disputes between a society and a member; in addition the Minister for the Environment is empowered to require societies to set up, either individually or jointly, an "ombudsman" type procedure for dealing with complaints from the public in relation to services they provide.

There are detailed provisions in the Act dealing with the accounts, the audit of societies, and the auditor, including the power which the Central Bank has to veto the appointment of an auditor. Additionally, duties are placed on an auditor to report certain matters independently to the Central Bank.

Societies are permitted, subject to certain procedures and approvals, to amalgamate with other societies and also to take a transfer of engagements from another society.

In addition, provision is made to apply to building societies the savings protection scheme pursuant to the Central Bank Act 1989, with provision made for shareholders to benefit as well as depositors. Various provisions are also made relating to the winding up of a society under the Companies Acts as if it were a company limited by shares.

A wide range of offences and penalties are specified in the 1989 Act. (See Appendix 1).

The Act repeals all previous building society legislation. However, the provisions of the Building Society Regulations 1987 (introduced under the Building Societies Act 1986) relating to redemption fees (partly), property insurance, valuation reports, legal charges and mortgage protection insurance are continued in force as far as housing loans are concerned. Many sections of the 1989 Act may be amended by regulations eg for a limited period, to remove any difficulty in bringing a provision into operation; or without limitation in time, to bring building society legislation into line with future relevant changes in company and banking law. In addition, some sections require regulations to be made to make the section effective eg in relation to a society providing a conveyancing service. (See Appendix 2).

THE GUIDE

A

a coelo usque ad centrum. [From heaven to the centre of the earth]. In principle, the extent of the ownership of property.

abandonment. The relinquishment or surrender of an interest, claim or thing. An easement (qv) may be lost by abandonment; evidence of abandonment must be supported by evidence of conduct or intention adverse to the exercise of the right: Carroll v Sheridan (1984) ILRM 451; O'Gara v Murray (1989) ILT & SJ 82.

abbreviated name. See NAME OF SOCIETY.

abroad. Outside the State. A building society is empowered, subject to its *adoption* of the power and the approval of the Central Bank, to exercise its powers under the BS Act 1989 outside the State (ibid ss.33(1) and 36(1)(g)). The Bank may impose conditions regarding the countries, the forms of security in any particular country, and requirements relating to currencies and to loans (ibid s.36(12)). The right of the Bank or an *authorised* (qv) person to require information, documents or other material, extends to a society's subsidiaries (qv) or associated bodies (qv) outside the State (ibid s.41(4)). See ADOPTABLE POWERS; ASSETS OUTSIDE THE STATE; INSPECTION.

abstract of title. A chronological statement of the instruments and events under which a person is entitled to land showing the links to his title. A vendor of land is bound to deliver an abstract to the purchaser, at the vendor's expense. See REQUISITIONS ON TITLE.

ACBSI. [Associate of the Chartered Building Societies Institute]. See CHARTERED BUILDING SOCIETIES INSTITUTE.

acceptance of bill. Signing a bill of exchange by the *drawee* in such a way as to signify acceptance of liability to pay the sum of money stated in the bill: Bills of Exchange Act 1882 ss.17-19. Acceptance may be a *general* acceptance which is an acceptance without qualification or a *qualified* acceptance which can be *conditional*, *partial*, *local*, qualified as to *time* or qualified as to *parties*. Acceptance for honour *supra protest* is acceptance of a bill in order to safeguard the drawee's good name (ibid ss.65-68).

It has been held that where a bank acted negligently in failing to safeguard its own interests, in mistakingly not awaiting notification of *acceptance* before discounting certain bills of exchange, the correction of this error on a short notice to the plaintiff company did not constitute a breach of the duty of care which it owed to the company: Hazylake Fashions Ltd v The Governor and Company of the Bank of Ireland (1989) ITLR (19 June 1989). See BILL OF EXCHANGE.

acceptance of deposits. See DEPOSIT.

acceptance supra protest. [Acceptance for honour]. See ACCEPTANCE OF BILL.

accident. An unlooked for mishap or an untoward event which is not expected or designed: Fenton v Thorley Co (1903) AC 443. Accident insurance policies usually provide cover for *injury by accident* or *injury caused by accidental means*. If a deliberate act on the part of the assured brings about an injury which is an unexpected and unforeseeable result of that action, his injury is caused by accident.

accidental omission. There are various provisions in the BS Act 1989 that ensure that proceedings or acts are not invalidated by the accidental omission to do something (eg to send a notice to a person entitled to receive one), or by the non-receipt of a notice by such person. For examples see 1989 Act ss.68(6), 74(8), 75(6).

It has been held in a particular UK case that the omission to give notice of a meeting was not accidental: Royal Mutual Benefit Building Society v Sharman & Ors (1963) 2 All ER 242.

accommodation party. A person who has signed a bill of exchange (qv) as drawer, acceptor or indorser, without receiving value therefor and for the purpose of lending his name to some other person. An accommodation party is liable on a bill to a *holder for value* (qv), and it is immaterial when such holder took the bill, whether he knew such party to be an accommodation party of not: Bills of Exchange Act 1882 s.28.

account payee. The addition of the words *account payee* on a cheque is an instruction to the collecting banker to collect only for the payee's account. The words put the bank on enquiry and it is negligence on the part of the banker, should adequate enquiry not be made: Home Property Co of London v London County and Westminster Bank (1915) 84 LJ KB 1846. A banker now includes a building society; see CHEQUE.

accountant. See AUDITOR, QUALIFICATIONS OF; INVESTIGATION.

accounting principles. The principles and rules governing the preparation of the annual accounts (qv) of a building society, which the Central Bank is empowered to prescribe by regulation: BS Act 1989 s.77(8)(c). See ACCOUNTING RECORDS. See also APPENDIX 2.

accounting records. A building society is required to cause proper accounting records to be kept on a continuous and consistent basis, and to establish and maintain systems of control of its business and records and systems of inspections and report thereon: BS Act 1989 s.76. This requirement also extends to subsidiaries (qv) of a society (ibid s.76(10)).

The accounting records must correctly record and explain the transactions of the society, disclose the financial position of the society at any time, enable the accounts to be readily audited, and enable the directors and the society to discharge their statutory functions (ibid s.76(2)).

The directors have a duty to ensure that there is in operation a system of control of the business and accounts of the society and that the controls are in operation (ibid s.76(5)-(7)). Failure to comply with these requirements could constitute an offence and could be sufficient grounds for a revocation or suspension by the Central Bank of *authorisation* (qv) (ibid ss.40 and 76(12)).

Accounting records must be preserved by the society for a period not less than 6 years after the latest dates to which they relate (ibid s.76(9)).

If a society, that is being wound up and is unable to pay all of its debts, has contravened its statutory obligation to maintain proper accounting records etc, every officer of the society who is in default is guilty of an offence, where the High Court considers the contravention has contributed to the society's inability to pay its debts or has resulted in substantial uncertainty as to its assets and liabilities or has substantially impeded its orderly winding up (ibid s.111).

The Registrar of Building Societies has reminded directors of building societies of their duty to be personally satisfied as to the adequacy of the system of control, inspection, and supervision; he further advised them that they should not hesitate to obtain appropriate professional advice: Report of Registrar (1984) p.13. See CONVEYANCING; AUDITOR, DUTY OF; AUDITOR'S REPORT; OFFICER; RECORDS. See APPENDIX I.

acknowledgment. Avowal or assent to. See TIERED INTEREST RATE.

act of a society. See ULTRA VIRES.

acting in concert. See SUCCESSOR COMPANY.

action. A civil proceeding commenced by summons or in such other manner as may be prescribed by the rules of court. An action against or by a building society before its conversion (qv) into a public limited company, may be prosecuted following conversion without any amendment in pleadings: BS Act 1989 s.107(2)(h).

acts of a director. See DIRECTOR.

actuary. A person who is an expert on mortality and insurance statistics. The evidence of an actuary is not only desireable but is necessary to enable a jury to arrive at anything like a reasonably accurate figure for damages for *future loss of earnings*: Long v O'Brien Cronin Ltd (1972) SC. Under recent legislation, any insurer which has its head office in the State and which has an authorisation to undertake life assurance, is required to appoint an actuary: Insurance Act 1989 s.34. The Minister for Industry and Commerce is empowered to prescribe the qualifications and experience of such actuary. See also Sexton v O'Keeffe (1966) IR 204. See INSURANCE.

administration of insurer. The taking over of the management of an insurer, on an order for administration made by the High Court, if the court considers (a) that the insurer has made inadequate provision for its debts or that the rights and interests of policy holders are being prejudiced or that the insurer is unable to comply with EEC insurance regulations and (b) that administration would be in the public interest.

The administrator so appointed is required to carry on the business as a going concern with a view to placing it it on a sound commercial and financial footing. There is provision for contribution from other insurers to an Insurance Compensation Fund and payment from that fund to the administrator. See Insurance (No 2) Act 1983; also In re PMPA Insurance Co (1986) ILRM 524 and (1988) ILRM 109.

administrator/administratrix. A person (male/female) appointed to manage the property of another. The person to whom the grant of administration of the estate of a deceased person is made. An administrator of an estate has the same rights and liabilities as if he were the executor of the deceased: Succession Act 1965 s.27. An attorney, acting under a power of attorney, may be an administrator:

RSC O.79 r.23. See EXECUTOR; EXECUTORSHIP.

adjudicator. See DISPUTES.

admissibility of evidence. Evidence may be received by a court only if it is both relevant and admissible. In general, all evidence relevant to *facts in issue* is admissible. Certain evidence is inadmissible eg evidence of privileged communications without the waiver of the person in whose favour the privilege exists. The admissibility of evidence is decided by the judge; the jury must be absent during arguments as to admissibility: The State v Treanor (1924) 2 IR 193; The People v Murray (1971) CCA.

A copy of any report of an inspector appointed by the Central Bank to investigate the affairs of a building society, is admissible in any legal proceedings as evidence of the opinion of the inspector in relation to any matter contained in the report: BS Act 1989 s.47(8). See INSPECTOR; PRIVILEGE.

adoptable powers. Powers which, under any provision of the BS Act 1989, must, in order to be exercisable, be *adopted* by the society (ibid s.2(1)). *Adopt* or *adopted* means adopt or adopted by agreement on the formation of the society or subsequently by a special resolution (qv) (ibid s.2(1)).

The powers which must be adopted by a society by *special resolution* and recorded in its memorandum (qv) are powers relating to: holding and developing land; unsecured or partly secured loans; investment in and support of bodies corporate; financial services; conveyancing services; auctioneering services and services relating to land; and the power to operate abroad (qqv) (ibid s.36).

Notice of such a *special resolution* must contain or be accompanied by a statement giving (a) a description of the activity in relation to which the power is to be exercised, (b) the reasons for adoption of each power, and (c) details of such other matters as the Central Bank may require (ibid s.36(3)).

The exercise of an adopted power is subject to the approval of the Bank (ibid s.36(4)). The decision of the Bank on an application for such approval must be made within 6 months and may be granted, refused, or granted subject to conditions, restrictions or exclusions as the Bank considers appropriate (ibid s.36(10)). See also Second Schedule, Part I, para 1(c). See ASSESSMENT OF SOCIETY; CEASING OF POWER; HIGH COURT; POWERS OF SOCIETY; PRELIMINARY VIEW. See APPENDIX I.

adult. A person who attains *full age*. See AGE OF MAJORITY.

adverse possession, title by. See LONG POSSESSION, TITLE BY.

advertisement. (1) For the purposes of planning legislation, means any word, letter, model, balloon, kite, poster, notice, device or representation employed for the purpose of advertisement, announcement or direction: LG(P&D) Act 1963 s.2(1). Advertisement structure means any structure which is a hoarding, scaffold, framework, poll, standard, device, or sign (whether illuminated or not) and which is used or intended for use for exhibiting advertisements. See 1963 Act s.54 and LG(P&D) Regulations 1977, third schedule, Part II (SI No 65 of 1977).

(2) As regards a building society, an advertisement includes every form of recommendation of any matter to which s.42 of the BS Act 1989 relates, including in

particular the display or publication of any such matter by way of leaflet, notice, circular, pamphlet, brochure, photograph, film, video, sound broadcasting, television, electronic communication or personal canvassing; and references to the issue of advertisements must be construed accordingly (ibid s.42(3)(a)).

The Central Bank is empowered to give a building society a *direction* (qv): (a) in relation to the matter or form of an advertisement and (b) to withdraw an advertisement or to cease advertising (ibid s.42(1)).

All 10 building societies in the State currently have permission to advertise for funds, the last permission having been given to the Metropolitan Building Society in April 1988. As regards the control of advertising under previous legislation, see Ireland Benefit Building Society v Registrar of Building Societies (1981) ILRM 73. See also Report of Registrar of Building Societies (1984) p.9. See ANNUAL PERCENTAGE CHARGE; AUTHORISATION; BUSINESS ASSOCIATE; HIGH COURT; NAME OF SOCIETY.

advertisement and disclosure. The publisher of an advertisement can be compelled to disclose the name and address of the person or his agent who procured the publication of an advertisement in relation to the supply or provision of any goods, services, living accommodation or facilities. See Consumer Information Act 1978 s.13; Restrictive Practices (Amendment) Act 1987 s.30. Advertisement in this context includes a catalogue, a circular and a price list (ibid 1978 Act s.l).

advertisement, misleading. An advertisement in relation to the supply or provision in the course or for the purpose of a trade, business or profession, of goods, services or facilities which is likely to mislead and thereby cause loss, damage or injury to members of the public to a material degree. It is an offence for a person to publish, or cause to be published, such an advertisement. Any person, including the Director of Consumer Affairs, may obtain an order from the High Court prohibiting the publication of such an advertisement. See Consumer Information Act 1978 s.8; European Communities (Misleading Advertising) Regulations 1988 (SI No 134 of 1988).

advertising order. An order which the Minister may make to compel inclusion of particular information in an advertisement of goods, services, living accommodation or facilities. It is an offence to publish an advertisement which fails to comply with the order. See Consumer Information Act 1978. s.ll.

advisory services. See FINANCIAL SERVICES; SERVICES RELATING TO LAND.

affirm. (1) To elect to be bound by a voidable contract. (2) To make a solemn declaration instead of an oath. See AFFIRMATION; PROPERTY TRANSACTION.

affirmation. A solemn declaration which a person may make instead of taking an oath, where the person states that he has no religious belief or that an oath is contrary to his religious belief: Oaths Act 1888. See OATH.

age of majority. The age at which a person attains *full age* ie when he attains the age of eighteen years, or, in case he marries before attaining that age, upon his marriage: Age of Majority Act 1985 s.2. See MINOR.

agent. A person who is employed for the purpose of bringing his principal (qv) into contractual relations with third parties. An agent does not make contracts on his own behalf and consequently it is not necessary that he should have full contractual capacity. When the agent has brought his principal into contractual relations with another, he drops out and the principal sues or is sued on the contract.

An agent may be a universal agent, a general agent or a special agent. A *universal* agent has authority to act for the principal in all matters eg under a universal power of attorney (qv). A *general* agent has authority to act in transactions of a class eg a solicitor, a managing director of a company; the scope of authority is that usually possessed by such agents. A *special* agent is one who is appointed for a particular purpose and his authority is limited to that purpose eg an auctioneer. An act done by an agent within the scope of his authority, binds his principal.

Agency may arise: (a) by express agreement, verbal or in writing, and will be limited by that agreement; (b) by implication or by conduct; (c) by necessity; (d) by ratification eg where a principal confirms and adopts a contract made by an agent who at the time of its making had no or insufficient authority.

An agency can be terminated by act of the parties (by agreement or by revocation) and by operation of law (death, bankruptcy or insanity of the principal or agent).

As regards agents and building societies, see AUCTIONEERING SERVICE; COMMISSION; EMPLOYEE; EXAMINATION; FINANCIAL SERVICES; FURNITURE; INSPECTION; INSPECTOR; INVESTIGATION.

agent, insurance. See INSURANCE AGENT.

agm. See ANNUAL GENERAL MEETING.

allonge. [Make longer]. A piece of paper attached to a bill of exchange (qv) as a continuation sheet for endorsements where there is no further room for them on the bill: Bills of Exchange Act 1882 s.32(1). The last endorsement on the actual bill should be made partly on the bill and partly on the allonge.

allotment, land. A piece of land, containing not more than one-quarter of a statute acre, let or intended to be let for cultivation by an individual for the production of vegetables mainly for the consumption of himself and his family: Acquisition of Land (Allotments) Act 1926 s.1 and Acquisition of Land (Allotments) (Amendment) Act 1934. For recovery of possession of an allotment, see the 1926 Act s.14 (1).

allotment, shares. The appropriation to a person of a certain number of shares in a company. Shares are said to have been alloted when a person acquires the unconditional right to be included in the company's register of members in respect of those shares: Companies Amendment Act 1983 s.2(2). A *return of allotments* must be made to the Registrar of Companies: 1963 Act s.58; 1983 Act s.31(2).

There is no requirement on a company into which a building society has become converted, to show in the list required to be delivered to the Registrar of Companies, the occupation of the person who immediately before the conversion date (qv) was a member of the society, if the register of members of the society did not contain this information: BS Act 1989 s.106(7). This exception applies for 5 years from the conversion date. See CONVERSION.

alteration. In relation to the *memorandum* (qv) or *rules* (qv) of a building society, *alteration* includes any addition to or variation of the memorandum or rules, the rescission of any provision of the memorandum or rules, whether with or without substitution of one or more than one provision in the memorandum or rules for any provision so rescinded, and cognate words must be construed accordingly: BS Act 1989 s.2(1).

alternative directors. Substitute directors. It has been held that the use of alternative directors was not in principle contrary to the basic structure or legal concept of building societies, nor was it prohibited by the BS Act 1976 (which Act is repealed by the BS Act 1989): Irish Civil Service Building Society v Registrar of Building Societies (1985) IR 167. There is no prohibition on alternative directors in the 1989 Act. See DIRECTOR.

amalgamation. The combination of two or more building societies by forming a society as their successor: BS Act 1989 s.95. In order to form a society as their successor, the amalgamating societies must (a) agree on the objects, memorandum, and rules of their successor, (b) each approve the terms of the amalgamation by *special resolution* (qv) including the memorandum and rules, and (c) make application jointly to the Central Bank for confirmation of the amalgamation (ibid ss.95(2) and 98). A notice in such form as the Bank may specify, giving particulars of the application and indicating that objections and representations relating to it may be made to the Bank, must be published in at least 2 newspapers (ibid s.98).

In relation to the special resolution, a statement, the contents of which have been approved by the Bank, must be sent by each society proposing to amalgamate to its members entitled to notice of a meeting of the society, showing specified matters eg the financial position of each society, the interest of the directors, any compensation or consideration proposed to be made, any changes in the terms governing outstanding loans, and details in relation to the employees (ibid s.97).

The special resolution approving an amalgamation must also approve any terms of the amalgamation which include provisions (a) for compensation to be paid to a director or other officer for loss of office or diminution of emoluments, or (b) for part of the funds to be distributed among any of the members (ibid s.99).

The Bank may confirm the amalgamation, in which case it registers the memorandum and rules of the successor society, issues a *certificate of incorporation* (qv) and specifies a date from which incorporation takes effect, from which date, all the property, rights and liabilities of each society stand transferred to and vested in the successor society and the amalgamating societies stand dissolved (ibid s.98(6)(a) and 95(3)-(7)).

The Bank may also refuse to confirm an amalgamation where eg it considers that the amalgamation would not be in the public interest or that information material to the members' decision was not made available to all those eligible to vote, or that some relevant requirement had not been fulfilled (ibid s.98(6)(b)).

In relation to the comments of the Registrar of Building Societies on the then proposed merger of the Educational Building Society and the Irish Permanent Building Society in 1985, see Report of Registrar (1984) p.14. See also AUTHORISATION; TRANSFER OF ENGAGEMENTS; STAMP DUTIES. See APPENDIX I.

amendment of resolution. See SPECIAL RESOLUTION.

ancient lights. The right to light which becomes absolute after 20 years of actual uninterrupted enjoyment of access to it, unless enjoyed by written consent: Prescription Act 1859 s.3. See LIGHT, RIGHT TO.

and company; & Co. The words marked on a cheque between two parallel traverse lines which have the effect of making the cheque payable only through a bank or a building society: Bills of Exchange Act 1882 s.79(2) and BS Act 1989 s.126. See CHEQUE, LIABILITY ON.

annual accounts. The accounts required to be prepared in respect of each financial year (qv) by the directors of a building society, whether as individual accounts or group accounts (qv), together with the notes to them: BS Act 1989 ss.2(1) and 77.

These annual accounts must consist of (a) an income and expenditure account giving a true and fair view of its income and expenditure for that year; (b) a balance sheet (qv) giving a true and fair view of the state of its affairs at the end of that year; and (c) a statement of the source and application of funds giving a true and fair view of the manner in which its business has been financed and in which its financial resources have been used during that year (ibid s.77(1)). The annual accounts must be in such form and contain such particulars as the Central Bank may direct; the Bank may also, by regulation, make further provision with respect to the annual accounts (ibid s.77(1) and (8)).

The annual accounts in respect of the last financial year must be laid by the directors before the agm and a copy must be sent to the Bank not later than 21 days before the agm (ibid s.82). A copy must also be made available to members and depositors at the society's offices and sent to them within 7 days on demand and on payment of a fee as may be fixed by the Bank (ibid s.82(3)). The Bank may direct a society to send any document comprised in the annual accounts free of charge to all members of the society (ibid s.82(4)). See ACCOUNTING PRINCIPLES; AUDITOR'S REPORT; CONVEYANCING; GROUP ACCOUNTS; REMUNERATION OF DIRECTOR. See APPENDIX I.

annual general meeting; agm. The meeting which a building society is required to hold in the State, in the first 4 months of each financial year (qv), and which must be specified as the *annual general meeting* in the notices calling it: BS Act 1989 s.67(1). An extension may be granted by the Central Bank upon application by a society (ibid s.67(3)); under the repealed enactments, the Registrar of Building Societies has granted extensions on a number of occasions: Report of the Registrar (1980) p.12 and (1982) p.9. If the society fails to do so, the Central Bank may call or direct the calling of the agm (ibid 1989 Act s.67(4)).

Matters to be laid before the agm include the annual accounts (qv), the summary financial statement, the directors' report (qv), and the auditor's report (qv). Particulars concerning business associates (qv) of the society and loans made to directors, must be available for inspection at the agm. The auditor of the society must be appointed at the agm, as must directors, unless elected by postal ballot (qv) before the agm. See AUDITOR, APPOINTMENT OF; DIRECTOR, ELECTION OF; DISCLOSURE OF LOANS; DISCLOSURE RE BUSINESS ASSOCIATE; FINANCIAL STATEMENT, SUMMARY; LOAN TO DIRECTOR; MEETING, PROCEDURE AT; NOTICE OF MEETINGS; RULES. See APPENDIX 1.

annual percentage charge; APR. The true cost of credit to consumers which must be shown in any advertisement which refers to the availability and the cost of credit: Consumer Information (Consumer Credit) Order 1987 (SI No 319 of 1987). The APR must be shown by way of example if no other means is practicable. Where the advertisement relates to the provision of goods or services, the cash price payable under the credit agreement and the number and amount of instalments must also be indicated. Similar provisions relating to APR apply to any notice or leaflet displayed at a place where a cash loan can be obtained or a credit purchase made.

The order does not apply to loans involving free credit. The exclusion of its applicability to banks, licenced under the Central Bank Act 1971 has been repealed: Consumer Information Act 1978 s.23; Restrictive Practices (Amendment) Act 1987 s.3.

The Director of Consumer Affairs has confirmed his intention to bring a test case to the High Court against a building society in order to clarify the way the cost of mortgages is displayed in advertisements; he is to seek a declaration by the Court as to the meaning of SI No 319 of 1987 (2nd June 1989).

annuity. An annual payment of a certain sum of money; it may be perpetual or be for the life of the annuitant or be statutory. If an annuity is charged on land, it amounts to a rent-charge (qv): Revenue Commissioners v Malone (1951) IR 269. There are *statutory annuities* which are charged on land in repayment of sums advanced to tenant farmers under the Land Purchase Acts eg Land Law Acts 1923 s.9; 1931 ss.4 and 7; 1953 s.4. Such annuities are burdens (qv) which affect registered land whether they are registered or not: Registration of Title Act 1964 s.72. A prior mortgage as regards building societies does not include certain specified annuities payable to the Land Commission: Land Act 1984. See PRIOR MORTGAGE.

annuity mortgage. A mortgage (qv) wherein the principal sum advanced by the mortgagee (lender) is intended to be repaid by the mortgagor (borrower) in regular, usually monthly, instalments which comprise both principal and interest on the principal outstanding. Compare with ENDOWMENT MORTGAGE. For example of a typical building society annuity mortgage, see APPENDIX 5.

ante-date. The date which a document bears which is a date before the date on which it was drawn. A bill of exchange (qv) is not invalid by reason only that it is antedated: Bills of Exchange Act 1882 s.13(2).

appeal. The transference of a case from an inferior to a higher tribunal in the hope of reversing or modifying the decision of the former. Where an appeal is provided for, generally only one appeal is allowable.

As regards appeals by a building society to the High Court against a decision of the Central Bank, see AUTHORISATION, REVOCATION OF; FORMATION; MEMORANDUM; REGISTRATION, CANCELLATION OF; RULES.

As regards appeals (by way of reference to the Central Bank) by a member against a decision of a building society, see COMMUNICATION WITH MEMBERS; ELECTION ADDRESS; RESOLUTION, PROPOSAL OF.

There is also provision for an appeal to the Supreme Court against a High Court order relating to the confirmation or cancellation of a conversion scheme (qv). See CONVERSION SCHEME, CANCELLATION OF.

As regards an appeal by a society against a judgment granted to a judgment creditor for a sum of money, see JUDGMENT CREDITOR.

appointment of auditor. See AUDITOR, APPOINTMENT OF.

appointment of director. See DIRECTOR, APPOINTMENT OF.

appraisement. The valuation of goods or property; in particular the valuation of goods seized in execution, or by distraint, or by order of the court. A person who is authorised to conduct auctions may act as an *appraiser* within the meaning of the Appraisers Act 1806 without being licenced under that Act: Finance Act 1950 s.8. See AUCTIONEER.

appurtenant. Belonging to; necessary to the enjoyment of a thing; annexed to a hereditament eg a right of way. See WAY, RIGHT OF.

APR. [Annual Percentage Charge (qv)].

aqua cedit solo. [Water passes with the soil]. Ownership of water generally goes with the ownership of the soil beneath the water. See Tennant v Clancy (1988) ILRM 214.

arbitration. The determination of disputes by the decision of one or more persons called *arbitrators*. Differences between arbitrators are decided by an *umpire*. An agreement to refer a dispute to arbitration is called an *arbitration agreement* (qv). Most contracts of insurance, partnership agreements, travel and building contracts, include an *arbitration clause* requiring that disputes be determined by an arbitrator. The decision of an arbitrator is called an *award*.

If legal proceedings are instituted in contravention of an arbitration agreement or clause, they may be *stayed* by either party, but only after an appearance has been entered and before delivering pleadings or taking any other *steps in the proceedings*: Arbitration Act 1980 s.5; Healy and Ors v Irish Mutual Building Society and Ors (1981) HC.

Where the rules of a building society provide that a *dispute* between the society and a member is to be determined by arbitration or by the Central Bank, the Arbitration Acts 1954 and 1980, subject to any necessary modification, apply to that dispute: BS Act 1989 s.91(3) and (4). However, in the case of determination of a dispute by the Bank, it is deemed to be a single arbitrator and the provisions relating to the appointment of additional arbitrators or umpires do not apply (ibid s.91(4)(b)).

An arbitration against or by a building society before its conversion (qv) into a public limited company, may be prosecuted following conversion without any amendment in documents: BS Act 1989 s.107(2)(h). See DISPUTES; GROUND RENT; STEP IN PROCEEDINGS.

arbitration agreement. A written agreement to refer present or future differences to arbitration whether an arbitrator is named therein or not: Arbitration Act 1954 s.2(1); an agreement in writing (including an agreement contained in an exchange of letters or telegrams) to submit to arbitration present or future differences capable of settlement by arbitration: Arbitration Act 1980 s.2.

The rules (qv) of a building society are deemed to be an *arbitration agreement,* where those rules provide that a dispute between a member and his society is to be determined by arbitration or by the Central Bank: BS Act 1989 s.91(3)(a) and (4)(a).

arbitrator. The arbitrator appointed to determine a dispute between a member and his building society, must be named and selected in accordance with the rules (qv) of the society, or if they make no such provision, one arbitrator must be named by the board of directors and one by the member: BS Act 1989 s.91(3)(b). An arbitrator must not be beneficially interested, whether directly or indirectly, in the funds of the society (ibid s.91(3)(c)). A society must also maintain a panel of arbitrators and keep a register of their names, which register must be kept available for inspection by members and the Central Bank (ibid s.91(3)(d)).

arms length, at. Removed from personal influence. As regards arms length relationships in building societies, see ASSESSMENT OF SECURITY; COMMISSION; DISCLOSURE OF INTEREST. See also AUCTIONEERING SERVICE; CONVEYANCING SERVICE.

arrears. Money not paid at the due date. The liability of a member of a building society is limited to the amount actually paid and in arrear on the shares he holds in the society: BS Act 1989 s.16(4). See In re Sheffield & South Yorkshire Permanent Building Society (in liquidation) (1889) 22 QBD 470. See MEMBER, LIABILITY OF.

articles of association. The regulations by which a company is to be governed and managed. The articles must be printed, divided into paragraphs numbered sequentially, be stamped in the same way as a deed and be signed by each subscriber to the *memorandum of association* and attested: Companies Act 1963 ss.11 - 15.

The articles of association of a *successor company* to a building society must include provisions to protect its independence for a period of 5 years after the conversion date: BS Act 1989 s.102(2). See SUCCESSOR COMPANY. See also MEMORANDUM OF ASSOCIATION.

artificial person. A body which is invested by law with a personality having rights and duties eg a corporation, a company, or a building society (qv).

assessment of security. A building society must make arrangements for assessing the adequacy of the security for loans to be secured by the mortgage of freehold or leasehold estate or interest; the valuation (qv) of the security and the assessment of the adequacy of the security are distinct functions which must be performed by different persons: BS Act 1989 s.25. An assessment must be made on the occasion of each loan; it must be carried out by an officer or employee of the society who has furnished to him a written report on the value of the security; and the officer or employee must have no financial interest in the disposition and must not be receiving a commission (ibid s.25(1) and (3)).

The Central Bank is empowered to

prescribe, by regulation, rules concerning the making available to a member, to whom a housing loan is to be made, of the report relating to the value of the security for the loan (ibid s.11(2)(b)(ii)). See COMMISSION; VALUATION OF SECURITY. See also APPENDIX 1; APPENDIX 2.

assessment of society. The Central Bank may commission an independent assessment of the capacity of a building society to exercise a power for which it has sought approval and the society must, if so directed by the Bank, defray the cost of such assessment: BS Act 1989 s.36(15). See ADOPTABLE POWERS.

assessor's report. It has been held that a building society was liable to a person who purchased a house (which turned out to be structurally defective) on the strength of an assessor's report which was printed upon the society's form and for which the person paid a fee: Martin v Irish Industrial Benefit Society (1960) Ir Jur Rep 42. See VALUATION REPORT.

assets, employment of. The Central Bank may impose, as a condition to an *authorisation* (qv) granted by it to a building society, limitations on the employment of assets: BS Act 1989 s.17(6)(a). See LIQUID ASSETS.

assets outside State. The Central Bank in exercise of any of its functions under the BS Act 1989 is not required to treat assets or liabilities of building societies held outside the State as if they were held in the State (ibid s.33(2)). See ABROAD; DEPOSIT; LIQUID ASSETS.

assign. To transfer property; an assignee ie the person to whom an assignment is made.

assignment of lease. The transfer of the total interest of the lessee under a lease (qv) to a new lessee. The *assignee* or new lessee takes subject to all the rights and liabilities of the former lessee. See Deasy's Act 1860 ss.9, 12,13; Landlord and Tenant (Amendment) Act 1980 s.66. See SUBLETTING.

assignment of mortgage. See MORTGAGES, SALE OF.

associated body. A body in which a building society holds shares or *corresponding membership rights*, ie such rights in relation to a body corporate (other than rights arising from the holding of shares) as are attributable to membership of the body: BS Act 1989 ss.2(1) and 28. A society is not permitted to invest in another body corporate whose objects enable it to undertake activities outside of the powers of the society or to invest in other bodies corporate (ibid s.28(2)).

Also the Central Bank may specify limits or restrictions on a body corporate in which a society invests, where the body is engaged in the business of accepting deposits or other repayable funds (ibid s.28(4)).

These provisions are to ensure that a society cannot transfer its main business to a subsidiary or to use subsidiaries to circumvent the requirements of the Act or of the Central Bank. However, a society may invest in and support a body for 3 months pending the alteration of the *objects* (qv) of that body and the Bank may grant a dispensation as it considers appropriate (ibid s.28(2)). See CONVERSION SCHEME; FINANCIAL SERVICES; OBJECTS CLAUSE; SUBSIDIARY.

associated employer. Any two employers are associated if one is a body corporate of which the other (directly or indirectly) has control or if both are bodies corporate of which a third person directly or indirectly has control; and the expression *associated employer* is to be construed accordingly: BS Act 1989 s.25(6). See FINANCIAL INTEREST.

association clause. The clause in a memorandum of association of a company in which the subscribers state that they desire to be formed into a company and agree to take the number of shares set opposite their names. See MEMORANDUM OF ASSOCIATION.

association of building societies. There are two industry associations which represent the interests of building societies in Ireland, the Irish Building Societies Association (qv) which represents the Irish Permanent, First National, Educational, and Irish Nationwide (sometimes referred to as the "big four"), and the Financial Services Industry Association (qv), representing the other six societies (sometimes incorrectly referred to as the "non-associated" societies).

assurance. (1) The documentary evidence of the transfer of land. (2) Insurance (qv): Insurance Act 1989 s.2(1).

assured. Insured (qv).

attachment. The enforcement of a direction to pay money. The property of a building society may not be attached while a direction (qv) under s.40 of the BS Act 1989 is in force, without the prior sanction of the High Court (ibid s.40(5)). See GARNISHEE.

attachment of funds. The Revenue Commissioners are empowered, with effect from lst October 1988, to attach amounts owed by a *financial institution* to a tax defaulter: Finance Act 1988 s.73. *Financial institution* includes a building society. See GARNISHEE.

attorney. See POWER OF ATTORNEY.

attornment. An acknowledgement by a person in occupation of land to be the tenant of the owner thereof. A mortgage may contain an *attornment clause* whereby the mortgagor attorns himself tenant of the mortgagee so that possession of the land may be obtained by way of ejectment (qv). See Deasy's Act 1860 s.94; Ulster Bank v Woolsey (1890) 24 ILTR 65; Portman Building Society (1951) All ER 191; Steyning and Littlehampton Building Society v Wilson (1951) Ch 1018. See MORTGAGEE, RIGHTS OF.

auction sales. A sale by auction is complete when the auctioneer announces its completion by the fall of a hammer or in other customary manner; until such announcement any bidder may retract his bid. A sale by auction may be notified to be subject to a *reserve* or *upset price* and a right to bid may also be reserved expressly by or on behalf of the seller. Where a sale by auction is not so notified, it is not lawful for the seller to bid himself or to employ any person (a *puffer*) to bid, or for the auctioneer knowingly to take any bid from the seller or any such person; a sale contravening this rule may be treated as fraudulent by the buyer. An *upset price* includes a price specifically named as the sum from which bidding may start.

In a *dutch auction* the property is put up at an excessive price and is offered at decreasing prices until someone closes. See SALE OF LAND.

auctioneer. A person who conducts sales by auction to the highest bidder. A person may not carry on or hold himself out or represent himself as carrying on the business of auctioneer except under and in accordance with a licence and no person may conduct an auction except with a licence or permit: Auctioneers and House Agents Act 1947 s.6.

An auctioneer's licence is granted by the Revenue Commissioners on application accompanied by a *certificate of qualifications*, a certificate of maintenance by the applicant of a deposit in the High Court, and the excise duty payable (ibid s.8). A certificate of qualifications is obtained on application to a district justice (ibid s.11; Auctioneers and House Agents Act 1967 s.12). An auctioneer must keep a *client account* (ibid s.5) and there are provisions governing proceedings in relation to deposits and banking accounts and bankruptcy (ibid ss.7-11).

The auctioneer is the agent of the seller, but becomes an agent of the buyer and seller for the purposes of providing a memorandum (qv) under the Sale of Goods Act 1893 and the Statute of Frauds. For the authority of an auctioneer as agent of the seller, see Law v Roberts & Co (1964) IR 292.

Any agreement in a contract relating to the sale, lease, or letting of property which makes the purchaser, lessee or tenant liable to pay the fees or expense of an auctioneer or house agent is void: Auctioneers and House Agents Act 1973 s.2. See also Attorney General v Manorhamilton Co-operative Livestock Mart Ltd (1966) IR 192. See APPRAISEMENT; AUCTIONEERING SERVICE; COMMISSION; DEPOSIT.

auctioneering service. Any business to which the Auctioneers and House Agents Act 1947 relates, including the business of a house agent (qv) within the meaning of that Act: BS Act 1989 s.32(6)(a). A building society is empowered to provide an *auctioneering service* and other *services relating to land*, subject to the *adoption* by the society of the power and approval of the Central Bank (ibid s.32(1)).

An auctioneer's licence is granted to a society by the Revenue Commissioners on application accompanied by: a copy of the Central Bank approval, a certificate of maintenance by the society of the required deposit in the High Court, and the excise duty payable (ibid s.32(2)).

The Minister for Justice is empowered to make regulations, governing the provision by societies of auctioneering services, which may include eg for prevention of conflicts of interests; for compensation against loss due to negligence, fraud or other dishonesty; for the qualifications and experience of the persons involved (ibid s.32(3)). Similar powers are given to the Minister for the Environment in respect of *services relating to land*. See BELOW COST SELLING; EMPLOYEE; LINKING SERVICES. See also APPENDIX 2.

audit. A detailed inspection of the accounts of a body and the systems of control of its business and records, carried out by a person known as an *auditor*. A building society must have an auditor. See AUDITOR, APPOINTMENT OF.

auditor, appointment of. A building society must, at each annual general meeting (qv), appoint an auditor or auditors to hold office from the conclusion of that meeting until the conclusion of the next agm: BS Act 1989 s.83(1). Where no such appointment is made, the Central Bank may appoint a person to fill the vacancy and his remuneration and expenses may be fixed by the Bank (ibid s.83(5)).

A society may also appoint by resolution at a general meeting, another person in place of an auditor who has been removed before his term of office expires, provided that that other person has been duly nominated, is qualified, and due notice has been given to the members and the Bank (ibid s.83(2)).

A casual vacancy may be filled by the directors or by the society in general meeting (ibid s.83(7)); in the latter case, at least 28 days notice of the resolution must be given to the society and to the Bank (ibid s.84(1)(d)).

Similar notice must be given in the case of a resolution appointing as auditor a person other than the retiring auditor or re-appointing as auditor a retiring auditor who was appointed by the directors to fill a casual vacancy (ibid s.84(1)(a) and (e)).

The Bank may, if it considers that the appointment of a particular person as auditor is not in the interest of the society, direct the society not to appoint or re-appoint that person (ibid s.83(9)). See DISQUALIFICATION; FIRM.

auditor, duty of. It is the duty of auditor to a building society to carry out such investigations in relation to the auditors' report (qv), as will enable him to form an opinion as to whether (a) the society has kept proper accounting records, and (b) the society has maintained satisfactory systems of control of its business and records, and systems of inspection and report thereon: BS Act 1989 s.88(4).

An auditor also has a duty to report to the Central Bank in writing if at any time he has reason to believe (a) that there exist circumstances which are likely to affect materially the society's ability to fulfil its statutory obligations, or (b) that there are material defects in the accounting records and systems of control, or (c) that there are material deficiencies in or omissions from any returns made by the society to the Bank (ibid s.89(1)).

He also has a duty to report to the bank where he proposes to qualify any report which he is to provide under the BS Act (ibid s.89(1)(d)). He must also, if requested by the Bank, furnish a report stating whether the society has complied with specified requirements; the Bank may require that in supplying information, the auditor shall act independently of the society (ibid s.89(2) and (4)(b)). See AUDITOR OF SUBSIDIARY; INDEMNIFY; INVESTIGATION.

auditor, liability of. See INDEMNIFY; LEGAL COSTS; RELIEF.

auditor of subsidiary. It is the duty of an auditor of a *subsidiary* (qv) or other *associated body* (incorporated in the State) of a building society to give to the society's auditors such information and explanation and such access to documents as the society's auditors may reasonably require: BS Act 1989 s.88(8).

auditor, qualifications of. An auditor of a building society must have the same qualifications as an auditor of a company as provided by the Companies Acts ie he must be a member of a recognised body of accountants or otherwise authorised by the Minister for Industry & Commerce: BS Act 1989 s.87(1).

A person is not qualified if he is:- an officer or employee of the society; a partner, employee, or employer of such officer or employee; a body corporate; a parent, spouse, brother, sister or child of an officer of the society; a former officer or employee of the society (if the accounts to be audited refer to a time during which he worked for the society); a person disqualified for appointment as an auditor of a subsidiary (qv) under the Companies Acts (1989 Act s.87(2)). An auditor must not act as auditor when he is disqualified (ibid s.87(3)). See DISQUALIFICATION. See APPENDIX I.

auditor, removal of. A building society may by resolution (qv) at a general meeting remove an auditor before his term of office expires: BS Act 1989 s.83(2). At least 28 days notice of the resolution must be given to the society and to the Central Bank (ibid s.84(1) and (2)). The society must not give notice of the meeting for 7 days after receipt of the resolution; this is intended to give the Central Bank an opportunity to make its views known if it so wishes (ibid s.84(4)).

The auditor is entitled to attend the next agm of the society and at the general meeting at which it is proposed to fill the vacancy caused by his removal, and to be heard at these meetings (ibid s.84(8)). He also has the right to have his written representations (of a reasonable length) sent by the society to its members unless the Bank is satisfied that this would substantially diminish public confidence in the society or that the auditor is seeking needless publicity for defamatory matter (ibid s.84(6)-(7)).

auditor, remuneration of. See REMUNERATION OF AUDITOR.

auditor, resignation of. An auditor of a building society may by a notice in writing served on the society and stating his intention to do so, resign from the office of auditor: BS Act 1989 s.85(1). The notice, a copy of which must be served on the Central Bank at the same time, must contain (a) a statement that there are no circumstances connected with his resignation that he considers should be brought to the notice of the members, depositors or creditors of the society, or (b) a statement of any such circumstances (ibid s.85(2)-(3)).

Where there are such circumstances stated, the society must within 14 days of the service, send a copy of the notice to every person entitled to notice of a general meeting of the society, unless the Bank decides otherwise eg where it is satisfied that the sending of the notice would be likely to diminish substantially public confidence in the society (ibid s.85(4)-(5)).

In addition, the resigning auditor may requisition the convening of a general meeting of the society for the purpose of receiving and considering such account and explanation of the circumstances connected with his resignation as he may wish to give to the meeting (ibid s.86). He may require, unless the Bank decides otherwise, that the society circulate to persons entitled to receive notice of the meeting, a further statement in writing prepared by him of the circumstances connected with his resignation which he considers should be brought to the notice of members (ibid s.86(3)-(4)). A resigning auditor also can attend and be heard at the next agm and at the meeting at which it is proposed to fill the vacancy created by his resignation (ibid s.86(5)).

The resignation of an auditor takes effect on the date on which notice of his resignation is properly served or at such later date as may be specified in the notice (ibid s.85(1)).

An auditor who decides not to make himself available for re-appointment must serve notice on the society at least 35 days before the agm at which his term of office is to expire and he must comply with the requirements placed on a resigning auditor pursuant to s.85(2) to (5): (ibid s.83(10) and (11)).

auditor, rights of. Every auditor of a building society has a right of access at all reasonable times to the books, accounts, records and vouchers of the society and to all other documents relating to its affairs as he thinks necessary for the performance of the duties of auditor: BS Act 1989 s.88(5). He is entitled to attend any general meetings of the society and to be heard on any part of the meeting which concerns him as auditor (ibid s.88(6)). See MISLEADING STATEMENT.

auditors' report. The report which the auditors of a building society are required to make to the members of the society on the accounts examined by them and on the annual accounts (qv) and the directors' report (qv) which are to be laid before the society at the agm during their tenure of office: BS Act 1989 s.88(1). The auditors' report must be read at the agm and be open to inspection by the members (ibid s.88(2)).

The report must indicate, inter alia, whether the auditors have received all the information and explanations they require; whether proper accounting records (qv) have been kept; whether the annual accounts (qv), the balance sheet (qv), the income and expenditure account, and statement of the source and application of funds, have been properly prepared and give a true and fair view of the business of the society (ibid s.88(3)).

The report must also state the opinion of the auditors that the director's report is consistent with the accounting records (ibid s.88(3)(f)). See also AUDITOR, DUTY OF; DISCLOSURE OF LOANS; FINANCIAL STATEMENT, SUMMARY.

authorisation. The right invested in a person or body by another allowing performance of an act. A building society is not permitted to raise funds or advertise for or otherwise solicit deposits or subscriptions for shares unless there is in force an *authorisation* granted by the Central Bank or deemed to be granted: BS Act 1989 ss.2(1) and 17. Existing societies, prior to the 1989 Act, with permission to advertise for funds are deemed to have been granted an authorisation by the Bank subject to any restriction imposed on that permission granted by the Registrar of Building Societies (ibid s.17(2)). Also, where all societies to an *amalgamation* (qv) are authorised on the date of incorporation of the successor society, the successor is deemed to be authorised from that date (ibid s.95(6)).

A society must not exercise any functions to which an authorisation relates unless it maintains a *deposit* in a specified amount with the Central Bank (ibid s.93).

An authorisation corresponds to a banking licence and gives effect to the 1st EC Banking Directive relating to the authorisation of credit institutions.

An authorisation is not required for (a) the acceptance of payments for particular deferred shares (qv); (b) the acceptance of payments for amounts due in respect of shares which represent interest on, or the repayment of, loans made to the holders of shares; or (c) certain borrowing with the prior written consent of the Bank (ibid s.17(3)).

There are specified procedures to be followed in applying for an authorisation and specified criteria to which the Bank must have regard in deciding on an application eg that the society has qualifying capital (qv) that is not less than the prescribed minimum (ibid s.17(4) and Third Schedule). See DEFERRED SHARES; DEPOSIT WITH CENTRAL BANK; DIRECTIVE EC; QUALIFYING CAPITAL; WARRANTY; WINDING UP. See APPENDIX I.

authorisation, revocation of. The Central Bank must revoke a building society's *authorisation* (qv) to raise funds in certain circumstances eg where the society so requests or where a *transfer of engagements* (qv) has taken place, or proceedings for the winding up (qv) of the society have been commenced: BS Act 1989 s.40(1).

The Bank may, as it thinks proper, revoke an authorisation in a wide range of circumstances eg where a society has ceased to pursue as one of its objects the making of housing loans (qv), or where a society has failed to comply with the requirements of the Act, or where it is expedient to do so in the public interest or to protect the funds of shareholders or depositors (ibid s.40(2)). Instead of revoking an authorisation, the Bank may give a direction (qv) to a society.

There are provisions governing representations to the Bank in relation to a proposed revocation and an appeal to the High Court within one month of the Bank's decision to revoke an authorisation (ibid Fourth Schedule). See LIQUIDATOR; REGISTER OF MEMBERS; WINDING UP.

authorised person. An officer of the Central Bank or any other person possessing appropriate qualifications or experience, authorised in writing by the Governor of the Bank to inspect or investigate a building society or its subsidiary (qv) or associated body (qv): BS Act 1989 s.41(1). See INSPECTION.

average clause. A term in a contract of insurance under which there is an apportionment of the loss between the insured and the insurer having regard to the extent to which the risk has been underinsured, eg in property insurance where the property is of greater value than the sum insured, the insured is in effect his own insurer of the difference and must bear a rateable share of any loss.

award. The finding or decision of an arbitrator. Unless a contrary intention is expressed therein, every arbitration agreement (qv) is deemed to contain a provision that the award will be final and binding: Arbitration Act 1954 s.27. Also unless an award otherwise directs, it carries interest as from the date of the award and at the same rate as a judgment debt (ibid s.34). The High Court has jurisdiction to set aside an arbitration award if there is an error in law on its face: Church & General Insurance Co v Connolly (1981) HC. See ARBITRATION.

B

bailment. The delivery of goods to another on the condition express or implied, that they shall be restored to the bailor, or according to his directions, as soon as the purpose for which they are bailed is answered: Coggs v Bernard (1703) 2 Ld Ray 909. The act of delivery is called a *bailment*, the person making the delivery is called a *bailor* and the person to whom it is made is called the *bailee*.

Where a building society becomes converted into a public limited company, all the rights and liabilities of the society as bailor or bailee of documents or chattels are vested and assumed by the company: BS Act 1989 s.107(2)(e). See CONVERSION.

balance sheet. The annual accounts (qv) of a building society must include a *balance sheet* which gives a true and fair view of the state of the society's affairs at the end of a financial year: BS Act 1989 s.77(1)(b). The balance sheet must be signed by two directors and by the chief executive (qv) (ibid s.81(1)). It must also have annexed to it the income and expenditure account, the statement of the source and application of funds and any group accounts (qv), as well as the auditors' and directors' report (qqv) (ibid s.81(2)). See FALSE INFORMATION. See APPENDIX I.

ballot. Any system of secret voting. As regards the ballot paper in a building society, see DIRECTOR, ELECTION OF; POLL; POSTAL BALLOT.

bank. A financial institution engaged in the acceptance of deposits of money, the granting of credits by loan or overdraft or otherwise, and engaged in other financial transactions such as the collection and payment of cheques and other money transmission services, the discounting of bills and the dealing in foreign exchange. It includes a body of persons, whether incorporated or not, which carries on the business of banking: Bills of Exchange Act 1882 s.2.

Banking business, for which a licence is required from the Central Bank, includes the business of accepting deposits payable on demand or on notice or at a fixed or determinable future date: Central Bank Act 1971 s.2 (as amended by the Central Bank Act 1989 s.29(a)). No company, association or partnership consisting of more than ten persons may be formed for the purpose of carrying on the business of banking unless it is registered as a company or is formed in pursuance of some other statute: Companies Act 1963 s.372.

A person must not carry on a banking business or hold himself out or represent himself as a banker unless he is the holder of a licence and maintains a deposit in the Central Bank: Central Bank Act 1971 s.7 (as amended by the Central Bank Act 1989 s.30). An authorisation (qv) of a building society by the Central Bank corresponds in many respects to a banking licence. Consumer protection in the Consumer Information Act 1978 now applies to licenced banks (ibid s.23; Restrictive Practices (Amendment) Act 1987 s.3).

The Registrar of Companies is required to notify the Central Bank of the delivery to him of any memorandum of association or articles of any company, which would in his opinion, be holding itself out as a banker or have one of its objects the carrying out of banking business, and he may not issue a certificate of incorporation to such a company unless the Central Bank indicates its willingness to issue a licence to the company or to exempt it: Central Bank Act 1971 s.15.

It is prohibited for a building society, an industrial and provident society, a friendly society, a credit union, an investment trust company or in a unit trust scheme (qv), to use in its name or description any of the words *bank*, *banker* or *banking* (ibid s.14). See also Central Bank Acts 1942 to 1989. See BANKER, DUTY OF CARE.

bank account. An account kept between a bank and a customer eg a current account (qv). See BANK ACCOUNT OF SOCIETY; DEPOSIT WITH BUILDING SOCIETY; DIRECTOR'S BANK ACCOUNT; FREEZE ASSETS; JOINT ACCOUNT.

bank account of society. The Central Bank may direct a bank, or any institution exempt under s.7 of the Central Bank Act 1971 (as amended by the Central Bank Act 1989 s.30) which holds an account of a building society to which a *direction* (qv) as regards an *authorisation* has been given by the Bank, to suspend the making of payments from the account without the prior authorisation of the Bank: BS Act 1989, Fifth Schedule, para 10(b).

bank holiday. Formerly a day on which banks were closed by statute: Bank Holidays Acts now repealed by the Central Bank Act 1989 s.4 and schedule. Now, in effect, a bank holiday is a public holiday as defined in the Holiday (Employees) Act 1973. Public holidays are Christmas Day, St Stephen's Day, 1st January (New Year's Day - SI No 341 of 1974), St Patrick's Day, Easter Monday, the first Monday in June and August, and the last Monday in October (SI No 193 of 1977).

A public holiday is a *non-business* day, as are Saturdays and Sundays; a bill of exchange (qv) which is due and payable on a non-business day, is payable on the next succeeding business day: Central Bank Act 1989 s.132. Special provision is made for a Saturday where the drawee of the bill is a banker and the drawee is normally open for business on that day.

A person is not compellable to make any payment or do any act on a public holiday which he would not be compellable to make or do on Christmas Day or Good Friday by virtue of any rule of law (ibid s.135).

banker, duty of care. The relationship between a banker and a customer who pays money into the bank is the ordinary relationship between debtor and creditor, with a super-added obligation, arising out of the custom of bankers, to honour the customer's drafts: Joachimson v Swiss Bank Corporation (1912) 3 KB 110.

A banker owes a duty to pay all cheques properly drawn on the customer's account, provided the account is in credit or within an agreed overdraft limit. The duty and authority of a banker to pay a cheque drawn on him is terminated by a *countermand* from the customer, or by notice of death or mental disorder of the customer, or notice of the presentation of a bankruptcy petition in respect of the customer, or notice of presentation of a petition to wind-up a company customer.

It has been held that the correction by a bank of an error in its procedures on a short notice to the plaintiff company did not constitute a breach of the duty of care which it owed to the company: Hazylake Fashions Ltd v The Governor and Company of the Bank of Ireland (1989) ITLR (19 June 1989). See also Reade v Royal Bank of Ireland (1922) 2 IR 46; Dublin Port & Docks Board v Bank of Ireland (1976) IR 118; Towey v Ulster Bank Ltd (1987)

ILRM 142; Banco Ambrosiano v Ansbacher & Co (1987) ILRM 669. See BANKERS' BOOKS; CHEQUE; BILL OF EXCHANGE.

banker and confidentiality. The relationship between banker and customer is a confidential one, subject to certain statutory exceptions. A court may make an order authorising a party to legal proceedings, to inspect, and take copies of, entries in the books of a bank: Bankers' Books Evidence Act 1879 s.7; RSC O.31 r.17; O.63 r.1(17). A court may also order a banker to reveal the affairs of a customer and has power to freeze the bank account of a customer who is a taxpayer: Finance Act 1983 s.18.

New powers are conferred on the Director of Consumer Affairs and Fair Trade and on the Fair Trade Commission to examine the accounts maintained by a *financial institution*, including banks, on the order of the High Court, which may so order if satisfied that it is reasonable to do so and is satisfied that the exigencies of the common good so warrant: Restrictive Practices (Amendment) Act 1987 s.41. *Financial institution* in this context is widely interpreted in the Act to include licenced banks, building societies, industrial and provident societies, friendly societies and credit unions (ibid s.41(4)(b)).

Under recent legislation, a court or judge is empowered to authorise a Garda to inspect and take copies of any entries in a banker's book for the purposes of investigation of an indictable offence, where the court or judge is satisfied that there are reasonable grounds for believing that such an offence has been committed and that there is material in the possession of the bank which is likely to be of substantial value to the investigation: Bankers' Books Evidence Act 1879 s.7A, as inserted by the Central Bank Act 1989 s.131(c). See ATTACHMENT.

bankers' books. A copy of an entry in a banker's book is prima facie evidence of the contents of the entry and of the matters recorded therein, on the copy being proved to be correct: Bankers' Books Evidence Act 1879 ss.3-5. See also Bankers' Books Evidence (Amendment) Act 1959; RSC O.31 r.17; O.63 r.1(17).

This provision is now extended to the books of a building society: BS Act 1989 s.126(1).

The definition of bankers' books and records which may be admissible in evidence in court proceedings has been extended to include computerised and other modern day recording media: Central Bank Act 1989 s.131(a). See INVESTIGATION.

bankers' draft. An order for the payment of money drawn by a bank upon itself. Payment on such a draft is certain; however an injunction may be granted to restrain a bank from honouring its own draft where there is evidence that such honouring would aid and abet a fraudulent transaction: Murphy v Allied Irish Banks and Deele Fuels (1988) HC.

The issue of drafts by a building society is a *financial service* (qv) which a society may be empowered to provide: BS Act 1989 s.29(2)(q).

banking law, changes in. See REGULATIONS.

banking licence. A licence granted under the Central Bank Act 1971 s.9 (as amended by the Central Bank Act 1989 s.32). See CONVERSION SCHEME, CONFIRMATION OF.

bankrupt. A debtor who has been adjudicated a bankrupt by the

High Court. See DISQUALIFICATION.

bankruptcy. *Bankruptcy is a law for the benefit and the relief of creditors and their debtors, in cases where the latter are unable or unwilling to pay their debts*: In re Reiman (1874) 20 Fed Cas 490. It is the compulsory administration of the estate of an insolvent person (known as a *bankrupt*) for the benefit of his creditors; it involves the distribution of the bankrupt's property among his creditors and relieves him of the unpaid balance of his liabilities.

A person is *adjudicated* a bankrupt on the petition of the debtor himself or more usually on the petition of the creditor when the debtor has committed an *act of bankruptcy*.

New legislation to revise, update and consolidate bankruptcy law came into force on 1st January 1989: Bankruptcy Act 1988. Under that Act the unpaid debt which constitutes an act of bankruptcy is £1,500 (ibid s.8(1)); the new legislation also provides for discharge of a bankrupt after 12 years in certain circumstances (ibid s.85); the Official Assignee is given primary responsibility in bankruptcy administration similar to a *liquidator* of a company; bankruptcy law is more closely aligned to the law on the winding up of companies, particularly in regard to disclaimer of *onerous property* , *fraudulent preferences* and *preferential payments* ; and provision is made for the winding up in bankruptcy of the estates of persons dying insolvent. See APPENDIX 5 clause 7(c)(iv); DISQUALIFICATION.

barring the entail. The conversion by the tenant in tail of an estate tail into a fee simple; it is achieved by a *disentailing deed.* The Official Assignee in bankruptcy is empowered to bar the entail: Bankruptcy Act 1988 s.64. See FEE TAIL.

barrister. Counsel; a member of the Honourable Society of King's Inns who has been called to the Bar. A practising barrister is one who holds himself out as willing to appear in court or to give legal advice and services to his client for reward. He has a right of audience in every court. As regards a barrister and building societies, see PRIVILEGE, LEGAL PROFESSIONAL

base fee. A particular kind of determinable *fee simple;* it continues only so long as the original grantor or any heirs of his body are alive and there is a remainder (qv) or reversion (qv) after it. A base fee arises where a tenant in tail attempts to convey a fee simple without *barring the entail* or when the tenant in tail disentails without the consent of the *protector of the settlement* (qv).

A base fee may be enlarged into a fee simple by a fresh disentailing deed by the former tenant in tail, or by the passage of time under the Statute of Limitations 1957, or by the owner of the base fee becoming the owner of the remainder or reversion in the fee simple immediately following the base fee.

bearer bill. A bill of exchange payable to bearer, or on which the only or last endorsement is an *endorsement in blank.* An *endorsement in blank* arises where the endorser merely signs his own name, or one which is payable to a fictitious or non-existent person. See Bills of Exchange Act 1882 ss.8(3) and 34. See ORDER BILL; BILL OF EXCHANGE.

below cost selling. There is a prohibition on the provision by a building society of auctioneering services (qv), conveyancing services (qv) and other services relating to land, at a charge for each service which is less than sufficient to meet all costs properly attributable to the provision of the service, taking one year with another: BS Act 1989 ss.31(12)(a) and 32(5)(a).

beneficial owner. The person who enjoys or who is entitled to the benefit of property ie on his own right rather than on behalf of someone else.

bill. (1) An account sent by a creditor to a debtor. (2) A written instrument eg a bill of exchange (qv).

bill of exchange. A form of negotiable instrument. An unconditional order in writing, addressed by one person to another, signed by the person giving it, requiring the person to whom it is addressed to pay on demand, or at a fixed or determinable future time, a sum certain in money, to, or to the order of, a specified person, or to bearer: Bills of Exchange Act 1882 s.3(1).

The person who gives the order to pay is the *drawer*; the person to whom the order to pay is made is the *drawee* and becomes the *acceptor* by writing his name across the face of the bill. The person to whom the payment is to be made is the *payee*; the payee must be named or indicated with reasonable certainty (ibid s.7(1).

If the payee is a fictitious or non-existing person, the bill may be treated as payable to bearer (ibid s.7(3)). A non-existent person is one whom the drawer did not know existed when he signed, whereas a fictitious person is one who does exist but was not the person intended by the drawer to receive payment: Clutton v Attenborough (1897) AC 90; Bank of England v Vagliano (1891) AC 107.

The definition of a *banker* in the Bills of Exchange Act 1882 s.2 has been amended to include a building society: BS Act 1989 s.126. See NEGOTIABLE INSTRUMENT; CHEQUE; ENDORSEMENT.

bill of exchange, acceptance of. See ACCEPTANCE OF BILL.

bill of exchange, discharge of. See DISCHARGE OF BILL.

bill of exchange, dishonour of. See DISHONOUR OF BILL.

bill of exchange, payment of. A bill of exchange is *payable on demand* if it is expressed to be payable on demand, or at sight, or on presentation, or where no time for payment is expressed, or where it is accepted or endorsed when overdue: Bills of Exchange Act 1882 s.10. A bill which is not payable on demand must be payable at a fixed or determinable future time; ie it must be payable at a fixed period after date or sight, or on, or at a fixed period after, the occurrence of a specified event which is certain to happen, though the time of happening may be uncertain (ibid s.11).

board of directors. A building society must have a board of directors of at least 3 directors: BS Act 1989 s.48(1). The rules (qv) of the society must provide for the powers and duties of the board of directors (ibid Second Schedule, Part II, para 5(h)). The board must as a board (a) appoint the chairman, the chief executive, and the secretary (qqv), and (b) decide on certain issues eg on the request by a member to communicate with other members. The board must take reasonable steps to ensure that the chief executive and secretary appointed are persons who have the knowledge and experience to discharge the functions (qv) of those offices (ibid s.49(3)).

The board must also, if it wishes to hold a premises (qv), for residential or commercial purposes, which is no longer required for its own business, resolve so to do. The board may by resolution, if the Central Bank consents, transfer the engagements of the society to another society. The board members also have responsibilities as individual directors (qv). See ARBITRATOR; COMMUNICATION WITH MEMBERS; DIRECTOR; TRANSFER OF ENGAGEMENTS.

body corporate. A succession or collection of persons having in the estimation of the law an existence and rights and duties distinct from the individual persons who form it from time to time eg a company registered under the Companies Acts, a building society, a local authority, a body established by charter. A body corporate is not permitted to be a director of a building society: BS Act 1989 s.48(2).

bona fide. In good faith; honestly; without fraud, collusion, or participation in wrongdoing. See LOAN TO DIRECTOR; PROPERTY TRANSACTIONS.

bond. (1) An agreement under seal whereby the *obligor* binds himself to the *obligee* to perform or refrain from an action. A *simple bond* is one without condition. A *common money bond* is one given to secure payment of money. (2) An interest bearing document, securing long term debt, usually issued by government or corporations.

The exemption from the requirements of the Insurance Acts 1909 to 1989 enjoyed by banks, in relation to the issue of certain bonds, securities and guarantees has been extended to building societies, which can provide these services as *financial services* (qv): BS Act 1989 s.30. The exemption applies to any bond or contract of suretyship or guarantee given by a society in the course of its business, or which is given by a person resident outside the State in the course of his banking business (ibid s.30(2)). See GUARANTEE; INSURANCE BOND.

Bord Pleanala, An. [The Planning Board]. The board which hears and determines appeals made to it against the decision of a planning authority (qv) in relation to planning permission for the *development* of land: LG(P&D) Act 1976 ss.2 and 3 and LG(P&D) Act 1983 s.5.

Any person may appeal to the board against the decision of a planning authority: LG(P&D) Act 1963 s.26(5) as amended by the 1976 Act s.14. The appeal must be made within the appropriate period, which in the case of the applicant, is one month beginning on the day of receipt by him of the decision, and 21 days, in the case of a third party, beginning on the day of giving of the decision (ibid 1963 Act s.26(5)(c)). The board must determine the application as if it had been made to them in the first instance and their decision, which must specify the reasons therefor, operates to annul the decision of the planning authority (ibid 1963 Act s.26(5)(b); 1976 Act ss.14(8) and 39(g)).

The board has an absolute discretion as to whether they will hold an oral hearing, although they may be directed so to do by the Minister (ibid 1976 Act s.109). Oral hearings are normally conducted by a person appointed by the board, who is known as an *inspector,* who is required to make a written report to the board which must include a recommendation on the matter (ibid 1976 Act s.23).

See Killiney and Ballybrack Development Association v Minister for Local Government (1974) HC; Geraghty v Minister for Local Government (1976) IR 153.

borrower. See BORROWING MEMBER; MORTGAGOR.

borrowing. A building society with an *authorisation* (qv) may raise funds, to be used for the objects of the society, by borrowing money and accordingly receiving deposits from any person: BS Act 1989 s.18(1). Such borrowing must not exceed the society's liabilities arising from its issue of shares, although the Central Bank may grant a dispensation from this requirement (ibid s.18(3)). A society must notify the Central Bank of all loans it receives from other societies (ibid s.18(8)). A society may give security for money borrowed, including the security of mortgages held by the society (ibid s.18(5)). See DEPOSIT; FOREIGN CURRENCY; ULTRA VIRES. See APPENDIX 1.

borrowing member. In relation to a *conversion resolution* (qv) in a building society, a person whose mortgage debt on a *housing loan* (qv) is not less than £500 or such other amount as the Central Bank may, from time to time, prescribe by regulation: BS Act 1989 s.71(2). A borrowing member, who was such at the end of the last financial year and continues to be so on the *voting date* (qv), is entitled to one vote on a conversion resolution (ibid s.69). This provision also applies in respect of house loans made under the *repealed enactments* (qv) (ibid s.71(2)(a)). See JOINT BORROWER, REPRESENTATIVE; LIQUIDATOR.

breach of confidence. See CONFIDENTIALITY.

breach of covenant. See APPENDIX 5 - TYPICAL MORTGAGE clause 7(c)(iii); COVENANT.

breach of duty. A breach of duty as regards a building society may be a ground for a *disqualification order*. Also an *indemnity* may not be given to exempt an officer (qv) or auditor (qv) of the society from liability for a breach of duty; however, *relief* may be given to such a person by the court and a proceedings may be withdrawn by a judge from a jury.

In a particular dispute, it was held that a society had been in breach of its duty to a member in regard to the unauthorised withdrawal of money from his stolen passbook: Hudson v Irish Permanent Building Society (1982) - Report of Registrar of Building Societies (1981) p.28. See also McMahon v Ireland, AG and Registrar of Friendly Societies (1987) HC. See DATA PROTECTION; DISQUALIFICATION ORDER; INDEMNIFY; NEGLIGENCE; RELIEF; WITHDRAWAL FROM JURY.

breach of trust. Some improper act, neglect or default of a trustee of which he is personally guilty; the measure of liability is the loss caused to the trust property: Trustee Act 1893 s.24. The trustee must replace misappropriated trust property with interest at 4%; if he has traded with the trust funds, the beneficiary can claim interest at 5% or the profits actually made.

In determining liability of a trustee for breach of trust, the court distinguishes between a breach of his duties, wherein utmost diligence is required (*exacta diligentia*), and a breach of a discretion, wherein he must act honestly and use the diligence of a prudent person.

As regards building societies and a breach of trust, see INDEMNIFY;

RELIEF; WITHDRAWAL FROM JURY.

bridging loan. A loan which a building society is empowered to make to a member of the society, before a mortgage is created, not exceeding the amount which the society has agreed to lend by way of a *housing loan* (qv): BS Act 1989 s.23(1)(b). A society is obligated to take all reasonable steps to ensure that the mortgage is created as soon as may be after the making of the bridging loan (ibid s.23(3)). See LOAN.

brochure. See ADVERTISEMENT.

building bye-laws. The bye-laws which sanitary authorities are empowered to make with respect:-to the structure and description of the substances used in buildings; to the sites and foundations of houses, buildings and other erections; to the sufficiency of space; and to the drainage: Public Health (Ireland) Act 1878 s.41. The proviso that this section was not to effect any building before the passing of the 1878 Act was repealed by the LG(P&D) Act 1963 s.86. It is the declared intention of successive governments that the building bye-laws will be replaced by building regulations.

It is usual in a building society mortgage to have a covenant (qv) whereby the borrower undertakes to comply with all bye-laws and with all enactments and regulations relating to planning and development eg see APPENDIX 5 - TYPICAL MORTGAGE clause 8(1). See BUILDING REGULATIONS.

building lease. A lease of land, situated in an urban area, or else demised for a term of at least 20 years, on which permanent buildings, which were not merely ancillary and subsidiary improvements, were erected by the lessee at the time of erection or under an agreement for the grant of the lease on their erection: Landlord and Tenant (Reversionary Leases) Act 1958 s.4; Southern Health Board v Reeves Smith (1980) IR 26. A building lease (although not now referred to as such), entitled to acquire the fee simple, is entitled to a reversionary lease (qv): Landlord and Tenant (Amendment) Act 1980 s.30. See PROPRIETARY LEASE.

building regulations. The regulations which the Minister is empowered to make for all or any of the matters set out in the Public Health (Ireland) Act 1878 s.41 (other than s.41(1)) and in the Public Health Acts Amendment Act 1890 s.23 (other than the last paragraph of s.23(1)): LG(P&D) Act 1963 s.86. Regulations made under this power will be effective irrespective of the age of any building. Regulations were drafted in 1983 but have not yet been made. See BUILDING BYE-LAWS.

building society. A building society incorporated or deemed to be incorporated under the BS Act 1989 (ibid s.2(1)). The registration or incorporation of a society under the *repealed enactments* (qv) is deemed to be a registration or incorporation under the 1989 Act (ibid s.124(2)). From the date of its incorporation a society is a body corporate (with the name contained in its memorandum (qv) and rules (qv)) having perpetual succession and a seal (qv) and the power to hold land (ibid s.10(6)). A society must have a board of directors (qv) of at least 3 directors, a chairman (qv), a chief executive (qv) and a secretary (qv) (ibid ss.48 and 49). See ASSOCIATION OF BUILDING SOCIETIES; CERTIFICATE OF INCORPORATION; CHARTERED BUILDING

SOCIETIES INSTITUTE; CUMANN FOIRGNIOCHTA; FORMATION; LIQUIDATOR; NAME OF SOCIETY; STATEMENT, DISPLAY OF.

business associate. A person is a *business associate* of a building society if that person (a) carries on a business which consists of or includes the provision of *relevant services*, (b) provides relevant services during that year to the society, and (c) is not a subsidiary (qv) of the society: BS Act 1989 s.60(2).

Relevant Services are conveyancing services, surveying and valuing land or other property, arranging for the provision of insurance against loss of or damage to property or on human life, advertising or public relations services, and any other services as may be specified as relevant services by the Central Bank from time to time (ibid s.60(5)). See DISCLOSURE RE BUSINESS ASSOCIATE.

burden. An encumbrance or liability affecting the ownership of land. The title of a registered owner of *registered land* is subject to (a) the burdens which appear on the register as affecting the land: Registration of Title Act 1964 s.69; (b) the burdens, though not registered, which affect all registered land (ibid s.72); (c) unregistered rights, which are enforceable personally against the registered owner who created them and against a volunteer transferee from the registered owner, but are not enforceable against a registered transferee for value.

The ownership of registered burdens is itself registered in the *register of leaseholds* where the burden is a lease, and in the *subsidiary register* for other burdens; except that a charge (qv) is usually registered in the register of the land on which the charge is a burden. See CAUTION; INHIBITIONS.

business tenant. The tenant of a *tenement* (qv). The rights of *business* tenants have been extended as regards alienation of their interest, as to improvement and change of use of the leased premises, as to acquiring a new tenancy and to compensation for disturbance and improvements: Landlord and Tenant (Amendment) Act 1980.

The tenant of a tenement has a right, subject to certain exceptions, to a new tenancy: (a) where the tenement was for three years continuously occupied by the tenant or his predecessors in title and bona fide used wholly or partly for the purpose of carrying on a *business*; a temporary break may be disregarded by the court if it considers it reasonable so to do; or (b) where the tenement was for the previous 20 years continuously in the occupation of the tenant or of his predecessors in title; or (c) where improvements have been made on the tenement that they account for not less than half of the letting value of the tenement (ibid s.13(1)).

Business includes trade, profession or business, whether or not carried on for gain or reward, and any activity for providing cultural, social or sporting services, for the public service, or for carrying out the functions of local authorities, health boards and harbour authorities. See Gatien Motor Co Ltd v The Continental Oil Co of Ireland (1979) IR 406; Irish Shell v John Costello Ltd (1981) ILRM 66; OHS Ltd v Green Property Co Ltd (1986) ILRM 451; Mealiffe v Walsh (1987) ILRM 301.

It is usual in a building society lease to have a provision whereby the borrower irrevocably appoints the secretary (qv) of the society to be his *attorney* in respect of specified matters under the 1980 Act eg see APPENDIX 5 - TYPICAL MORTGAGE clause 12. See CHARGE; IMPROVEMENTS, COMPENSATION FOR; DISTURBANCE, COMPENSATION FOR.

bye-laws. See BUILDING BYE-LAWS.

C

camera, in. See IN CAMERA.

cancellation of conversion scheme. See CONVERSION SCHEME, CANCELLATION OF.

cancellation of registration. See REGISTRATION, CANCELLATION OF.

candidate. As regards a candidate for election as a director of a building society, see CANVASSING; DIRECTOR, NOMINATION OF; ELECTION ADDRESS; POLL; SUPERVISOR OF ELECTIONS.

canvassing. It is an offence for an employee of a building society to solicit support for a candidate for election as a director or to invite a member of the society to appoint as his proxy any particular person to vote in an election: BS Act 1989 s.51(8). To constitute the offence the soliciting or invitation must take place at the place of employment of the employee or at a meeting of the society. The offence does not apply to an employee who is an officer (qv) of the society or is himself a candidate. See APPENDIX I.

canvassing, personal. See ADVERTISEMENT.

capital. See QUALIFYING CAPITAL.

caretaker. A person who has been put into possession of any lands or premises by the owner thereof and who agrees to give up possession when requested by the landlord. So long as the relationship of caretaker exists, the caretaker cannot acquire a title under the Statute of Limitations: Musgrave v McAvey (1907) 41 ILTR 230. A caretaker is estopped from disputing or disclaiming his landlord's title: Gowrie Park Utility Society Ltd v Fitzgerald (1963) IR 436. See also Deasy's Act 1860 s.86.

case stated. A statement of the facts in a case submitted for the opinion of a higher court, clearly identifying the point of law upon which opinion is sought. As regards building societies and stating a case in relation to the determination of a dispute, see ARBITRATION; CIRCUIT COURT.

cash card. A card issued by a bank (qv) or a building society (qv) to a person by means of which cash may be obtained by the person from an automated teller machine. See FINANCIAL SERVICES.

casting vote. The second and deciding vote which a chairman may have power to give when there is an equality of votes. See CHAIRMAN.

casual vacancy. There are provisions in the BS Act 1989 governing the filling of casual vacancies in the office of director or appointment of auditor. For discussion on *casual vacancy* see Healy and Ors v Irish Mutual Building Society (1982) - Report of Registrar of Building Societies (1981) p.32. See AUDITOR, APPOINTMENT OF; DIRECTOR, APPOINTMENT OF.

cause of action. The facts which give rise to a right of action in a court of law. A cause of action existing against or in favour of a building society prior to its conversion into a company, may be prosecuted against or in favour of the company without amendment to any writ or pleading: BS Act 1989 s.107(2)(h).

caution. A warning. An entry in the register of the Land Registry to protect unregistered rights on registered land from being defeated by the registration of a subsequent transferee for value: Registration of Title Act 1964 ss.97-98. It is a requisition to the Registrar requiring notice to be given to the *cautioner* before registration of any dealing by the registered owner of specified land.

CBSI. [Chartered Building Societies Institute (qv)].

ceasing of power. Where an *adoptable power* (qv) ceases to be exercised by a building society, this fact must be annexed to its memorandum (qv): BS Act 1989, Second Schedule, Part I, para 4.

Central Bank. The Bank established to be the principal currency authority in the State and with regulatory functions in relation to banks and building societies: Central Bank Acts 1942 to 1989; BS Act 1989. The Bank is conducted and managed by a board of directors consisting of a Governor (qv) and other directors: Central Bank Act 1942 s.5 as amended by the Central Bank Act 1989 s.14.

The Bank is required to administer the system of regulation and supervision of building societies provided for by or under the BS Act 1989 with a view to (a) the protection by each society of the funds of its shareholders and depositors, and (b) the maintenance of the financial stability and well being of societies generally (ibid s.37). The Bank is required to include in its Annual Report, a report in relation to building societies.

The Bank has wide powers to control the exercise by building societies of their *adoptable powers* (qv) including: imposing conditions as to whom a service may be provided (eg to members (qv) or non-members); whether a service must be through a subsidiary or by the society itself; the amount of funds to be devoted to the activity; whether approval is required for individual investments; the qualifications of the personnel employed to provide the service; the keeping of separate accounting records; charges to be made for a service; arrangements to prevent conflicts of interests; and specifying general requirements relating to eg asset size, capital ratios etc, which a society must meet before it can exercise any particular power (ibid s.36). See CONFIDENTIALITY; DERIVATIVE ACTION; DISPUTES; GOVERNOR OF CENTRAL BANK; INDEMNIFY; REGISTRAR OF BUILDING SOCIETIES; WARRANTY.

certificate of incorporation. The certificate issued by the Central Bank to a building society when it registers the memorandum (qv) and rules (qv) of the society; a society is said to be incorporated on the issue of the certificate: BS Act 1989 s.10(1) and (3). A certificate of incorporation is sufficient evidence, unless the contrary is shown, that all the requirements of the Act in respect of registration have been complied with and that the society is duly registered and incorporated (ibid s.10(7)).

It has been held that the court has no power to declare a certificate of incorporation void on the ground that it has been obtained irregularly: Glover v Giles (1881) 18 Ch D 173. It has also been held that a mistake did not nullify the incorporation of the Irish Life Building Society under a similar section in previous legislation (BS Act 1976 s.11(7)) as the plaintiffs had failed to prove their case: Irish Permanent Building Society v Registrar of Building Societies (1981) ILRM 242. However, see

REGISTRATION, CANCELLATION OF. See AMALGAMATION; DOCUMENTS, PRESUMPTIONS AS TO; FORMATION; INCORPORATION. See also REGISTRATION AS COMPANY.

certificate of reasonable value. The certificate, granted by the Minister for the Environment, which the applicant for a specified loan from lending institutions, including local authorities, in respect of a new house, must furnish to the institution before the specified loan may be made: Housing (Miscellaneous Provisions) Act 1979 s.18. It is for the Minister to determine whether the price of the house represents reasonable value; there is an appeal to the Circuit Court from his decision not to issue a certificate (ibid s.18(3) and 18(5)).

A certificate is required to qualify for relief from stamp duty on conveyances, transfers and leases of newly erected houses or flats: Housing Act 1966 s.52. The Minister may issue a *certificate of exemption* if it appears to him that a new house is not being provided for sale. See also RSC O.101.

certificate of registration. The certificate which the Central Bank must send to an applicant building society when it registers a conversion scheme (qv) and conversion resolution (qv); the certificate is sufficient evidence, unless the contrary is proved, that the statutory requirements in relation to the conversion scheme have been complied with: BS Act 1989 s.104(5). See DOCUMENTS, PRESUMPTIONS AS TO. See also REGISTRATION CERTIFICATE.

cestui que vie. The person for whose lifetime another holds an estate or interest in land. See LIFE ESTATE.

chain of title. The instruments which show the successive conveyances from the original source to the present owner. See MARKETABLE TITLE.

chairman. Person who regulates the proceedings of a meeting. At a general meeting of a company, the chairman has the duty of ensuring that the business before the meeting is properly conducted. His rulings on points of order and related matters are deemed prima facie to be correct (see John v Rees [1970] Ch 345). He normally has a casting vote where there is an equality of votes; it has been held that the casting vote of a chairman who has been invalidly appointed is void: Clark v Workman (1920) 1 IR 107.

In a building society, the directors (qv) must appoint from among their number a chairman of the board of directors: BS Act 1989 s.48(3). The chairman must not also be the chief executive (qv) of the society except with the consent of the Central Bank (ibid s.48(4)). However, the chairman of a *special meeting* (qv) of a society, called to consider the affairs of the society, must be appointed by the Central Bank (ibid s.45(4)(b)). See INVESTIGATION; SPECIAL RESOLUTION.

charge. A form of security for the payment of a debt or performance of an obligation. A charge created by a company may be *fixed* or *floating*. Any charge purported to be created on the deposit maintained by a building society with the Central Bank, is void, except a charge created by the Bank: BS Act 1989 s.93(8). See DEPOSIT WITH CENTRAL BANK. See CHARGE, REGISTRATION OF; CHARGE ON LAND; FIXED CHARGE; FLOATING CHARGE; LIEN.

charge, registration of. The systems which exist to register charges on a person's property to enable others to determine the assets which are mortgaged. The systems often impute notice of the existence and the content of the charges registered. Special procedures exist for registering mortgages on land, mortgages on ships, farmers' chattle mortgages, and company charges. See Registration of Title Act 1964; Mercantile Marine Act 1955 s.50; Agricultural Credit Act 1978 s.26. See CHARGE ON LAND; FIXED CHARGE; FLOATING CHARGE; SEARCHES.

charge card. A card issued by a promoter to an individual having an address in the State by means of which goods, services or cash may be obtained by the individual, and amounts in respect of the goods, services or cash may be charged to the individual's account: Finance (No 2) Act 1981 s.17(2)(a). See FINANCIAL SERVICES.

charge on land. A charge which the registered owner of land can create to secure an advance of money; the charge must be registered as a charge on the land and the chargeant must be registered as the owner of the charge. The registered owner of the charge has all the powers of a mortgagee (qv) by deed within the meaning of the Conveyancing Acts: Registration of Title Act 1964 s.62.

It has been held that a provision in a deed of charge permitting the registered owner to take possession in the event of certain defaults of the chargor need not be registered on the folio separately from the deed of charge: Gale & Gale v First National Building Society (1985) IR 609.

The deposit of a certificate of charge, or of a land certificate (qv) has the same effect as the deposit of title deeds of unregistered land. Money charged on land in the State must be construed, unless otherwise described, as being in the currency of the State: Northern Bank v Edwards (1986) ILRM 167.

It is usual in a building society mortgage to have a provision whereby money paid by the society in completing unfinished buildings on the mortgaged property or in repairing or insuring the property will be a *charge* on the property. Also provision is usually made in such mortgages for money expended by the society as *attorney* for the borrower in certain landlord and tenant proceedings to be a charge on the property. See APPENDIX 5 - TYPICAL MORTGAGE clause 5(b), 8(i) and 12. See DEPOSIT OF TITLE DEEDS.

charities. Trusts in favour of legally *charitable objects*. Such trusts, unlike private trusts, are not subject to the rule against perpetuities (qv) and they do not fail for uncertainty.

A charity must confer a benefit on the public or on a sufficiently wide section of the public. Charitable objects are classified into four main divisions (a) relief of poverty; (b) advancement of education; (c) advancement of religion;(d) other charitable purposes: Income Tax Special Purposes Commissioners v Pemsel (1891) AC 531; Barrington's Hospital v Commissioner of Valuations (1957) IR 299.

The general administration of charities is the responsibility of the Commissioners of Charitable Donations and Bequests for Ireland, a statutory body, appointed by the government. See Charities Acts 1961 and 1973. See CY-PRES; DEPOSIT INTEREST RETENTION TAX; TRUST; TRUST CORPORATION.

Chartered Building Societies Institute. The professional institute, founded in the UK in 1934, to provide education and social activities for building society staff in order to promote the highest personal standards of competence and practice. The Institute was granted a Royal Charter in 1979 which provides for the Institute's services and activities to extend to persons concerned with the provision of finance for home ownership and the encouragement of personal savings.

A Republic of Ireland Centre of the Chartered Institute (the first outside the UK) was established on 24th February 1988 affiliated to the North-Western Group of the Institute. The Centre held seminars, meetings, and education courses in its inaugural year.

Membership of the Chartered Institute comprise: *subscribing members* who wish to maintain the benefits of contact with the Institute; *certificated members* who have successfully completed the "Certificate in Building Society Practice"; *students* who are studying for the "Associateship Examination"; *associates* (ACBSI) who have passed the "Associateship Examination"; and *fellows* (FCBSI) who are elected by the Council of the Institute from the senior *associates*. [CBSI, 19 Baldock Street, Ware, Hertfordshire SG12 9DH, UK].

chattel. Generally property other than freehold. *Chattels real* are leasehold and other interests in land which are less than freehold. *Chattels personal* are movable tangible articles of property eg goods (qv) and choses in possession (qv). See CHOSE; FURNITURE.

chattel mortgage. When used without qualification, it means an instrument under seal made between a recognised borrower of the one part and a recognised lender of the other part which is (a) a floating chattel mortgage, or (b) a specific chattel mortgage, or (c) both a floating and specific chattel mortgage: Agricultural Credit Act 1978 s.23(1). A *floating chattel mortgage* is an instrument under seal whereby the borrower charges stock from time to time on the borrower's land with the payment of any money advanced or to be advanced to the borrower. A *specific chattel mortgage* is one which charges specific stock (wherever situate). A register of chattel mortgages must be kept and maintained in every Circuit Court office (ibid s.26).

A registered specific chattel mortgage operates and has the effect of prohibiting the mortgagor from selling or otherwise transferring ownership or possession of the stock without giving notice in writing to the mortgagee, and of prohibiting the mortgagor from selling at less than a fair and reasonable price (ibid s.27). A registered floating chattel motgage creates an ambulatory and shifting charge on all stock the property of the mortgagor from time to time on the land to which the chattel mortgage relates (ibid s.30). Priority of chattel mortgages is in accordance to the times at which they are respectively registered (ibid s.34). See also Chattel Mortgages (Registration) Order 1928 (SR & O No 40 of 1928).

cheque. A bill of exchange (qv) drawn on a banker (or now a building society), payable on demand: Bills of Exchange Act 1882 s.73. The person making the cheque is the *drawer* and the person to whom it is payable is the *payee*. When a cheque bears across its face the words *and Company*, or any abbreviation thereof, between two parallel traverse lines, it is said to be *crossed generally*, and when it bears across its face the name of a banker, it is said to be *crossed specially* (ibid s.76).

A generally crossed cheque can be paid only through a bank (or now a building society) and a specially crossed cheque only through the bank so specified. A cheque which is crossed *not negotiable* cannot give to the transferee a better title than the holder of the cheque had (ibid s.81). It is not open to a drawer of a cheque to question the value of his own cheque: Private Motorists Provident Society v Moore (1987) HC.

The definition of *banker* in the Bills of Exchange Act 1882 s.2 has been amended to include a building society: BS Act 1989 s.126. This amendment is to permit building societies to provide a cheque service. The acceptance of deposits of money for current accounts (qv), the collection of cheques and the payment of cheques drawn on a society, are *financial services* (qv) which a society may be empowered to provide (ibid s.29(2)(f)). See also Cheques Act 1959. See ACCOUNT PAYEE; COLLECTION OF CHEQUES; DAYS OF GRACE; ENDORSEMENT; MONEY TRANSMISSION; NAME OF SOCIETY; PAYMENT; TRAVELLERS CHEQUES.

cheque, countermand of payment. Revocation by the drawer of the authority to pay a cheque. A banker (or building society) is liable if he wrongly pays a countermanded cheque. See Bills of Exchange Act 1882 s.75. See Reade v Royal Bank of Ireland (1922) 2 IR 22.

cheque, drawing of. Drawing a cheque implies three statements - (a) that the drawer has an account with that bank or building society, (b) that he has authority to draw on it for that amount, and (c) that the cheque, as drawn, is a valid order for that amount (ie that the present state of affairs is such that, in the ordinary course of events, the cheque will on its future presentation be duly honoured).

cheque, issue. A cheque is *issued* at the time of its first delivery complete in form to the person who takes it as a holder: Bills of Exchange Act 1882 s.2.

cheque, liability on. A banker (or building society) who pays a cheque drawn on him in good faith and in the ordinary course of business, is not liable to the true owner if an endorsement is forged: Bills of Exchange Act 1882 s.60; BS Act 1989 s.126. Also, where a banker pays the holder of a cheque, in good faith and without notice that the holder's title is defective, the payment is valid and the banker is entitled to debit the customer's account (ibid 1882 Act s.59).

In order to obviate the long established practice by which bankers refused to pay a cheque unless it was endorsed at the bank by the party presenting it, the law was changed in 1959 to provide that *where a banker in good faith and in the ordinary course of business pays a cheque drawn on him which is not endorsed, or is irregularly endorsed, he does not in doing so, incur any liability by reason only of the absence of, or irregularity in, endorsement, and he is deemed to have paid it in due course*: Cheques Act 1959 s.1.

A collecting banker is protected from liability to the true owner of a cheque where the banker receives payment of the cheque for a *customer*, who has no title, or a defective title to the cheque, provided the banker acts in good faith and without negligence: Cheques Act 1959 s.4. A collecting banker is also protected if he becomes a *holder for value* (qv) or an *holder in due course* (qv). See also CHEQUE, PRESENTMENT BY NOTIFICATION.

cheque, overdue. A cheque which has been in circulation for an unreasonable time. It can only be negotiated subject to any defect of title affecting it at its maturity. See Bills of Exchange Act 1882 s.36(2) and (3). See MATURITY.

cheque, post-dated. A cheque which bears a date subsequent to the actual date on which it was drawn, and issued before the date it bears. A cheque is not invalid by reason only that it is post-dated: Bills of Exchange Act 1882 s.13(2). See Royal Bank of Scotland v Tottenham (1894) 71 LT 168.

cheque, presentment by notification. Recent legislation provides for the presentment for payment by a collecting banker of a cheque *by notification* to the drawee banker of the *essential features of the cheque* other than by its physical presentment: Bills of Exchange Act 1882 s.45A, as inserted by the Central Bank Act 1989 s.132(c). Presentment by notification includes presentment by the transmission of an electronic message.

A cheque paid on presentment by notification is deemed to have been paid in the *ordinary course of business* but this does not relieve the collecting banker or the drawee banker from the liability they would have been subject to if the cheque had been physically presented for payment. The drawee banker can request the physical presentment of the cheque and this does not constitute *dishonour* of the cheque for non-payment.

The *essential features of the cheque* include: the serial number of the cheque; the identification code number of the drawee banker; the account number of the drawer of the cheque; and the amount of the cheque.

cheque, stale. A cheque which is *out of date* ie one bearing a date of twelve (or, in some cases, six) months prior to presentation. See London County Banking Co v Groome (1881) 8 QBD 288.

cheque card. A card issued by a bank (or building society) and presented with a cheque to a supplier of goods or services, who as a consequence is assured of payment by the bank to a stated maximum amount. The drawer of the cheque represents that he has authority from the bank to use the card so as to oblige the bank to honour the cheque. See Metropolitan Police Comr v Charles (1977) AC 177.

chief executive. The person appointed by the board of directors of a building society, who is responsible under the immediate authority of the board, for the conduct of the business of the society: BS Act 1989 s.49. A society must have a chief executive but the offices of chief executive and that of secretary may not be held by the same person except with the consent of the Central Bank (ibid s.49(2)); a similar prohibition applies in the case of chief executive and chairman (ibid s.48(4)). Where the chief executive is also a director he may be referred to as the managing director (ibid s.49(7)), and, unlike other directors, he is not required to retire as a director every three years (ibid s.50(10)). See CONTRACT OF SERVICE; DIRECTOR'S EMPLOYMENT CONTRACT; DIRECTORS, REGISTER OF; DISQUALIFICATION; FINANCIAL STATE-

MENT, SUMMARY; OFFICER.

chief office. A building society is required to have an office in the State (to be known as its *chief office*) to which all communications and notices (qv) may be addressed: BS Act 1989 s.15. Notice of any decision to change the location of the chief office must be sent by the society to the Central Bank. The manner in which a society may change its chief office must be provided for in its rules (qv) (ibid Second Schedule, Part II, para 5(b)). See NAME OF SOCIETY.

chose. A thing. A *chose in possession* is a movable chattel in the custody or control of the owner or the right to which can be enforced by taking physical possession eg of one's own goods. A *chose in action* is a right of proceeding in law to procure the payment of a sum of money or to recover pecuniary damages for a wrong inflicted or the non-performance of a contract. A *legal chose in action* is a right of action which could be enforced in a court of law eg debts; an *equitable chose in action* is a right which formerly could only be enforced in a court of chancery eg an interest in a trust.

Circuit Court. The court above the District Court (qv) in the hierarchical system of courts. The country is divided into eight circuits; a Circuit Court judge is assigned to each circuit and travels to several towns in that circuit to hear cases, sitting alone in civil cases and with a jury in criminal cases when the accused is so entitled. There are permanent circuit courts in Dublin and Cork. On civil matters, the court can award damages of up to £15,000; it can deal with proceedings relating to the execution of trusts where the trust estate (in so far as it relates to land), does not exceed £200 rateable valuation. On criminal matters the Circuit Court hears *indictable* (qv) offences sent to it by the District Court.

Where the rules of a building society so provide, the Circuit Court may hear and determine a dispute between a member and the society, arising out of the rules (qv) of the society or provisions of the BS Act 1989, which determination is final and binding on the parties, but the court may, at the request of a party to the dispute, state a case to the High Court on a point of law (ibid s.91(2)). See CERTIFICATE OF REASONABLE VALUE; DISPUTES.

circular. See ADVERTISEMENT.

clog on equity of redemption. The equitable doctrine which does not permit the equity of redemption (qv) to be fettered or unreasonably restricted by any provision which would make it difficult for the mortgagor (qv) to redeem a mortgage after the date for repayment of the mortgage debt.

close. Enclosed land. See WAY, RIGHT OF.

coinage. See LEGAL TENDER.

co-ownership. The concurrent ownership of two or more persons in the same property. See JOINT TENANCY; TENANCY IN COMMON.

collection of cheques. The charges imposed by the holder of a banking licence on a building society which has an authorisation (qv) is subject to the approval of the Central Bank: Central Bank Act 1971 s.26 as amended by the BS Act 1989 s.29(5). See CHEQUE.

collection of rent. See SERVICES RELATING TO LAND.

commencement. The time at which an Act, regulation, statutory instrument, or section or part thereof, comes into operation.

Provision is made in the BS Act 1989 for the Act to come into operation on such day or days as may be fixed by order of the Minister, either generally or with reference to a particular purpose or provision, and different days may be so fixed (ibid s.1(2)). See also Interpretation Act 1937 s.12 sch. See APPENDIX 2, P.177.

commercial purposes. A building society is empowered, subject to having adopted the power by special resolution and recorded in its memorandum (qv), to acquire, hold, dispose of and develop or participate in the development of land where the land is to be used for *commercial purposes*: BS Act 1989 ss.21(1) and 36. See ADOPTABLE POWERS; DEVELOPING LAND.

commission. The remuneration of an agent or an employee.

As regards auctioneer's commission, the test applied by the court in relation to a dispute over commission is whether the event contracted for by the principal actually happened and whether the agent was the cause of the happening. It has been held that a *sole agent* is not entitled to commission where the exertions of the sole agent had not played any part in effecting a sale and the agency agreement did not contain any express term prohibiting the principal from negotiating a sale during the continuance of the agency: Murphy, Buckley & Keogh Ltd v Pye (Ireland) Ltd (1971) IR 57.

As regards insurance, recent legislation empowers the Minister for Industry and Commerce to reduce the commissions paid to insurance intermediaries (qv), where he is of the opinion that these are excessive: Insurance Act 1989 s.37. He is also empowered to prohibit, by order, commission payments in the form of benefits-in-kind or loans (ibid s.38). A life assurance policy which is in contravention of these provisions is voidable at the instance of the policyholder within one month of conviction of the insurer and the premium will be refunded together with interest (ibid s.42).

As regards a building society, a commission includes any gift, bonus, fee, payment or other benefit: BS Act 1989 s.2(1). Any person who is engaged by a society in making reports on the value of securities or in connection with the assessment of the adequacy of securities or the authorisation of the making of loans must not accept any commission for or in connection with any loan made by the society (ibid s.25(4)). A person is disqualified from authorising the making of a loan, who receives a commission for introducing the parties, or who has a financial interest (qv) in the disposition (ibid s.25(3)). Proceedings were initiated by the DPP in relation to mortgage commissions under the repealed enactments (qv), resulting in the acquittal of the person charged: Report of Registrar of Building Societies (1982) p.9 and (1984) p.10. See also ASSESSMENT OF SECURITY; VALUATION OF SECURITY.

committee of inspection. See LIQUIDATOR; WINDING UP OF SOCIETY.

common. A right of common is the right to take some part of any natural product of the land or water belonging to another. It may be created by grant or claimed by prescription (qv). The principal rights of common are: pasture, piscary, estovers and turbary (qqv).

common, tenancy in. See TENANCY IN COMMON.

communication with members. Where a member of a building society wishes to communicate with other members on a subject relating to its affairs, he may request the board of directors of the society to transmit information to other members, and the board is required to comply with the request where it is satisfied, having regard to the interests of members as a whole and to other relevant circumstances, that the request is made in good faith: BS Act 1989 s.65(4)(a). The applicant is liable for any costs incurred by the society in complying with the request and the society may require the applicant to give security for payment of costs (ibid s.65(4)(b)).

A decision on the request must be notified to the applicant within one month from the day of receipt and the grounds for a refusal given, if that be the case (ibid s.65(5)). An appeal (by way of referral) lies against a refusal to the Central Bank (ibid s.65(5) and (7)). See also MEMBERS, REGISTER OF.

company. An association of persons formed for the purpose of some business or undertaking, carried on in the name of the association, each member having the right to assign his shares to any other person, subject to the regulations of the company. Companies are either incorporated or unincorporated. An *unincorporated* company has no existence separate from its members who are individually liable for its debts without limit eg a partnership. An *incorporated* company is a legal entity distinct from its members. Companies are incorporated (1) by charter (2) by statute and (3) by registration.

Companies are limited or unlimited, depending on whether the liabilities of their shareholders is limited or not. A *limited* company may be either a *private* company or a *public* company. A private limited company must include *limited* or *teoranta* in its name. A public limited company must include *public limited company* or *cuideachta phoibli theoranta* in its name. The transferability of the shares of a private limited company is restricted but is not restricted in the case of a public limited company. A private company must have at least two members whereas the minimum number in a public company is seven.

The statute law relating to companies is mainly contained in the Companies Act 1963 and the Companies Amendment Acts 1977, 1982, 1983, and 1986; Stock Transfer Act 1963; Registration of Business Names Act 1963; Mergers, Take-Overs and Monopolies Control Act 1978. There is provision in the BS Act 1989 by which a building society may convert itself into a public limited company (plc). See COMPANY, PUBLIC LIMITED.

company law, application of. See REGULATIONS; SUBSIDIARY; WINDING UP.

company, public limited. [plc]. A public company limited by shares with a minimum of seven members, which complies with specific requirements of the Companies Acts. To become and remain a plc, the company must have a minimum authorised share capital of at least £30,000; at least one-quarter of the nominal amount must have been paid up on its issued share capital, together with any premium on its shares; it must not have allocated any shares it offered for subscription when the offer was *under-subscribed*; it must not have allocated shares for service contracts, or for contracts that can be performed more than five years from the allotment date; an independent valuation must have been made of non-cash consideration transferred in order to acquire shares in it, and of major transactions between it and its first members during its first two years' commercial existence; shares taken by its subscribers must have been paid for in cash; any lien or other charge on its own shares is void; and it may not pay a dividend if it is insolvent in that its net assets are less than its called up share capital and its undistributed reserves: Companies Amendment Act 1983 ss.5(2), 17(1), 19(1), 22, 26(2), 28-35, 44 and 46.

There is provision in the BS Act 1989 by which a building society may convert itself into a public limited company (plc). See CONVERSION.

compensation. A payment to make amends for loss or injury to person or property, or to compensate for some deprivation. There are provisions in the BS Act 1989 requiring disclosure of the compensation to be paid to a director or other officer of a society in the event of an *amalgamation* with another society, or the *transfer of engagements* to another society, or on a *conversion* of a society to a public limited company. There are also provisions to provide by regulation for compensation to be paid to persons arising from the provision by societies of auctioneering and conveyancing services. The Registrar of Building Societies has prepared guidelines on payments to directors for loss of office: Report of Registrar (1984) p.13. See AMALGAMATION; AUCTIONEERING SERVICE; CONVERSION RESOLUTION; CONVEYANCING; REMUNERATION OF DIRECTOR; TRANSFER OF ENGAGEMENTS.

complaints. The Minister for the Environment may, by regulations, require a building society to establish or join in establishing a scheme or schemes for the investigation of complaints against the society or any of its subsidiaries or other associated bodies in relation to a prescribed matter of complaint: BS Act 1989 s.92. It is intended that such a scheme, if established, would be to deal primarily with complaints concerning the services provided by a society, rather than disputes between a member and his society, for which there is separate provision. See DISPUTES.

compound interest. For compound interest to be chargeable, provision for such interest must be provided for in the mortgage deed: Eastern Counties Building Society v Russell (1947) 1 All ER 500. It is now general practice for building societies to carry forward annually, the total outstanding indebtedness of the borrower in one sum (which may include arrears in accrued interest) and to charge the borrower with interest on that one sum for the ensuing account period, which arrangement may include an element of compound interest. See APPENDIX 5 - TYPICAL MORTGAGE clause 3(d); INTEREST.

compulsory acquisition. See COMPULSORY PURCHASE.

compulsory purchase. The power given by statute to certain bodies to acquire land compulsorily eg local authorities and health boards. It is usual for a building society mortgage to require the borrower to assign to the society the benefit of any compensation arising from the compulsory purchase of the mortgaged property. It is also usual for the principal money advanced by the society and remaining unpaid to become due forthwith on such compulsory purchase. See APPENDIX 5 - TYPICAL MORTGAGE clause 5(c)(iii) and (d). See also POWER OF ATTORNEY.

computer. See BANKERS' BOOKS; FALSIFICATION; RECORDS.

conacre. A licence to enter land and to till the land, sow crops and reap the harvest. Such a licences does not create the relationship of landlord and tenant.

concert party. See SUCCESSOR COMPANY.

concessions. It is usual to have a provision in a building society mortgage whereby any *concessions* granted by the society as regards the payment of any money by instalment or otherwise will not affect the power of sale or other powers provided by the mortgage or by statute or otherwise eg see APPENDIX 5 - TYPICAL MORTGAGE clause 14.

concurrent ownership. The co-ownership of two or more persons in the same property. See JOINT TENANCY; TENANCY IN COMMON.

conditions of sale. The terms under which a purchaser is to take property sold by auction. The usual terms state: the number of years title to be shown; the title which is to be a good *root of title* (qv); the time within which *requisitions on title* are to be made; the rescission by the vendor on onerous conditions being made; the deposit and conditions for forfeiture; the compensation for misdescription; the payment of the purchase money and the interest thereon. It is usual to adopt the standard form of conditions issued by the Incorporated Law Society. See AUCTION SALES; SALE OF LAND.

Confederation of Irish Industry. See FINANCIAL SERVICES INDUSTRY ASSOCIATION.

confidentiality. Disclosure of confidential information may amount to a breach of contract where so provided in such a contract. In the absence of contract, the donee of confidential information may be under a duty, in equity, not to use that information to the donor's detriment. There is no absolute confidentiality where the parties concerned are a government and a private individual: The AG for England and Wales v Brandon Books (1987) ILRM 135. See also House of Spring Gardens v Point Blank (1984) IR 611.

There is a prohibition on the disclosure of any information concerning the business of any building society or its subsidiaries (qv) or associated companies; the prohibition is placed on the Governor, a Director, officer or servant of the Central Bank, in relation to any information which may come to his knowledge by reason of his office or employment unless such disclosure is to enable the Bank to carry out its functions: BS Act 1989 s.44.

Exceptions are made in respect of certain specified disclosures eg where required by a court in connection with criminal proceedings; where made with the consent of the person to whom the information relates; where made in a manner so framed as not to enable information relating to any particular body or person to be ascertained from it; where made to an institution of the European Communities for the purpose of the State's membership (ibid s.44(2)).

Exceptions are also provided in the case of the *conversion* of a building society into a public limited company (ibid s.107(2)(g)(i)). For further provisions regarding building societies and confidentiality, see BANKER AND

CONFIDENTIALITY; DATA PROTECTION. See also APPENDIX I.

confidential communications. Communications which are privileged from disclosure or discovery eg professional communications between counsel or solicitor and client. See PRIVILEGE, LEGAL PROFESSIONAL.

confirmation of conversion scheme. See CONVERSION SCHEME, CONFIRMATION OF.

conflict of interest. See AUCTIONEERING SERVICE; CENTRAL BANK; CONVEYANCING.

connected person. A person is *connected* with a director of a building society if he is (a) that director's spouse, parent, brother, sister or child, or (b) a body corporate with which the director is associated, or (c) a trustee of a trust whose beneficiaries include the director, his spouse or any of his children, or (d) a person acting as partner of the director or of any person who is connected to the director: BS Act 1989 s.52(1). A director is *associated* with a body corporate where he owns one-fifth of that body's equity share capital or controls the exercise of more than one-fifth of its voting power (ibid s.52(2)). A child includes a step-child. See DISCLOSURE OF INTEREST; GUARANTEE AND DIRECTOR; PAYMENT ON BEHALF OF DIRECTOR; PROPERTY TRANSACTIONS.

consideration. Some valuable benefit received by a party who gives a promise (*promisor*) or performs an act, or some detriment suffered by a party who receives a promise (*promisee*). *Some right, interest, profit or benefit accruing to one party, or some forbearance, detriment, loss, or responsibility given, suffered or undertaken by the other*: Currie v Misa (1875) 10 Ex 153. Consideration is necessary to the validity of every *simple contract*, including those in writing. Consideration must be *real*; it need not be adequate to the promise, but it must have some ascertainable value. Consideration must be *legal*. Consideration must move from the promisee; a person may be a party to a contract but a stranger to the consideration.

Consideration may be *executed* or *executory* but not *past*. Consideration is *executed* when the act constituting the consideration is performed; consideration is *executory* when it is in the form of a promise to be performed at a future date. A *past* consideration is one which is wholly executed and finished before the promise is made. For consideration to support a bill of exchange, see HOLDER FOR VALUE. See CONTRACT; VALUABLE CONSIDERATION.

consolidation of mortgages. The equitable doctrine that a mortgagee (qv) who holds two or more mortgages made by the same mortgagor (qv) on different properties, can consolidate them into one and refuse to be redeemed as to one without payment of what is due to him on all. The time for repayment on the mortgages being consolidated must have passed.

However a restriction on consolidation is imposed by s.17(1) of the Conveyancing Act 1881 but the restriction does not apply where a contrary intention is expressed in the mortgage deed. It is common practice to have a provision in building society mortgages excluding the application of s.17 and providing that the mortgage is to be a security for all moneys owing by the borrower to the society, now or hereafter from time to time, and that no property held by the society as security for the moneys advanced will be released or discharged until the whole of the moneys owing has been repaid eg see APPENDIX 5 - TYPICAL MORTGAGE clause 10.

It has been held that the rules of a building society may provide that the mortgagor will not be entitled to redeem a security without at the same time redeeming every other security held by the society: Andrews v City Permanent Building Society (1881) 44 LT 641. Consolidation may also apply where more than two mortgages exist, but it does not necessarily follow that the right to consolidate can be invoked as between each and every one of the mortgages: Huges v Britannia Permanent Benefit Building Society (1906) 2 Ch 607.

consumer, dealing as. A party to a contract is said to *deal as a consumer* in relation to another party if (a) he neither makes the contract in the course of a business nor holds himself out as doing so, and (b) the other party does make the contract in the course of a business, and (c) the goods or services supplied under or in pursuance of the contract are of a type ordinarily supplied for private use or consumption: SGSS Act 1980 s.3. A buyer dealing as a consumer is given the protection of certain implied conditions which cannot be excluded.

A buyer is not regarded as dealing as consumer on a sale by competitive tender, or a sale by auction of goods of a type or by or on behalf of a person of a class, defined by the Minister for Industry & Commerce. It is for those claiming that a party does not deal as consumer to show that he does not (ibid s.3(3)). See O'Callaghan v Hamilton Leasing (Ireland) Ltd (1984) ILRM 146; Cunningham v Woodchester Investment Ltd (1984) HC.

contingent. Something which awaits or depends on the happening of an event. See LIABILITY; LIQUID ASSETS.

contingent remainder. A remainder (qv) where the grantee is unascertained or where the title depends on the occurrence of a specified event eg *to A (a bachelor) for life, remainder to his first child to reach 21 years.* A contingent remainder is saved if it is one which can be treated as a legal remainder and if it does not offend against the rule against perpetuities: Contingent Remainders Act 1877. Contingent remainders are alienable *inter vivos* by deed: Real Property Act 1845 s.6; and are devisable by will: Succession Act 1965 s.76. See PERPETUITIES, RULE AGAINST.

contra proferentem. The doctrine that the construction least favourable to the person putting forward an instrument should be adopted against him, provided that this works no wrong. This doctrine has been used in contracts of insurance to lighten the effects of a non-disclosure of material facts; ambiguous expressions will be held against those using them: In re Sweeney & Kennedy Arbitration (1950) IR 85. See also Brady v Irish National Insurance (1986) ILRM 669.

contract. A legally binding agreement. A *speciality contract* is one which is in writing and is sealed and delivered; it is also known as a *deed* or a *contract under seal.* A *simple contract* is one which is not under seal; all simple contracts require *consideration* (qv) to support them. A contract by deed does not require consideration to support it.

An *implied contract* arises from the assumed intention of the parties. A *quasi-contract* arises by operation of law, irrespective of the intention of the parties. A *contract of record* arises from obligations imposed by a court of record eg a recognisance.

References in contracts and other instruments to the payment of money are references to Irish pounds unless some other currency is specified: Central Bank Act 1989 s.25.

contract, disclosure of interest in. See DISCLOSURE OF INTEREST.

contract for services. A contract with an independent contractor ie a person who contracts to perform a particular task for another and is not under the other person's control as to the manner in which the task is performed. An employer is not normally liable for the *torts* of an independent contractor, unless the employer has been negligent himself eg in supervising the work. The distinction between an employee (qv) and an independent contractor is important in relation to taxation, social welfare and employment protection legislation. See Walshe v Baileboro Co-operative (1939) 73 ILTR 232; Lynch v Palgrave Murphy (1964) IR 150.

As regards building societies and contract for services, see DIRECTOR'S EMPLOYMENT CONTRACT.

contract of employment. A contract of employment may generally be created by deed, or be in writing or be verbal. In certain employments, the employer is required to give to each employee a written statement setting out the conditions under which he is employed: Minimum Notice and Terms of Employment Act 1973 s.9. A contract of employment in restraint of trade is generally void. See CONTRACT OF SERVICE; DIRECTOR'S EMPLOYMENT CONTRACT; EMPLOYEE.

contract of service. A contract of employment. A building society is required to keep at its chief office (qv) a register containing a copy of the *contract of service* of each director who has such a contract with the society or with a subsidiary (qv); the provision does not apply to any contract which has less than 3 years to run or which can be terminated by the society within 3 years without payment of compensation: BS Act 1989 s.55. Where the contract of service is not in writing, a memorandum setting out the terms of the contract must be kept in the register. Every such copy and memorandum must be open to the inspection of any member of the society without charge (ibid s.55(3)). See also DIRECTOR'S EMPLOYMENT CONTRACT; EMPLOYEE. See APPENDIX I.

contravention. Includes failure to comply: BS Act 1989 s.2(1). See OFFENCES.

contribution. Payment of a proportionate share of a liability which has been borne by one, or some only, of a number of persons liable eg where there are a number of insurance policies in respect of a particular risk and one insurer pays out on that risk, he may bring an action against the other insurers for a rateable contribution.

contributory. Every person liable to contribute to the assets of a company in the event of the company being wound up. As regards a building society, see OFFICER; WINDING UP.

controlled dwelling. A house which is subject to statutory rent control, let as a separate dwelling, or a part so let, of any house, whether or not the tenant shares with any other persons any portion thereof or any accommodation, amenity or facility in connection therewith: Housing (Private Rented Dwellings) Act 1982.

For such a dwelling to be subject to control, there must be a letting of not greater than year to year. There is no control where the rateable valuation exceeds certain limits; where the dwelling is erected on or after 7th May 1941 or let by local authorities or furnished; or is subject to a service letting, or where let bona fide for *temporary convenience* or to meet a temporary necessity; or in certain cases where it is a separate and self-contained flat. See also Housing (Private Rented Dwellings) Act 1983.

The amount of the landlord's income is only a relevant factor in determining the tenant's rent if the landlord seeks to make it so: Quirke v Folio Homes (1987) SC. See RSC O.112. See Housing (Rent Tribunal) Regulations 1983 and 1988 (SIs 222 of 1983 and 140 of 1988).

conversion. A building society may convert itself into a *public company limited by shares* (a plc) by approving a conversion scheme (qv) by a conversion resolution (qv); by obtaining *confirmation* of the Central Bank to the conversion scheme; and by having the society registered as a company under the Companies Acts and the provisions of the BS Act 1989 (ibid s.101(1)-(2)).

A society proposing to convert must consult with the Bank at least 6 months prior to the moving of a conversion resolution (ibid s.101(4)). The conversion scheme must be confirmed by the Bank and there is provision by which a petition may be made to the High Court to cancel a conversion scheme. The Minister for the Environment is empowered to make further provision by regulations in relation to the conversion of a society into a company (ibid s.108).

In April 1989, the second largest building society in the UK, Abbey National, with £34,000m in assets and 8.2m members, became the first building society in the UK to vote in favour of conversion into a plc pursuant to the UK BS Act 1986. The conversion, which included an offer of 100 free shares to members, was unsuccessfully opposed by an association of members named the Abbey Members Against Floatation.

In November 1986, South Africa's largest building society, United, with assets of R12,000 (IR£3,300m), became the first society to demutualise in that country pursuant to its Equity BS Act 1986; United has since been listed on the Johannesburg Stock Exchange as UBS Holdings. This conversion did not include any free shares; the scheme offered all members with a minimum of R1000 (IR£270) in their share account at a qualifying date the right to purchase one share at a price of R2 per share for every R10 in their account, subject to a minimum of 100 shares; 71% of the qualifying members took up their entitlement and this represented 90% of the capital raised. Other South African societies to convert have been the Natal, the Allied, and the Saambou. See REGISTER OF MEMBERS, COMPANY; REGISTRATION AS COMPANY; STAMP DUTIES.

conversion date. The date on which a building society becomes converted and is registered as a company: BS Act 1989 s.100.

conversion grant. See LEASE FOR

LIVES RENEWABLE FOREVER.

conversion resolution. A resolution of a building society which has been passed by a majority of such members of the society as, being entitled to do so, vote in person or by proxy (qv) on a poll on the resolution at a meeting of the society of which notice specifying the intention to move the resolution as a *conversion resolution* has been duly given: BS Act 1989 ss.2(1) and 71. There is provision also for a *postal ballot* (qv) on a conversion resolution (ibid s.71(1)(b)).

A *conversion scheme*, wherein a society proposes to convert itself into a public limited company, must be approved by a conversion resolution, in which *borrowing members* (qv) have a right to vote along with other members (ibid s.101).

Before a conversion resolution is moved, a statement, the contents of which have been approved by the Central Bank, must be sent by the society to every member entitled to notice of the meeting (ibid s.103). The statement must, inter alia:- summarise in sufficient detail the proposals and the reasons for conversion; specify any proposed changes in the principal activities of the society and its policy in relation to the making of loans and the determination of the rate of interest; state the financial position of the society and its subsidiaries; state the interest (if any) of the officers of the society in the conversion and any compensation payable; and state that a copy of the conversion scheme (qv) may be obtained free of charge from the society. See CONVERSION SCHEME; JOINT BORROWER, REPRESENTATIVE; NOTICE OF RESOLUTIONS; VOTING.

conversion scheme. A scheme drawn up by the board of directors of a building society for the conversion of the society into a public limited company: BS Act 1989 s.100. The conversion scheme must be approved by the Central Bank and must, inter alia, state the name of the proposed *successor company* (qv), its proposed authorised and issued share capital; the names of its first directors and auditors; the entitlement of members of the society to shares or to subscribe for shares; the changes proposed to the society's investments in its subsidiaries (qv) or associated bodies (qv); the terms on which shareholdings of members of the society will be held as deposits by the successor company; the terms of any distribution of funds of the society in connection with the conversion; and the rights of members of the society to a distribution of the assets of the company in the event of it being wound up within 5 years of the conversion date (qv) (ibid s.101(3)-(5)).

The right of members of a society to acquire shares in the successor company or to any distribution of the funds of the society is restricted to members who held shares in the society throughout the two years prior to notice being given to members of the conversion resolution (qv) (ibid s.101(6)). This provision, which applies to persons who became members after 21st December 1988, must be included as a term of the conversion scheme. See CONVERSION.

conversion scheme, cancellation of. The High Court may on a petition being made to the Court, make an order confirming or cancelling a conversion scheme (qv) on such terms as it thinks fit;

however, in exercising its power, it must have regard only to the rights and interests of the members of the society, or any class of them: BS Act 1989 s.105(5)-(6).

The petition may be made (a) by not less than 100 members who were qualified to vote on the conversion resolution (qv) approving the conversion scheme, or (b) with the approval of the Court, by any member of the society (ibid s.105(1)). The petition must be made within one month after the date the Central Bank published notice of its registration of the conversion scheme (ibid s.105(2)). Also any appeal from the High Court order must be made within one month from the date of perfection of the order (ibid s.105(7)). See VOTING.

conversion scheme, confirmation of. The Central Bank must confirm a conversion scheme (qv) on the application of a building society made within 14 days of the meeting at which the society approved the scheme, unless it is of the opinion that (a) confirmation would be contrary to the public interest, or (b) some information material to the member's decision was not made available to all the members eligible to vote, or (c) some relevant requirement of this Act or of the rules was not fulfilled, or (d) there is a substantial risk that the successor company (qv) will not be granted a *banking licence* (qv) under the Central Bank Act 1971 s.9: BS Act 1989 s.104. See CERTIFICATE OF REGISTRATION. See also CONVERSION SCHEME, CANCELLATION OF.

conveyance. The transfer of the ownership of property; the instrument effecting the transfer. The deed of conveyance will contain the date, names of the parties, narrative recitals or introductory recitals, testatum, operative clause, parcels, habendum, and testimonium (qqv). The Law Reform Commission has proposed changes in the law to simplify conveyancing, including reducing the period of title which has to be investigated from 40 to 20 years: Ninth Report of LRC (1986/87). See MARKETABLE TITLE; OVERREACHING CONVEYANCE; VOLUNTARY CONVEYANCE.

conveyancing services. Conveyancing for any fee, gain or reward is primarily restricted to solicitors (qv): Solicitors Act 1954 s.58. However, the Minister for Justice is empowered to make regulations authorising building societies to provide conveyancing services: BS Act 1988 s.31(1). *Conveyancing services* are the preparation of transfers, conveyances, contracts, leases or other assurances in connection with the disposition or acquisition of estates or interests in land (ibid s.31(13)). Except in a conveyance by way of mortgage, a society will not be permitted to provide conveyancing services to both the disponer and the disponee in the one conveyance thereby providing a ban on a society acting for both the vendor and purchaser of property.

Provision is made for the regulations to deal with other matters eg other potential conflicts of interest; the availability of compensation for negligence, fraud or other dishonesty; and the extent to which societies will be required to employ solicitors to provide the conveyancing services. Also societies will be required to maintain separate accounting records for the conveyancing services and to ensure that the income from the services is not less than sufficient to meet its costs (ibid s.31(12)). A statement attesting the correctness of these accounts must be signed and attached to the annual accounts (qv). See BELOW COST SELLING; BUSINESS ASSOCIATE; LINKING SERVICES; PRIVILEGE. See also APPENDIX 2.

co-option. The directors of a building society may, if its rules (qv) so provide, co-opt as a director to fill any vacancy on the board of directors, any person who appears to them to be fit and proper to be a director, and who is not otherwise disqualified: BS Act 1989 ss.50(11) and 64. The person however must not have failed to be elected at any director election held within the preceding 16 months. A society is required to notify the Central Bank of the proposed co-option of persons as directors as least 14 days before the date of appointment (ibid s.50(15)). See DIRECTOR, APPOINTMENT OF; DIRECTOR, RETIREMENT OF.

corporeal property. Property which is visible or tangible eg land and goods. See OWNERSHIP.

corresponding membership rights. See ASSOCIATED BODY.

counterpart. A lease is generally prepared in two identical forms, one called a lease and the other a counterpart, the lease being signed by the lessor and the counterpart by the lessee and then exchanged and signed. The contents of a lease may be proved by its counterpart: Deasy's Act 1860 s.23. See Jagoe v Harrington (1882) 10 LR Ir 335.

covenant. A clause, usually in a deed, which binds a party to do some act or to refrain from doing some act. No technical words are necessary to constitute a covenant: Lant v Norris (1757) 1 Burr 287.

Covenants in building society mortgages usually include (a) to repay the loan by instalments of principal and interest; (b) to repair and maintain the premises; (c) to retain adequate insurance cover; (d) not to let the property without the consent of the society; and (e) where the property is a leasehold interest, to observe and perform the terms and conditions of the lease. See Municipal Permanent Investment Building Society v Smith (1888) 22 QBD 70. See APPENDIX 5 - TYPICAL MORTGAGE clause 3, 5, 7(c)(iii), and 8.

Usual covenants in a lease refer to the covenant of the landlord that the tenant will have quiet enjoyment; and refer to the covenants of the tenant to pay the rent and rates; to keep the premises in repair and to deliver them up at the end of the tenancy in good repair; to permit the landlord to enter and inspect the premises from time to time. *Restrictive* covenants in certain leases, absolutely prohibiting a change in use or improvements, are to be construed as prohibiting same without the licence or consent of the lessor, which shall not be unreasonably withheld: Landlord and Tenant (Amendment) Act 1980 ss.64-69. There may be a refusal of consent based on valid estate management grounds: OHS Ltd v Green Property Co Ltd (1986) ILRM 451.

A covenant is said to *run with the land* when the advantage or liability of it passes to the assignee of the land. Covenants may be registered as burdens affecting registered land: Registration of Title Act 1964 s.69. See also Deasy's Act 1860 ss.41-42. See also Belmont Securities Ltd v Crean (1989) ILT & SJ 22.

cover note. A document issued by an insurer to the insured covering risks until issue of a policy of insurance. It is a separate contract distinct from the policy and is usually operative for a specific period. See Mackie v European Assurance Society (1869) 21 LT 102.

credit. The time which a creditor allows his debtor to pay a debt; the total amount he permits the debtor to borrow or to owe.

credit, letter of. See LETTER OF CREDIT.

credit, provision of. Arranging the provision of credit, including the joining of credit card companies, is a *financial service* (qv) which a building society may be empowered to provide: BS Act 1989 s.29(2)(a). See FINANCIAL SERVICES.

credit by fraud, obtaining. The misdemeanour (qv) committed by a person who, in incurring any debt or liability, has obtained credit under false pretences, or by means of any other fraud: Debtors (Ireland) Act 1872 s.13(1). It is also an offence for a *bankrupt* or *arranging debtor*, to obtain credit without disclosing the fact that he is a bankrupt or arranging debtor: Bankruptcy Act 1988 s.129.

credit card. A credit instrument issued to an individual by a bank (qv) or other body by means of which cash, goods or services may be obtained by the individual on credit on production of the instrument, the issuer undertaking to pay the supplier of the cash, goods or services in return for payment to him (the issuer) by the individual. A credit card is also a card issued by a bank to an individual having an address in the State whereby the amounts in respect of the goods, services and cash supplied may be charged to the account of the individual: Finance (No 2) Act 1981 s.17(1)(a). See Diners Club Ltd v Revenue Commissioners (1987) HC; Eurocard International v Controller of Trade Marks (1987) HC. See CREDIT, PROVISION OF.

credit instruments. See DISCOUNTING.

credit transfer system. The activity of a credit transfer system is a *financial serive* (qv) which a building society may be empowered to provide: BS Act 1989 s.29(2)(p).

creditor. A person to whom a debt is owing. A *secured creditor* is one who holds a mortgage (qv), or charge (qv), or lien (qv) on the debtor's property. An *unsecured creditor* is one who does not so hold. A *judgment creditor* is a person in whose favour a judgment for a sum of money has been entered against the debtor. See DISQUALIFICATION ORDER; DISTRIBUTION OF ASSETS; FALSE INFORMATION; JUDGMENT CREDITOR; OFFICER; SECURITY FOR COSTS.

crossing of cheque. See CHEQUE.

crystallisation. See FLOATING CHARGE.

cuideachta phoibli theoranta. cpt. [Public limited company (qv)].

cumann foirgniochta. [Building society (qv)].

currency. See LEGAL TENDER.

currency exchange rates. See HEDGE.

current account. A running account kept between parties with debits and credits eg a current banking account. The acceptance of deposits of money for current accounts is a *financial service* (qv) which a building society may be empowered to provide: BS Act 1989 s.29(2)(f).

curtilage. A courtyard, garden, yard, field, or piece of ground lying near and belonging to a dwellinghouse.

cy-pres. [As near]. The doctrine by which a trust, which discloses a general charitable intention, will not be permitted to fail because the particular mode of application specified by the testator cannot be carried out; the law will substitute another mode *cy-pres*, that is, as near as possible to the mode specified by the testator. See CHARITIES.

D

data protection. The statutory protection provided to protect the privacy of individuals with regard to automated personal data; it entitles individuals to establish the existence of automated *personal data* kept in relation to them, to have access to the data (with some exceptions), and to have inaccurate data rectified or erased: Data Protection Act 1988 ss.3-6.

Various obligations are imposed on persons who keep automated personal data eg that the data must be accurate, be kept for lawful purposes, not be disclosed in any manner incompatible with those purposes and be protected by adequate security measures (ibid s.2). Persons keeping such data, ie data controllers (qv) and data processors (qv), owe a *duty of care* to the data subjects (qv) concerned to the extent that the law of *torts* (qv) does not already provide (ibid s.7).

The legislation provides for the appointment of a Data Protection Commissioner. Certain categories of persons and bodies who keep personal data are required to register with the Commissioner eg those who keep particularly sensitive data (political opinions, health, criminal convictions etc), the public sector and financial institutions (ibid s.16 and Third Schedule).

The legislation does not apply to (a) personal data kept for State security purposes or kept by an individual only for recreational purposes; (b) personal data kept on manual files; or (c) non-personal data eg data concerning companies and partnerships (ibid s.1(4)). The legislation applies to financial institutions, which include building societies (ibid s.1(1)). See also SI Nos 349, 350 and 351 of 1988.

days of grace. Days allowed for making a payment or doing some other act after the time limited for same has expired. Three days of grace were added to the period in which a *bill of exchange* had to be paid, unless the bill provided to the contrary eg where it was payable on demand or was a fixed dated bill: Bills of Exchange Act 1882 s.14. As a *cheque* is a bill payable on demand, the drawer thereof was not entitled to any days of grace (ibid ss.14 and 73; M'Lean v Clydesdale Banking Co (1883) 9 App Cas 95). *Days of grace* as regards bills of exchange have now been abolished: Central Bank Act 1989 s.132. See BANK HOLIDAY; BILL OF EXCHANGE.

Deasy's Act. [Landlord and Tenant (Ireland) Act 1860]. The consolidating Act, which introduced the notion that the relationship of landlord and tenant is one of contract; so called after Serjeant Deasy, then Attorney General for Ireland, who piloted the Act through parliament. It continues as the foundation of the law of landlord and tenant in Ireland.

death of depositor. See DEATH OF SHAREHOLDER.

death of shareholder. Where a shareholder in a building society dies, the society is empowered to pay to such person who appears to the society to be entitled to receive it, the funds of the deceased shareholder, up to such amount as is fixed from time to time by the Central Bank: BS Act 1989 s.19. Under previous legislation the amount fixed by the Registrar of Building Societies was £3000.

The society must satisfy itself by evidence contained in a statutory declaration (qv) as to the death of the shareholder and the entitlement of the person claiming, and where the person is not the executor (qv) of the deceased shareholder, the society must notify the President of the High Court in writing of the payment. Such a payment will be valid and effectual against any demand against the funds of the society. Identical provisions apply where the deceased is a depositor.

It has been held that the death of a member operates as an immediate withdrawal, so that the personal representative of a member who dies before the start of a winding up does not have to give notice of withdrawal to gain priority: In re West London & General Permanent Benefit Building Society (1898) 78 LT 393.

debenture. An instrument, often but not necessarily under seal, issued by a corporate or public body as evidence of a debt or as security of a loan of a fixed sum of money upon which interest is payable. It is usually called a *debenture* on the face of it and it contains a promise to pay the amount mentioned on it. Debentures do not form part of the capital of a corporate body; debenture holders are creditors of the body and not shareholders. See SUCCESSOR COMPANY.

debt. A sum of money which one person is bound to pay to another. Debts are: (a) *simple* contract debts; (b) *specialty* debts, created by a document under seal; (c) debts of *record* eg recognisances and judgment debts; (d) *secured* debts, for which security has been given; (e) *preferential* debts. A contract by way of guarantee to pay for the debts of another must be evidenced in writing: Statute of Frauds (Ireland) 1695 s.2. See SHARES.

debt instruments. See SHARES.

debts, sale and purchase of. See FINANCIAL OBLIGATIONS.

deceit. The tort of fraud (qv).

declaration of interest. See DISCLOSURE OF INTEREST.

deed. An instrument which is in writing, sealed and delivered, to prove and testify the agreement of the parties whose deed it is, as to its contents. It is usually signed. The seal is usually fixed to the deed before execution. The deed is sealed by placing a finger on the seal with the intention of sealing it; delivery is effected by handing the deed to the other party or by words indicating an intention to deliver it.

A deed takes effect from the date of delivery. It is known as an *escrow* (qv) when it is delivered subject to a condition. Certain contracts must be made under seal eg contracts made without consideration. See Empson's Case (1870) LR 9 Eq 597.See DISPUTES; INVESTIGATION; TITLE DEEDS.

deed of conveyance. The deed to effect the transfer of property. It often includes : recitals; testatum; parcels; operative words; habendum; tenendum; reddendum; conditions; powers; covenants; testimonium (qqv).

deeds, registration of. The system which provides for the registration of deeds, conveyances and wills at the Registry of Deeds situated in Dublin: Registration of Deeds (Ireland) Act 1707. The document registered continues to be the evidence of title, unlike the system of registration of title. Registration is voluntary and a wide variety of documents dealing with interest in land may be registered. Failure to register may mean a *loss of priority* against other interests charged against the land.

A search in the Registry of Deeds will inform a purchaser of certain transactions affecting the title of the *unregistered* land, with the assurance that all transactions which were capable of being registered but which were not registered, will be treated as fraudulent and void, unless actual notice of them was brought to the attention of the purchaser. See Fullerton v Provincial Bank of Ireland (1903) IR 483. See LAND REGISTRATION; MEMORIAL; OFFICIAL SEARCH.

defamation. The tort (qv) consisting of the publication of a *defamatory* statement concerning another without just cause or excuse, whereby he suffers injury to his reputation. A *defamatory statement* is a false statement which exposes the person to hatred, ridicule or contempt, or which causes him to be shunned or avoided, or which tends to injure him in his office, calling or business. The test is whether the words tend to lower the person in the estimation of right-thinking members of society. Defamation may be a *libel* (qv) or a *slander* (qv). See Defamation Act 1961. See DEFAMATORY MATTER; REFER TO DRAWER.

defamatory matter. There are provisions in the BS Act 1989 which are intended to prevent the publication of defamatory matter; see AUDITOR, REMOVAL OF; ELECTION ADDRESS; RESOLUTION, PROPOSAL OF.

default. See INDEMNIFY; RELIEF; WITHDRAWAL FROM JURY.

default by borrower. Where there is default by a borrower in respect of payment required to be made pursuant to a mortgage by deed, the mortgagee (lender) may have the following remedies: (a) a court order for possession of the mortgaged property; (b) sale of the mortgaged property without the intervention of the court; (c) a court order for sale of the property; (d) the mortgagee going into possession of the property and taking the rents and profits from it; (e) the appointment of a receiver (qv); (f) foreclosure (qv). See APPENDIX 5 - TYPICAL MORTGAGE clause 7(c); MORTGAGEE, RIGHTS OF.

defence. There are a number of instances in the BS Act 1989 which provide that it is a defence to a charge of failing to take reasonable steps to comply with the Act, that the person charged had reasonable grounds for believing and did believe that a competent and reliable person was charged with the duty of ensuring such compliance and was in a position to discharge that duty eg re accounting records s.76(12); annual accounts s.77(9); directors' report s.78(4).

deferred shares. As regards a building society, shares that (a) are not redeemable or are redeemable only in circumstances approved by the Central Bank, (b) bear rights to participate in distributions of interest, profits or assets only after the claims of other shareholders are met, (c) are issued on terms that they will be used in full to meet any loss or deficit in the funds of a society before the funds of other shareholders are called upon, and (d) are issued in accordance with such other requirements as may be specified by the Bank for such shares: BS Act

1989 s.17(10).

An *authorisation* (qv) to raise funds, granted by the Bank, is not required for the acceptance of payments by way of subscription for *deferred shares* unless the aggregate of the payments exceeds £250,000 or such higher amounts as may be specified by the Bank (ibid s.17(3)a).

The rules (qv) of a society must provide for whether any deferred shares are to be issued and, if so, within what limits (ibid Second Schedule, part II, para 5(d)). See QUALIFYING CAPITAL; SHARE.

deficiencies. See AUDITOR, DUTY OF; DEFERRED SHARES.

defraud. See FRAUD.

demand a poll, right to. See POLL.

demise. The grant of a tenancy or lease; to let or lease land. Land which is let or leased is often referred to as *demised premises*.

de-mutualise. See CONVERSION.

deposit. (1) In a contract for the sale of land, a part-payment of the purchase price; it is a usual condition of such sale that where the purchaser makes default, the vendor may forfeit the deposit and resell the land, and recover any deficiency and expenses on resale from the purchaser, being allowed this amount or the deposit, whichever is the greater. In auction sales, the conditions usually require the deposit to be paid to the auctioneer, who holds as stakeholder. In the absence of agreement to the contrary, a deposit paid to the vendor's solicitor is treated as paid to him as the vendor's agent rather than as a stakeholder. See Leemac Overseas Investments Ltd v Harvey (1973) IR 160; Desmond and Boyle v Brophy (1986) ILRM 547. See LOAN.

(2) As regards financial institutions, a deposit is generally understood to mean a sum of money paid on terms whereby it will be returned with or without interest. "There is no definition in Irish law as to what is or is not a deposit": In re Irish Commercial Society Group Ltd (in receivership and in liquidation) (1987) HC p.828. See also DEPOSIT WITH BUILDING SOCIETY; DEPOSIT WITH CENTRAL BANK.

deposit interest retention tax. The taxation at source of interest paid or credited on *relevant deposits* with banks, building societies and certain other bodies: Finance Act 1986 ss.31-40. A relevant deposit is any deposit other than an *exempted deposit*; an exempted deposit includes eg a deposit in respect of which no person ordinarily resident in the State is beneficially entitled to any interest ie deposits from persons ordinarily resident abroad (ibid s.31(1)). Apart from companies chargeable to corporation tax, only three classes of persons may claim repayment of retention tax: incapacitated persons, persons aged 65 or over, and charities (ibid s.39).

deposit of title deeds. The delivery of title deeds to lands which creates an *equitable mortgage* (qv) thereon. The title deeds may be deposited to secure a debt antecedently due, or a sum then advanced or future advances; the depositee acquires a right to hold the deeds until the debt is paid and also acquires an equitable interest in the lands. Where the title deeds are accompanied by a memorandum of deposit signed by the mortgagor (qv), the mortgagee (qv) can protect his interest by registering the memorandum in the Registry of Deeds (qv). The mortgagee's remedy to obtain repayment of debt and interest is by way of mortgage suit (qv). See CHARGE, REGISTERED; FAMILY HOME; LAND CERTIFICATE; TITLE DEEDS.

deposit with building society. A building society with an *authorisation* (qv) may raise funds, to be used for the objects of the society, by borrowing money and accordingly receiving deposits from any person: BS Act 1989 s.18(1). Such borrowing must not exceed the society's liabilities arising from its issue of shares, although the Central Bank may grant a dispensation from this requirement (ibid s.18(3)). The requirement is intended to ensure that societies continue to have recourse to retail funds for prudential reasons and to continue the *mutual* status of societies.

The Central Bank may impose, as a condition to an *authorisation* (qv) granted by it to a building society, limitations on the acceptance of deposits (ibid s.17(6)(a)).

A reference in any enactment to the deposit of money or the keeping of an account in a bank, is to be construed, unless the context otherwise requires, as including the deposit of money with or the keeping of an account in a building society; such deposit or account may be held in the form of a shareholding in the society (ibid s.127). This provision gives to societies the same status in law as banks as repositories of funds eg for payment of wages, and maintaining client accounts.

A *deposit* is defined in the 1989 Act as including loans and cognate expressions are to be construed accordingly (ibid s.2(1)). Interest bearing deposits in certain designated building societies are authorised trustee investments pursuant to section 2 of the Trustee (Authorised Investments) Act 1958. See ASSOCIATED BODY; BORROWING; CURRENT ACCOUNT; REGISTRATION AS COMPANY; SAVINGS PROTECTION SCHEME; TRUSTEE INVESTMENTS.

deposit with Central Bank. A building society is required to maintain on deposit with the Central Bank an amount equal to 0.2 per cent of the society's total liabilities in respect of shares and deposits denominated in Irish pounds, and such other shares and deposits as may be prescribed by regulations, issued or held by the society at its offices in the State, but not less than £20,000: BS Act 1989 s.93(2). This proportion may be amended by regulation. Also, certain shares and deposits are to be excluded in the calculation to be made by the Bank (ibid s.93(4)).

The deposit carries interest as may be determined by the Bank; it cannot be subject to any form of execution in satisfaction of a claim or be the subject of a charge (qv), except in respect of the *savings protection scheme* (qv) (ibid s.93(7), (8) and (9)). For transitional provisions, pending the coming into force of the *savings protection scheme*, see ibid s.6(5). See AUTHORISATION; LIQUID ASSETS; SAVINGS PROTECTION SCHEME.

depositor. The Central Bank (qv) has a statutory duty to protect the funds of depositors with a building society and it may revoke an authorisation (qv) of a building society where it is expedient to do so. A depositor is entitled to receive on demand a copy of the annual accounts (qv) of his society. For priority of depositors in a winding up of a society, see WITHDRAWALS. See also AUDITOR, RESIGNATION OF; AUTHORISATION, REVOCATION OF; SAVINGS PROTECTION SCHEME; SUCCESSOR COMPANY.

depositor, death of. See DEATH OF

SHAREHOLDER.

depreciation of security. It is common practice to have a provision in a building society mortgage giving the society certain powers in the event that any building on the mortgaged property is pulled down, removed or injured so as materially to depreciate the value of the security. See APPENDIX 5 - TYPICAL MORTGAGE clause 7(c)(v).

derelict site. Includes any land (a) on which there are no buildings or all of the buildings (other than sheds, huts or other temporary structures) are in a ruinous, dilapidated or dangerous condition and none of the buildings is being used as a dwelling, and (b) which is or is likely to become injurious to health or to the amenities of the neighbourhood by reason of its objectionable or neglected condition or by reason of the deposit or collection therein of debris, rubbish or insanitary material: Derelict Sites Act 1961 s.1.

Local Authorities may acquire compulsorily any derelict site situate in their functional area. They may also require the owner by notice to carry out such works as are necessary to prevent the land from continuing to be a derelict site (ibid s.3). They may also enter on the site themselves, carry out the works and recover the expenses of so doing from the owner (ibid s.2).

derivative action. A company's action, the right to which is derived from the company, brought by a *minority shareholder* or shareholders. It is an exception to the rule that the proper plaintiff in respect of a wrong alleged to be done to a company is, prima facie, the company. It arises where the company is controlled by the defendant and the only way in which the wrong can be remedied is to allow any member to bring suit on the company's behalf. See Prudential Assurance Co v Newman Industries Ltd (1981) 1 Ch 229. See DERIVATIVE ACTION, BUILDING SOCIETY.

derivative action, building society. The Central Bank may bring proceedings in the name of a building society, where it appears to the Bank that proceedings ought in the public interest be brought by the society, following consideration by the Bank of an inspector's report into the affairs of the society: BS Act 1989 s.47(6). The proceedings which may be brought include those for damages in respect of any fraud (qv) misfeasance (qv) or other misconduct in connection with the promotion or formation (qv) of the society or the management of its affairs, or for the recovery of any property misapplied or wrongfully retained. See INDEMNIFY; INVESTIGATION.

destruction. See FALSIFICATION.

determinable fee. See FEE SIMPLE.

developing land. A building society is empowered, subject to having *adopted* the power by special resolution and recorded in its memorandum, to acquire, hold, dispose of, and develop or participate in developing land where the land is to be used (a) for residential purposes and purposes ancillary or incidental thereto, or (b) for other commercial purposes: BS Act 1989 ss.21(1), 21(4) and 36. This power must not be exercised by a society except with the approval of the Central Bank and in accordance with the terms and conditions of such approval (ibid s.36(4)).

A distinction is made between residential and commercial property in that a society does not have to adopt the power, in order to acquire, hold and dispose of land for residential purposes, if the acquisition and holding is to enable the society to make loans on the security of equitable interests in the land in circumstances authorised by the Central Bank (ibid s.21(2)).

A society must dispose of land held under s.21 if the Central Bank so directs (ibid s.21(3)). See ADOPTABLE POWERS; EQUITABLE MORTGAGE; PREMISES.

direction. The Central Bank is empowered under the BS Act 1989 to give directions to building societies in relation to a wide range of matters eg in relation to the form and content of the annual accounts (qv); in relation to a special meeting (qv); in relation to prohibiting the appointment or re-appointment of a particular person as auditor (qv).

It is also empowered to give a direction in writing to a society to suspend, for a period not exceeding 6 months, the raising of funds, the making of payments, and/or the acquisition or disposal of other assets or liabilities: BS Act 1989 s.40(2) and Fifth Schedule. The circumstances under which the direction may be given are the same as apply where the Bank has a discretion regarding the revocation of an authorisation (qv) of a society. Where such a direction is in force, the commencement of winding up proceedings, or the appointment of a receiver may not take place, and the property of the society may not be attached, sequestered or otherwise distrained, except with the sanction of the High Court (ibid s.40(5)).

A society to whom a direction has been given under s.40(2) may apply to the High Court for an order setting aside the direction, and the Bank may apply to the court for an order extending the period of operation of a direction (ibid Fifth Schedule, para 2-5).

Under previous legislation, the Registrar of Building Societies suspended payments by the Irish Benefit Building Society: Report of the Registrar (1982) p.8. See ADVERTISEMENT; AUTHORISATION, REVOCATION OF; HIGH COURT; ULTRA VIRES. See APPENDIX I.

directive, EC. Legislation of the EEC which states an objective which each member state must realise within a prescribed period eg the 1st EC Banking Directive relating to the authorisation (qv) of credit institutions. Where the provisions of a directive appear, as far as their subject matter is concerned, to be unconditional and precise, individuals may rely on those provisions in the absence of implementing measures adopted within the prescribed period as against a national provision incompatible with the directive: McDermott & Cotter v Minister for Social Welfare (1987) ILRM 324.

director. A member of the board of directors of a corporate body with powers and duties to manage the business of the body. In a building society, it includes any person occupying the position of director, by whatever name called: BS Act 1989 s.2(1). A society must have at least 3 directors (ibid s.48(1)). The board of directors must appoint a chairman (qv), a chief executive (qv) and a secretary (qv) (ibid ss.48(3) and 49(1)). The board must take reasonable steps to ensure that the chief executive and secretary appointed are persons who have the knowledge and experience to discharge the functions (qv) of those offices (ibid s.49(3)).

A director does not have to be a member of the society, if its rules (qv) so provide (ibid s.50(5)); however, its rules may impose a condition for eligibility that a director hold shares of not less that £500 in value (ibid s.50(6)). Also, the acts of a director are valid notwithstanding any defects which may afterwards be discovered in his appointment or qualifications (ibid s.50(14)). The powers and duties of the board of directors must be provided for by the rules of the society (s.10 and Second Schedule, Part 11, para 5 (h)). For transitional provisions on the 1989 Act coming into force, see s.124(11)-(13).

It has been held that there was nothing in the BS Act 1976 (since repealed) which required that all directors must be of the same class or that the method of appointing or removing them should be uniform for all directors: Irish Civil Service Building Society v Registrar of Building Societies (1985) IR 167. See ALTERNATE DIRECTOR; BOARD OF DIRECTORS; BODY CORPORATE; CO-OPTION; DIRECTOR'S BANK ACCOUNT; DISQUALIFICATION; GUARANTEE AND DIRECTOR; LEASE TO DIRECTOR; LOAN TO DIRECTOR; OFFICER; PAYMENT ON BEHALF OF DIRECTOR; PROPERTY TRANSACTIONS; REMUNERATION OF DIRECTORS; WINDING UP.

director, appointment of. The rules (qv) of a building society must provide for the manner of appointing directors (including the filling of casual vacancies): BS Act 1989, Second Schedule, Part II, para 5(i). See CO-OPTION.

director, election of. A director of a building society must be elected to office either (a) at an annual general meeting of the society, or (b) by postal ballot before the agm: BS Act 1989 s.50(1). A contested election at the agm must be by poll (qv). A candidate for election as a director must be nominated or be deemed eligible for election without nomination.

A *supervisor of election* (qv) must be appointed by the society in accordance with its rules. The Central Bank may, following consideration of the report of the supervisor, apply to the High Court for an order setting aside the result of an election and directing the society to hold another election (ibid s.51(7)). All ballot papers and all the documents and records of a society relating to an election must be retained by the society for one year from the date of the election (ibid s.51(6)). See also ibid s.10 and Second Schedule, Part 11, para 5(i).

In a particular dispute, it was held that the election of directors was valid: Healy and Ors v Irish Mutual Building Society and Ors (1982) - Report of Registrar of Building Societies (1981) p.38. See CANVASSING; CO-OPTION; DIRECTOR, NOMINATION OF; ELECTION ADDRESS; POLL; SUPERVISOR OF ELECTION; VOTING.

director, managing. See MANAGING DIRECTOR.

director, nomination of. The rules (qv) of a building society must not require as conditions of the validity of a person's nomination for election, (a) that more than 20 members join in nominating him; (b) that a nominating member be a member for more than 2 years before the date of the nomination or hold, or have at any time during that period held, shares in the society to a value greater than £250; or (c) that more than £250 be deposited with the society in connection with his candidature.

The rules may however impose as a condition of a person's eligibility to be nominated for election as a director, a requirement that he holds shares of not less than £500 in value (ibid s.50(6)). The Central Bank may by regulation (qv) substitute other numbers, amounts or period for those above (ibid s.50(6) and (9)).

A society must give notice of the latest date for receipt of nominations by publishing it in at least 2 daily newspapers not earlier than 42 days and not later than 21 days before the latest date, or alternatively by sending it to members not earlier than the notification of the preceding year's agm (ibid s.51(1)). The society must also notify the Bank of all valid nominations as soon as possible after the closing date for nominations (ibid s.50(15)(a)).

In a particular dispute, it was held that the delivery of nominations after close of business was not invalid where the rules (qv) did not require that delivery take place before close of business: Healy and Ors v Irish Mutual Building Society and Ors (1982) - Report of Registrar of Building Societies (1981) p.38. See DIRECTOR, RETIREMENT OF; MINOR.

director, removal of. The rules (qv) of a building society must provide for the manner of removing directors: BS Act 1989, Second Schedule, Part II, para 5(i). The Central Bank may impose, as a condition to an *authorisation* (qv) granted by it to a building society, the removal of any director or other officer (qv) (ibid s.17(6)(c)). See also DISQUALIFICATION.

director, remuneration of. See REMUNERATION OF DIRECTOR.

director, retirement of. A director of a building society must retire from office not later than the end of the third agm of the society following the date of his election: BS Act 1989 s.50(10). This requirement does not apply to a director who is also the chief executive (qv). The rules of the society may require an earlier retirement. A retiring director is eligible for election without nomination.

A person who has been co-opted as a director ceases to hold office at the end of the next agm following his appointment and is eligible for election without nomination (ibid s.50(12)). However that agm is disregarded for this purpose, if the co-option takes place after the closing date for nomination of candidates.

The claim by a former director of a building society that his resignation was induced by duress, was dismissed by consent: Farrell v Irish Permanent Building Society (1989) HC. See CO-OPTION.

Director of Public Prosecutions; DPP. The independent office established by statute by which all serious crimes are prosecuted in the name of the People: Prosecution of Offences Act 1974. The holder of the office is a civil servant and is independent in the exercise of his function. The function of the DPP in deciding whether or not to prosecute an individual for the alleged commission of a criminal offence is an executive one, and it is not reviewable by the courts, as this would interfere with his independence: The State (McCormack) v Curran (1987) ILRM 225.

As regards a building society, the Central Bank must refer a matter to the DPP, where it appears to the Bank that a person has (in relation to a society, the affairs of which have been investigated) been guilty of any offence for which he is criminally liable: BS Act 1989 s.47(4).

Also the DPP may make an application to the Court for a *disqualification order* (qv) against a person, disqualifying the person in relation to a building society (ibid s.64(5)). See also 1937 Constitution, art.30(3). See CONFIDENTIALITY; INDICTMENT; INVESTIGATION; SUMMARY PROCEEDING.

director's bank account. A director or past director of a building society is required to produce to an inspector of a society whose affairs the inspector is investigating, all documents relating to his bank account in certain circumstances: BS Act 1989 s.46(3). These circumstances include where money has been paid into or out of the bank account, which has been connected with any act or omission, which constituted misconduct (whether fraudulent or not) by that director towards the society or its members, or related to a transaction which should have been and had not been disclosed in the register for that purpose.

A *bank account* in this connection includes an account with any person who is exempt from holding a licence by virtue of the Central Bank Act 1971 s.7(4).

director's contract of service. See CONTRACT OF SERVICE.

director's employment contract. Any term by which a director's employment with a building society is to continue for a period exceeding 5 years is void, unless the term is first approved by a resolution of the society in general meeting, if the employment cannot be terminated by the society by notice, or can be terminated only in specified circumstances: BS Act 1989 s.54. A written memorandum setting out the proposed agreement, incorporating the term, must be available for inspection by members of the society. Employment in this instance includes a contract for services, eg consultancy services which a director might provide. See CONTRACT FOR SERVICES.

director's name. A building society is required to state the name of every director in legible characters in all business letters, on or in which the society's name appears, and which are sent by the society to any person: BS Act 1989 s.63. The Central Bank may grant an exemption from this obligation if special circumstances exist.

directors, register of. Every building society is required to keep at its chief office (qv) a register containing particulars of the name, residential address, place and date of birth, nationality, business occupation, and other directorships within the preceding 5 years, of each director, the chief executive and secretary of the society: BS Act 1989 s.66. A society is required to send a return of these particulars to the Central Bank (within 14 days of any change) and a member (or any other person) is entitled to have sent to him a copy of the register or to inspect the register.

directors' report. The report which the directors of a building society are required to prepare in respect of each financial year (qv) of the society and of its subsidiaries, and which must contain a fair view of the development of its business during the financial year and of its position at the end of it: BS Act 1989 s.78. The report, which must be signed by two directors, other than the chief executive, must also give such information relating to such aspects of its business, including its future development, as the Central Bank may specify (ibid s.78(1)(b) and 78(2)). See AUDITORS' REPORT. See APPENDIX I.

DIRT. Deposit interest retention tax (qv).

discharge of bill. Release from the obligations of a bill of exchange which occurs when all the rights and obligations attached to it are released, in one of the following ways: by payment in due course; by remuneration; by cancellation; by material alteration; by delivery up. See Bills of Exchange Act 1882 ss.59 and 61-64. See PAYMENT IN DUE COURSE.

discharge of mortgage. See REDEMPTION.

disclosure of information. See BANKER AND CONFIDENTIALITY; CONFIDENTIALITY; DATA PROTECTION; PRIVILEGE.

disclosure of interest. It is the duty of a director of a building society who is in any way, whether directly or indirectly, interested in a contract or proposed contract, (including any transaction or arrangement) with the society to declare the nature of his interest at a meeting of the directors of the society: BS Act 1989 s.53(1) and (8). A general notice given by a director is deemed to be a sufficient declaration of interest, where it is to the effect that he is a member of a specified company or firm and is to be regarded as interested in any contract which may be made with that company or firm or with a specified person who is *connected* with him. (ibid s.53(5)).

A copy of every declaration made and notice given must within 3 days (excluding a Saturday, Sunday or a public holiday) be entered into a register, which must be open for inspection, without charge, by any officer, auditor or member of the society at the chief office (qv) and at every general meeting of the society (ibid s.53(7)).

The Registrar of Building Societies has had occasion to remind societies and directors of their obligations in relation to similar requirements in the repealed enactments: Report of Registrar (1984) p.11-12. See CONNECTED PERSON; DIRECTOR'S BANK ACCOUNT.

disclosure of loans. A building society is required to maintain a register containing the details of the loans to, payments on behalf of, leases or hirings of property to, or guarantees provided to a director or to a *connected person* where the value is in excess of £1000, whether provided by the society itself or through arrangements between the society and another institution: BS Act 1989 s.59. The register must include transactions or arrangements during the current financial year (qv) and any of the preceding 10 financial years, but excluding years prior to 1989.

A society is required to make available for inspection by members of the society, a statement containing *requisite particulars* (as may be specified by the Central Bank) of such transactions and arrangements. The statement must be available at the chief office (qv) of the society for 15 days prior to the agm and at the agm and must have annexed to it a report of the auditors to the society. Two copies must be sent to the Bank, one of which will be maintained on the public file (qv) of the society. See DIRECTOR'S BANK ACCOUNT.

disclosure re business associate. A building society is required to maintain at its chief office (qv) a register containing the aggregate of fees paid to a *business associate* (qv) of the society in the last complete year and each of the 5 financial years preceding that year but excluding years prior to 1989: BS Act 1989 s.60(3) and (4).

This requirement arises where during a financial year of the society, a person is both an officer of the society and is, or is a director of or a partner in, a *business associate* of the society (ibid s.60(1)). An exemption is provided where the volume of business does not exceed £5,000 or such other sum as may be specified by the Central Bank (ibid s.60(7)). A statement, containing the particulars required to be kept in the register as respects the last complete financial year preceding the agm, must be made available for inspection by members of the society at its chief office for 15 days prior to the agm and at the agm (ibid s.60(8)). See DIRECTOR'S BANK ACCOUNT.

discounting. Discounting of credit instruments is a *financial service* which a building society may be empowered to provide: BS Act 1989 s.29(2)(e).

disentailing deed. See FEE TAIL.

dishonesty. See AUCTIONEERING SERVICE; CONVEYANCING SERVICE.

dishonour of bill. A *bill of exchange* is dishonoured if the drawee refuses to accept it or having accepted it fails to pay it: Bills of Exchange Act 1882 s.47. *Dishonour* gives the holder an immediate right of recourse against the drawer and endorsers of the bill; but notice of such dishonour must be given to those whom the holder wishes to hold liable. Where a *foreign bill* is dishonoured, formal notice of dishonour must be given by the process of *noting and protesting* (qv). See Walex & Co v Seafield Gentex Ltd (1978) IR 167; Spicer-Cowan Ireland Ltd v Play Print Ltd (1980) HC. See CHEQUE, PRESENTMENT BY NOTIFICATION.

dispose. See DISPOSITION.

disposition. The passing of property, whether by act of parties or act of law. As regards building societies, *dispose* and *disposition* in relation to any property, include the granting of any interest in or right over it: BS Act 1989 s.2(1). See DEVELOPING LAND; DIRECTION; FINANCIAL INTEREST; SERVICES RELATING TO LAND.

disputes. There is provision made in the BS Act 1989 for the settlement of disputes between a building society and a member in his capacity as a member, in respect of any matter, rights or obligations arising from the rules (qv) of the society or any provision of the Act or statutory instrument (qv) under it, other than the construction or effect of a mortgage deed or of any contract comprised in or based on a document other than the rules of the society (ibid s.91).

The rules (qv) of a society must provide for the settlement of disputes by reference either to the Circuit Court (qv), the Central Bank, or arbitration (qv) (ibid s.10, Second Schedule, Part II, para 5(s)).

In relation to the Bank as an arbitrator, the Minister may by regulations, provide that the functions of the Bank devolve on an adjudicator under a statutory or non-statutory scheme for the adjudication of complaints (ibid s.91(5)). See COMPLAINTS.

disqualification. A deprivation of a right, power or privilege. A person who has been adjudicated bankrupt (qv) and whose bankruptcy still subsists or who has been convicted of an indictable offence (qv) in relation to a building society or involving fraud or dishonesty or against whom a *disqualification order* (qv) has been made shall not be qualified to be appointed or act as an officer, auditor, receiver, liquidator or to be in any way, whether directly or indirectly, concerned with or to take part in the promotion, formation, direction or management of a society: BS Act 1989 s.64(1). See also FINANCIAL INTEREST. See APPENDIX I.

disqualification order. An order made by a court disqualifying a person, where it is satisfied in any proceedings or as a result of an application made to it, that the person has been guilty of any fraud or breach of duty in relation to a building society, its members or creditors; or whose conduct makes him unfit to be concerned with the management of the society; or where he has been persistently in default in relation to certain reporting requirements: BS Act 1989 s.64(2) and (13). It is also an order made under s.184 of the Companies Act 1963 (ibid 1989 Act s.64(4)).

An applicant must give not less than 10 days notice of his intention to make the application to the person who is the subject of the application (ibid 1989 Act s.64(7)). A person who is the subject of a disqualification order may apply to the High Court for relief (ibid s.64(8)). See SECURITY FOR COSTS.

disregard clause. Generally understood to mean a clause in a lease (qv) whereby the review of rent provided for in the lease must not take into consideration any future rent reviews, notwithstanding that provision may have been made for such reviews to be carried out on a regular basis. See RENT REVIEW CLAUSE.

dissolution of society. Breaking up or bringing to an end of a society. A building society is dissolved when it is *wound up*, or is *amalgamated* with another society, or where it *transfers its engagements* to another society. A society ceases to be incorporated as a society on its registration as a company following *conversion* (qv) to such company. See AMALGAMATION; DISTRIBUTION OF FUNDS; REGISTRATION AS COMPANY; REGISTRATION, CANCELLATION OF; TRANSFER OF ENGAGEMENTS; WINDING UP.

distrain. To seize goods by way of distress (qv). The property of a building society may not be distrained while a direction under s.40 of the BS Act 1989 is in force, except with the prior sanction of the High Court (ibid s.40(5)). See DIRECTION.

distress. The act of taking movable property out of the possession of a wrongdoer, to compel the performance of an obligation, or to procure satisfaction for a wrong committed. As to goods the subject of a hire-purchase agreement, see the Law of Distress Amendment Act 1908 s.4 and the Hire-Purchase Act 1946 s.17. Distress may not be levied on the goods of a bankrupt (qv) or an arranging debtor (qv) after the date of adjudication or order for protection: Bankruptcy Act 1988 s.139. Distress is a form of legal *self-help* eg distress for rent due. Distress also refers to the goods seized. Generally the law does not look favourably on distress. See DISTRAIN.

distribution of funds. The rules (qv) of a building society must provide for the right of members to participate in the distribution of surplus assets after the payment of creditors on the winding up or dissolution of the society: BS Act 1989, Second Schedule, Part II, para 5(u). See also AMALGAMATION; CONVERSION SCHEME; TRANSFER OF ENGAGEMENTS.

disturbance, compensation for. The compensation payable to a business tenant (qv) with a business equity of renewal, who is not entitled to a new tenancy in certain specified circumstances eg where the landlord is to pull down and rebuild or reconstruct the property or where the landlord requires vacant possession to carry out a scheme of development for which he has planning permission: Landlord and Tenant (Amendment) Act 1980. The amount of compensation will usually be the pecuniary loss, damage or expense which the tenant sustains or incurs or will sustain or incur by reason of his quitting the tenement (ibid s.58).

documents, presumptions as to. Where a document, which is at least 30 years old, is produced from proper custody, there is a presumption in law that the signature and handwriting thereon is genuine; attestation (qv) or execution need not be proved. Where a deed has been proved to have been signed and attested, it is presumed to have been sealed and delivered, even though no impression of seal appears thereon. An alteration in a deed is presumed to have been made prior to execution, and in a will is presumed to have been made after execution. There is no presumption about documents not under seal, except the presumption of legality ie that they were made so as not to commit an offence.

A certificate of incorporation (qv) or of registration (qv) or other document relating to a building society, purporting to be duly signed, is deemed to be duly issued and must be received in evidence in the absence of evidence to the contrary: BS Act 1989 s.116(1). Similar provisions apply to a printed document certified to be a copy of the memorandum (qv) or rules (qv) of the society (ibid s.116(2)).

documents, production of. For the provisions in the BS Act 1989 dealing with the requirements to produce documents or to give information, see ABROAD; AUDITOR OF SUBSIDIARY; AUDITOR, RIGHTS OF; INSPECTION; INVESTIGATION; PRIVILEGE, LEGAL PROFESSIONAL.

donatio mortis causa. A gift of personal property in anticipation of death. To be a valid gift it must be made in contemplation of the donor's death, be intended to take effect from his existing illness (unless the donor indicates otherwise) and be completed by delivery at the time to the donee. See In re Beaumont (1902) 1 Ch 889.

It has been held that shares in a building society which were evidenced by a share certificate were not the proper subject matter of a *donatio mortis causa*: In re Weston, Bartholomew v Menzies (1902) 1 Ch 680. It was held however that delivery of a building society pass book (the more modern method of providing evidence of share ownership) can be the subject of a donatio mortis causa, as can building society deposits: Griffith and Abbey National Building Society (1947) Reg Rep May 23; Tyler v Tyler (1935) LJ CCA 137.

double insurance. Insurance by the insured, with more than one insurer, of the one risk on the same interest in the same subject-matter. See Zurich Insurance v Shield Insurance (1987) SC.

DPP. Director of Public Prosecutions (qv).

draft. (1) An order for the payment of a sum of money. (2) A rough copy of a document. See BANKERS' DRAFT.

drawee. The person to whom a bill of exchange (qv) is addressed.

drawer. The person who signs a bill of exchange (qv) as the maker thereof.

drawing of cheque. See CHEQUE, DRAWING OF.

dry rent. See RENT SECK

duty, breach of. See BREACH OF DUTY.

duty of auditor. See AUDITOR, DUTY OF.

dwelling, inviolability of. See INVIOLABILITY OF DWELLING.

E

easement. A right enjoyed by the owner of land over the lands of another eg a right of way, right to water, right to light, or right of support. An easement cannot exist *in gross* ie independently of property, otherwise it may amount to a mere licence; it is a right which is annexed to property, in alieno solo (qv), rather than to an individual. The *dominant* tenement is the land owned by the possessor of the easement, and the *servient* tenement is the land over which the right is enjoyed.

education. See CHARTERED BUILDING SOCIETIES INSTITUTE.

ejectment. The recovery of possession of land. In the Circuit Court, ejectment is usually obtained by *ejectment civil bill* on the title or for overholding, where the rateable valuation of the land does not exceed £200. Ejectment can be obtained for non-payment of rent but this is not usually sought as the defendant in any such proceedings may, at any time before the decree for possession is executed, pay all rents and arrears and costs due and as a consequence the proceedings will be stayed: RCC O.22 r.15; O.35. Similar provisions for ejectment apply in the District Court which has jurisdiction where the rent does not exceed £2500 per annum: DCR r.176. See Deasy's Act 1860 ss.52 and 72; Courts Act 1981 ss.2(1) and 6(a)(ii).

election. See DIRECTOR, ELECTION OF; SUPERVISOR OF ELECTION.

election address. It is the duty of a building society to send, at its expense, the election address of a duly nominated candidate for election as a director of the society, to each member who is entitled to notice of the election: BS Act 1989 s.51(2). The election address of not more than 300 words must be furnished to the society by the candidate before the closing date for nominations. The society is not required to circulate an address where its contents do not relate directly to the affairs of the society or would be likely to diminish substantially public confidence in the society, or seeks needless publicity for defamatory matter or is for frivolous or vexatious purposes (ibid s.51(2) and (3)).

The society must notify the candidate within 7 days of receipt of the election address, if it refuses to circulate the address and there is provision for an appeal (by way of reference) to the Central Bank within 7 days of the refusal (ibid s.51(4)).

electronic communication. See ADVERTISEMENT.

eligibility for nomination. See DIRECTOR, NOMINATION OF.

emblements. The profits from sown land; the crops or products as are the result of agricultural labour. The right to emblements is lost where a tenancy is ended by the tenant's own act.

emigrant. For exchange control purposes, means a person who departs from the State to take up *permanent* residence (ie residence for three years or more) elsewhere, having been resident in the State for at least the three preceding years: Central Bank Exchange Control Notice Ex 10. Emigrants, on following a specified procedure, are permitted to transfer the entire amount of their *net* Irish assets (ie total Irish assets less total Irish liabilities) out of the State on emigration.

The procedure involves submission of a specified form to a *financial institution*, which in this context includes a building society. The approval of the Central Bank is required to be obtained by the financial institution where the total net assets exceed £100,000.

The financial institution should also provide the emigrant with a letter for presentation to Irish customs if more than the equivalent of £1,200 is being exported on the person or in the baggage of the emigrant; in such circumstances there is a maximum limit of the equivalent of £1,200 per person in foreign currency notes and of £150 per person in Irish currency notes in denominations not exceeding £20. Any funds in excess of these amounts must be in a form other than currency notes eg traveller's cheques, bank drafts or letters of credit (qqv). See EXCHANGE CONTROL.

employee. A person who is under a *contract of service* to an other person, called the employer, under which the employer has the right to direct the employee not only as to what is to be done but as to how it is to be done: Roche v Patrick Kelly & Co Ltd (1969) IR 100. For income tax purposes, an employee is any person in receipt of emoluments: Income Tax Act 1967 s.124.

The parties cannot alter the truth of the employer/employee relationship by putting a different label on it: Lamb Bros Dublin Ltd v Davidson (1979) HC; Massey v Crown Life Insurance Co (1978) 2 All ER 576. An employee generally has access to employment protection legislation.

An employee of a building society, a subsidiary (qv) or other associated body (qv), is prohibited from acting as an agent for the subsidiary or body which provides an *auctioneering service* (qv) or *other services relating to land* (qv): BS Act 1989 s.32(4).

Where a society converts itself into a public limited company, each employee of the society becomes an employee of the company, his service is deemed to be unbroken and his terms and conditions will, until varied, be identical with the terms and conditions of his employment with the society immediately before the conversion date (qv) and be capable of variation in the same manner (ibid s.107(2)(i)). See AMALGAMATION; ASSESSMENT OF SECURITY; AUDITOR, QUALIFICATIONS OF; CANVASSING; DIRECTOR'S EMPLOYMENT CONTRACT; MISLEADING STATEMENT; OFFENCES; TIME TO COMPLY.

employment contract. See DIRECTOR'S EMPLOYMENT CONTRACT.

encroachment. Unauthorised extension of the boundaries of land; unauthorised entrance upon another's rights or possessions. An encroachment by a tenant on another person's land generally enures for the landlord's benefit, unless the conduct of the landlord or the tenant indicates a contrary intention: Meares v Collis (1927) IR 397. See LONG POSSESSION, TITLE BY; TRESPASS TO LAND.

encumbrance. A charge or liability which burdens property eg a mortgage, lease, easement, restrictive covenant. An *encumbrancer* is a person who has the right to enforce an encumbrance.

endorsement. A signature, usually on the reverse side of a document, generally operating as a transfer of rights arising from the document. Endorsement is a mode of transferring bills of exchange.

An *endorsement in blank* is an endorsement by the endorser of his own signature without specifying the name of the transferee, under which the bill becomes payable to the bearer. A *special endorsement* is one which specifies the name of the person to whom or to whose order the bill is to be made payable. A *conditional endorsement* is one which is subject to the fulfilment of a specific condition. A *restrictive endorsement* prohibits further transferability (eg *pay John Murphy only - signed ...*).

An endorser of a bill agrees to compensate the holder or any endorser subsequent to his own endorsement who is compelled to pay it if the bill is dishonoured when duly presented for payment. See Bills of Exchange Act 1882 ss.32-35. See BILL OF EXCHANGE; CHEQUE.

endowment mortgage. A mortgage wherein the principal sum advanced by the mortgagee (lender) is intended to be repaid by means of a *life-endowment insurance policy* effected by the mortgagor (borrower). The endowment policy from an insurance company will typically provide for the payment of the principal sum at a specified date or on the mortgagor's death, whichever is earlier. If the policy is a *with profits* one, it will provide for the mortgagor to participate in the profitability of the insurance company. The mortgagor pays a regular premium to the insurance company, and interest to the mortgagee on the principal sum advanced. The mortgage deed usually provides that the repayment of the principal sum advanced by the mortgagee is suspended, so long as the endowment policy is kept up and the mortgagor continues to pay interest on that principal sum. See APPENDIX 5; MORTGAGE.

enlargement. Increasing an estate eg the enlargement of a base fee (qv) into a fee simple (qv). See GROUND RENT.

entail. See FEE TAIL.

entry, right of. It is usual for a building society mortgage to specify the right of the society to enter into the possession of the mortgaged property and for the principal money outstanding to be due and payable forthwith on such right becoming enforceable. It is also usual for the mortgage to give the society the right to withdraw from possession. See APPENDIX 5 - TYPICAL MORTGAGE clause 7 (a) and (f). However, for limitations on the right to enter into possession, see MORTGAGEE, RIGHTS OF.

environment assessment directive. The directive of the European Economic Community, done at Luxembourg on 27 June 1985, which requires developers to produce *environment impact assessments* of a wide range of projects. The assessment is required to identify the direct and indirect effects of a *project* on human beings, fauna, and flora; soil, water, air, climate and landscape; the inter-action between these factors; material assets and the cultural heritage (ibid art.3). A project means the execution of construction works or of other installation or schemes, or other interventions in the natural surroundings and landscape including those involving the extraction of mineral resources (ibid art.2).

Subject to certain exemption provisions, an environment impact assessment is mandatory for projects of the class listed in Annex 1 (ibid art.4); these projects include crude oil refineries, power stations, integrated chemical installations and waste disposal installations.

Member states were required to implement the directive by 3rd July 1988. It was implemented in this State by means of circular letters issued by the Department of the Environment on 1st July 1988 to local authorities, other government departments, and state sponsored bodies.

equitable charge. See EQUITABLE MORTGAGE.

equitable lien. A lien (qv) which exists independently of possession and which is binding on all who acquire the property with notice of the lien eg a vendor's lien for unpaid purchase money; a purchaser's lien for prematurely paid purchase money.

equitable mortgage. The mortgage which arises in equity (qv) by: (a) the agreement to execute a legal mortgage; or (b) the formal mortgage of the *equity of redemption*; or (c) the deposit of title deeds, with or without a memorandum of deposit. A legal mortgage takes priority over an equitable one, even if created after the equitable one, under the equitable maxim *where the equities are equal, the law prevails*. See DEPOSIT OF TITLE DEEDS; EQUITY OF REDEMPTION; MORTGAGE.

equity. Fairness, impartiality, natural justice. The doctrines and procedures which developed alongside the common law and statute law, administered originally by the Court of Chancery to remedy some of the defects of the common law, and which became fused together by the amalgamation of the courts by the Judicature (Ireland) Act 1877. This Act provided that where there is any conflict between the rules of law and equity, equity is to prevail.

equity of redemption. The sum total of the mortgagor's (borrower's) rights in equity; it is an equitable estate which can be assigned, devised or mortgaged again. It exists from the moment the mortgage is made. It includes the equitable right to redeem the mortgage when the legal right has been lost by failure to pay the mortgage debt by the due date. There must be no *clogs* (qv) on the equity of redemption. A formal mortgage of the equity of redemption creates an equitable mortgage.

The equity of redemption is lost by: (a) sale by a court in lieu of foreclosure; (b) sale out of court by a mortgagee under an express power of sale given in the mortgage deed or by statutory power of sale given by the Conveyancing Act 1881 s.19; (c) lapse of time under the Statute of Limitations 1957. See FORECLOSURE; MORTGAGE; PUISNE MORTGAGE; REDEMPTION.

escheat. The *reversion* of land to the lord of the fee or the State on failure of heirs of the owner. It derived from the feudal rule that where an estate in fee simple came to an end, the land reverted to the lord by whose ancestors or predecessors the estate was originally created. Abolished by the Succession Act 1965 s.11. In default of next-of kin, the State takes the estate as ultimate intestate successor (ibid s.73).

escrow. A deed delivered to a person who is not a party to it, to be held by that party until certain conditions are performed eg the payment of money, after which it is delivered and takes effect as a deed. See DEED.

estate. An interest in land. An estate may be of *freehold* or less than freehold. Freehold estates are those of fee simple, fee tail and a life estate; less than freehold estates are leases and tenancies (qqv).

estate agent. See AUCTIONEER; HOUSE AGENT.

estate management. See COVENANT.

estate tail. See FEE TAIL.

estovers, common of. The right to cut wood, gorse or furze on the lands of another. See PROFIT A PRENDRE.

eviction. Dispossession; recovery of land by due process of law. See EJECTMENT.

examination. Interrogation of a person on oath. An inspector (qv) appointed to investigate the affairs of a building society is empowered to examine on oath the officers, members and agents of the society and administer an oath (qv) accordingly: BS Act 1989 s.46(2).

excess clause. A clause in an insurance policy whereby the insured is to bear the first specified amount of any loss. See INSURANCE.

exchange, bill of. See BILL OF EXCHANGE.

exchange control. The restricting of certain outward movement of funds from the State and ensuring that funds accruing to Irish residents from external sources are not withheld from the country's external reserves: Exchange Control Acts 1954 to 1986. The 1986 Act continued controls in force to 1990.

The primary purpose of exchange control is to safeguard the national external reserves and to regulate the effect of capital movements on the exchange rate of the Irish pound. Certain restrictions and obligations are imposed on all residents of the State, regardless of where they may be at the time of the transaction, in relation to any gold, foreign currency and securities they may own or acquire and in respect of payments which they may wish to make abroad. Permitted transactions are derived from regulations made by the Minister for Finance and are specified in notices published by the Central Bank of Ireland.

Exchange controls were relaxed from 1st January 1988; persons were then permitted to invest up to £5000 in foreign shares; the limit on property purchased outside the EEC was increased to £50,000; the £40,000 limit on assets which an individual could take abroad when emigrating was abolished; the limit on cash flow which banks, insurance companies and pension funds could invest abroad was increased to 12.5%; and the personal travel allowance was increased to £1200.

Further relaxation of exchange controls was introduced from 1st January 1989; the purchase of medium and long-term foreign securities funded with Irish pounds was permitted, as was the purchase of short-term foreign securities funded by foreign currency borrowing.

The government has announced its intention to abolish exchange controls as regards EC member states by 1992. See also EMIGRANT.

excise duty. A duty chargeable on certain goods and licences. The government is empowered to impose, vary or terminate excise duties by order, provided the order is validated by confirmation by the Oireachtas (qv): Imposition of Duties Act 1957; McDaid v Judge Sheehy (1989) HC - ITLR (13 Feb 1989). See AUCTIONEERING SERVICE.

executor. An *executor* is the person to whom the execution of a will, ie the duty of carrying its provisions into effect, is confided by the testator. The duties of an executor are: to bury the deceased; to prove the will; to collect the estate and, as necessary, to convert it into money; to pay the debts in their proper order; to pay the legacies and to distribute the residue among the persons entitled. The executor may bring actions against persons who are indebted to the testator or are in possession of property belonging to the estate. When several executors are appointed and only some of them prove the will, they are called the *proving* or *acting executors*.

It is the duty of an executor to notify a spouse in writing of the right of election between the spouse's *legal right* and any rights under the will: Succession Act s.115. See DEATH OF DEPOSITOR; EXECUTORSHIP; PERSONAL REPRESENTATIVE.

executorship. Executorship is a *financial service* which a building society may be empowered to provide: BS Act 1989 s.29(2)(n). See FINANCIAL SERVICES.

executor's year. The period allowed for the personal representative of a deceased to distribute the estate. An action for failure to distribute within this year is not permissable without leave of the court. This does not affect the right of creditors to bring proceedings. See Succession Act 1965 s.62.

executory interest. A future interest in land which is not a reversion (qv) or a remainder (qv).

exempted developments. Developments for which planning permission (qv) is not required: LG(P&D) Act 1963 s.4. These include: (a) development consisting of the use of any land for the purpose of agriculture or forestry; (b) development by a planning authority within its functional area; (c) development consisting of the carrying out of works for the maintenance, improvement or other alteration of a structure which affects only the interior of the structure (with exceptions) or which do not materially affect the external appearance of the structure so as to render its appearance inconsistent with the character of the structure or of neighbouring structures; (d) development consisting of the use of any structure or other land within the curtilage of a dwellinghouse for any purpose incidental to the enjoyment of the dwellinghouse as such (ibid s.4 and LG(P&D) Act 1976 s.43(1)(c)).

The Minister is empowered to make regulations providing for any class of development being an exempted development: 1963 Act s.4(2) and LG(P&D) Regulations 1977, Part III (SI No 65 of 1977). The question as to what constitutes an exempted development is to be decided by An Bord Pleanala: 1976 Act s.14(9)(b). See also SI No 403 of 1983; SI No 1 of 1984; SI No 348 of 1984; SI No 130 of 1985. See SPECIAL AMENITY ORDER.

explanatory memorandum. A memorandum which sometimes accompanies a Bill with the purpose of explaining the proposed legislation. It may be examined by the court to discover the purpose of an enactment: McLoughlin & Ors v Minister for the Public Service (1986) ILRM 28. An explanatory memorandum was issued with the BS Bill 1988 which Bill was later enacted, with amendments, as the BS Act 1989.

extinguishment. The ceasing of a right or obligation eg an easement (qv) is extinguished when the *dominent* and *servient* tenements are united in the same person. See also CONSOLIDATION; MERGER.

F

false information. It is an offence for a person recklessly (or knowing it to be false) to provide an answer or explanation, to make a statement or to produce lodge or deliver, any return, report, certificate, balance sheet or other document which is false in a material particular: BS Act 1989 s.120(1).

There are more severe penalties where the court is of opinion that the offence substantially contributed to a society being unable to pay its debts, or prevented or seriously impeded the orderly winding up (qv) of a society, or substantially facilitated the defrauding of the creditors of the society or the creditors of any other person (ibid s.120(2)). See APPENDIX I.

falsification. As regards a building society, where any register or record is required to be kept, and is not kept by making entries in a bound book but by some other means (eg in computer or fiche form), there is a duty imposed to guard against falsification and to facilitate the discovery of any such falsification: BS Act 1989 s.117(4).

An officer of a building society who destroys, mutilates, or falsifies, or is privy (qv) to the destruction, mutilation or falsification of any record or document affecting or relating to the property or affairs of the society, or makes or is privy to the making of a false entry therein, is guilty of an offence, unless he proves he had no intention to defeat the law (ibid s.120(3)). See APPENDIX I.

family home. A dwelling in which a married couple ordinarily reside; it includes a dwelling in which a spouse whose protection is in issue ordinarily resides, or if that spouse has left the other spouse, ordinarily resided before so leaving: Family Home Protection Act 1976. It includes any building, or any structure vehicle or vessel (whether mobile or not), or part thereof, and includes a garden.

If a spouse conveys any *interest* in the family home to a person other than the other spouse, such conveyance is void unless the prior consent in writing of that other spouse has been obtained (ibid s.3(1)). If both spouses join in the sale of the family home, one spouse cannot subsequently object to the sale on the ground that a consent in writing of that spouse had not been obtained: Nestor v Murphy (1979) IR 326.

If a spouse omits or refuses to consent to a disposal of the family home, the court may order the dispensing of such consent eg where the non-owning spouse has deserted the other spouse (ibid s.4; R v R (1978) HC). Also, the court may make such order as is just and equitable, where it appears to the court on the application of a spouse, that the other spouse is engaging in such conduct as may lead to the loss of any interest in the family home, or may render it unsuitable for habitation as a family home with the intention of depriving the applicant spouse or a dependent child of his residence in the family home: S v S (1983) ILRM 387.

The provisions of the 1976 Act apply only where one spouse has any estate, right, title or other interest, legal or equitable in the family home (ibid s.1(1)). It has been held that a house, owned by a company in which the husband was the major shareholder, was a family home: LB v HB (1980) HC; C v C (1983) HC. Also, a spouse's prior consent is not required to render a *judgment mortgage* (qv) effective against a family home: Containercare (Ireland) Ltd. v Wycherley (1982) IR 143; Murray v Diamond (1982) 2 ILRM 113. However, the deposit of title deeds of a family home in 1975 did not provide a lender with security for the repayment of advances made after the passing of the 1976 Act: Bank of Ireland v Purcell (1988) ILRM 480.

As from 1st January 1989, any disposition of the property of a bankrupt (qv), an arranging debtor (qv), or a person dying insolvent, which comprises a family home without the prior sanction of the court, is void: Bankruptcy Act 1988 s.61(4) and 61(5). See also Family Law Act 1981 s.10. See MATRIMONIAL PROPERTY; MORTGAGEE, RIGHTS OF.

FCBSI. [Fellow of the Chartered Building Societies Institute]. See CHARTERED BUILDING SOCIETIES INSTITUTE.

fee. (1) The term used in land law to denote that an estate is capable of being inherited. (2) Payment for a service; there are various provisions under the BS Act 1989 by which the Central Bank may fix a fee for copies of documents relating to a building society to be made available to members or others eg see ANNUAL ACCOUNTS. See also DISCLOSURE RE BUSINESS ASSOCIATE; REDEMPTION FEE; PUBLIC FILE.

fee farm grant. A *fee simple* estate with a rent reserved to the grantor. Since the Renewable Leasehold Conversion Act 1849, a *lease for lives renewable forever* (qv) operates as a fee farm grant if the lessor is capable of making such a grant. A fee farm grant creates the relationship of landlord and tenant between the parties: Deasy's Act 1860. A fee farm rent, whether rent seck (qv) or rent charge (qv) may be recovered by various remedies: Conveyancing Act 1881 s.44. See FEE SIMPLE; PRIOR MORTGAGE..

fee simple. An estate of freehold being the most extensive that a person can have. A fee simple estate may be: (a) a *fee simple absolute*, which is an estate which continues forever; (b) a *determinable fee*, which is a fee simple which will automatically determine on the occurrence of some specified event which may never occur; (c) a *fee simple upon condition*, which may be upon a condition precedent or a condition subsequent; (d) a *base fee*, which is a particular kind of determinable fee; and (e) a *fee farm grant* which is a fee simple with a rent reserved to the grantor.

To convey a fee simple estate it is essential to use the correct words of limitation: *to A and his heirs* or *to A in fee simple*; or *to A and successors* in the case of a grant to a corporation sole. No words of limitation are required in a devise by will or a grant to a corporation aggregate (eg a limited company). For determination of the purchase price of the fee simple, see Landlord & Tenant (Amendment) Act 1984 s.7. See also Conveyancing Act 1881 s.51. See BASE FEE; SHELLEY'S CASE, RULE IN; GROUND RENT.

fee tail. An entail; an estate tail; a freehold estate which continues for as long as the original tenant and any of his descendants survive. It is created by the words of limitation *heir* followed by some words of procreation eg *To A and the heirs of his body*, or *to A in tail* since the Conveyancing Act 1881. An estate tail may be created by will only by the same words of limitation as those required in a deed: Succession Act 1965 s.95.

The owner of the estate tail is known as the *tenant-in-tail*. A *tail male* or a *tail female* are entails where the property descended to males or females exclusively. In order to *bar* the entail and create a fee simple (qv) estate, it is necessary for the tenant-in-tail to execute a *disentailing deed* which must be enrolled in the Central Office (qv) within six months of execution: Fines and Recoveries Act 1833. An entail cannot be barred by will. See In re Fallon (1956) IR 268; Bank of Ireland v Domville (1956) IR 37. See BARRING THE ENTAIL; PROTECTOR OF THE SETTLEMENT.

fiduciary. A person who has been entrusted with powers for the benefit of others but who in the exercise of those powers is not subject to the direct and immediate control of those others eg building society directors, trustees, liquidators, executors and court appointed receivers (qqv). The general rule is that a person in a fiduciary position is not entitled to make a profit and he is not allowed to put himself in a position where his interest and his duty conflict. See INDEMNIFY.

film. See ADVERTISEMENT.

final certificate. Often refers to the certificate of an architect pursuant to a standard building contract, which provides that the certificate is conclusive evidence that the works have been properly carried out and completed in accordance with the contract. See Elliot & Co v Minister for Education (1987) ILRM 710.

finance house, liability of. A finance house is deemed to be a party to the sale of goods to a buyer *dealing as consumer*, and the finance house and the seller of the goods are *jointly and severally* answerable to the buyer for any breach of contract and for any misrepresentation made by the seller with respect to the goods, where the buyer has entered into an agreement with the finance house for the repayment to the finance house of money paid by the finance house to the seller in respect of the price of goods. See SGSS Act 1980 s.14. See CONSUMER, DEALING AS.

financial interest. A person is taken to have a *financial interest* in the disposition (qv) of any security if he would on a disposition of that security, be entitled to the whole or part of the proceeds of the disposition: BS Act 1989 s.25(7). A person who has a financial interest in a disposition is disqualified from making an assessment (qv) of the adequacy of the security for certain loans or from making a valuation (qv) of the security; any director, other officer or employee of that person or of an *associated employer* (qv) is similarly disqualified (ibid s.25(2) and (3)).

financial obligations. The sale and purchase of financial obligations, debts and securities, is a *financial service* (qv) which a building society may be empowered to provide: BS Act 1989 s.29(2)(c).

financial planning. The provision of advice relating to financial planning is a *financial service* (qv) which a building society may be empowered to provide: BS Act 1989 s.29(2)(i).

financial services. Any of the following activities - arranging the provision of credit, including the joining of credit card companies; the giving of guarantees and indemnities; the sale and purchase of financial obligations, debts and securities; investment services; the discounting of credit instruments; the acceptance of deposits of money for current accounts, the collection of cheques and the payment of cheques drawn on the society; insurance; the maintenance of a company's register of members; the provision of advice relating to taxation and financial planning; financing hire-purchase; leasing; money transmission; trusteeship; executorship; foreign exchange; the operation of a credit transfer system; the issue of drafts, travellers cheques and letters of credit; or other activities of a similar nature (including advisory services) that appear to the Central Bank to be financial services: BS Act 1989 s.29(2).

A building society is empowered, subject to *adoption* of the power and the approval of the Bank, to provide, as principal or as agent, *financial services*; such services do not include the making of loans (qv) for which there is separate provision under the 1989 Act. See ADOPTABLE POWERS; LINKING SERVICES.

Financial Services Industry Association. The industry association, within the structure of the Confederation of Irish Industry, which represents the interests of the financial services industry in Ireland, including over 120 banks, building societies, insurance companies, venture capital companies, charge card companies and other financial services companies.

The building society members of the FSIA are those six societies which are not currently members of the Irish Building Societies Association (qv) and sometimes referred to as the *non-associated* societies, viz ICS, Irish Life, Irish Mutual, Norwich Irish, Midland & Western, and Metropolitan.

The objectives of the FSIA are: to promote the development of the financial services industry in Ireland; to interpret and assess national and international developments which affect the industry, to formulate an industry response, and to prepare the industry for change; and to promote the development of internationally traded services based in Ireland. The *non-associated* societies group has become the Irish representative in the European Community Mortgage Federation. [FSIA, Confederation House, Kildare Street, Dublin 2].

financial statement, summary. The statement as regards a building society, derived from the annual accounts (qv) and the directors' report (qv), which must be prepared by the directors, be signed by 2 directors and the chief executive, be sent to members of the society entitled to notice of the annual general meeting and to the Central Bank, not later than 21 days before the date of the agm, and include a statement from the auditors as to its consistency with the annual accounts and the directors' report: BS Act 1989 s.79. The Central Bank may specify the form and content of the summary financial statement (ibid s.79(4)).

financial year. The financial year of a building society is the period of 12 months ending on a 31st day of December: BS Act 1989 s.113. The *initial* financial year is such period as expires with the end of the calendar year in which the society is formed.

firm. Persons who have entered into partnership with one another; the name under which their business is carried on is called the firm name: Partnership Act 1890 s.4. In the event that partners trade under names other than their own, they must comply with the Registration of Business Names Act 1963. An action may be brought by or against a firm in the name of the firm. See RSC O.14.

The appointment of a firm by the name of the firm to be the auditor of a building society shall be deemed to be an appointment of those persons who from time to time during the period of the appointment are the partners in that firm as from time to time constituted and are qualified to be auditors of the society: BS Act 1989 s.83(8). See AUDITOR, QUALIFICATIONS OF.

fixed charge. A specific charge on specific property of say a corporate body eg on land and buildings of the body, as security for a loan, as contrasted with a *floating charge*. A *fixed charge* invariably involves the vesting of a legal interest in the vendor of the loan at the time of the transaction. See CHARGE; DEBENTURE; FLOATING CHARGE; CHARGE, REGISTRATION OF.

fixtures. Personal chattles annexed to the freehold by a temporary occupier and which are removable by him. A chattle which, judging from the mode in which it is affixed and all the surrounding circumstances, was affixed by the occupier to be enjoyed as a chattle is removable. If it was affixed to constitute an improvement to the house or land, it is not. See Sanders v Davis (1885) 15 QBD 218; Norwich Union Life Insurance Society v Preston (1957) 1 WLR 813. See also Deasy's Act 1860 s.17. See FURNITURE.

flat. Colloquially, a suite of rooms in a building, usually on one floor of a building which has a number of floors. A leasehold or freehold interest may be created in a flat; there is no reason at common law why the owner of land cannot convey horizontal slices of the air space above it to others, whether by way of lease or freehold interest: Humphries v Broghen (1850) 12 QB 739.

A flat is entitled to vertical support from the lower part of the building and to the benefit of such lateral support as may be of right enjoyed by the building itself: Dalton v Angus (1881) 6 App Cas 740. There is provision for the registration of land which is a *flat or floor, or part of a flat or floor, of a house*: Land Registration Rules 1972 r.30(1)(a). See MULTI-STOREY BUILDINGS.

floatation. See CONVERSION.

floating charge. An equitable charge or mortgage on the assets for the time being of a going concern. It attaches to the subject charged in the varying conditions it happens to be in from time to time. The charge remains dormant or *floats over* the assets until the undertaking ceases to be a going concern, or until the person in whose favour the charge is created (the *chargee*) intervenes.

A floating charge becomes a fixed charge, and is said to *crystalise*, when a receiver is appointed, or a winding up commences, or if the chargee intervenes when entitled so to do. An *automatic crystallisation clause* is one stipulating that a floating charge will crystalise on some specific event occurring. Debentures issued by a corporate body are often secured by a floating charge on the property, present and future, of the body. See CHARGE; FIXED CHARGE.

forebearance. Refraining from enforcing a right eg for a debt. A forebearance to sue may be adequate consideration (qv) to support a contract. See Fullerton v Bank of Ireland (1903) AC 309. See CONCESSIONS.

foreclosure. The forfeiture by a mortgagor (qv) of his *equity of redemption* (qv). The mortgagee's right to foreclosure is the right to apply to the court for an order directing the mortgagor to redeem his mortgage within a certain time or in default to be deprived of his right to redeem forever. Although available as a remedy, foreclosure has fallen into disuse in Ireland: Antrim County Land, Building & Investment Co Ltd v Stewart (1904) 2 IR 357. See MORTGAGE SUIT.

foreign bill. See INLAND BILL.

foreign currency. A building society is empowered to make *housing loans* (qv) and other *loans* (qv) in a currency other than the currency of the State, with the approval of the Central Bank: BS Act 1989 ss.22(1) and 23. It may also, with approval, raise funds in a foreign currency to be used for the objects (qv) of the society by the issue of shares (qv) and by borrowing money (ibid s.18). See FOREIGN EXCHANGE.

foreign exchange. A foreign exchange service is a *financial service* (qv) which a building society may be empowered to provide: BS Act 1989 s.29(2)(o). See EXCHANGE CONTROL.

forfeiture. The deprivation of a person of his property as a penalty for some act or omission. Forfeiture may take place by agreement or by operation of law eg a forfeiture clause in a lease may enable the lessor to determine the lease. Forfeiture of the lands and goods of a felon was abolished by the Forfeiture Act 1870. A covenant for the forfeiture of a lease on the bankruptcy (qv) of the lessee is, from 1st January 1989, void as against the Official Assignee (qv): Bankruptcy Act 1988 s.49(1). See LEASE, DETERMINATION OF.

forged endorsement. See CHEQUE, LIABILITY ON.

formation. A building society may be formed by any 10 or more persons who are not otherwise disqualified, by (a) agreeing the objects (qv) of the society and on the extent of its powers in a memorandum (qv), (b) agreeing on rules (qv) for the regulation of the society and (c) delivering to the Central Bank 3 copies of the memorandum and rules: BS Act 1989 s.10(2). A society is not incorporated until it has been issued with a *certificate of incorporation* (qv) (ibid s.10(1)).

The Central Bank must register the memorandum and rules and issue the society with a certificate of incorporation if it is satisfied on a number of grounds (eg that registration would not be prejudicial to the orderly and proper regulation of societies generally);

it may also refuse registration if it has reason to believe that the society would not obtain an authorisation (qv) to raise funds (ibid s.10(3)). An appeal lies to the High Court against a decision to refuse registration (ibid s.10(4)). See DISQUALIFICATION; FINANCIAL YEAR; REGISTRATION, CANCELLATION OF.

four unities. See JOINT TENANCY.

fraud. A tort (qv) arising from a false statement of fact made by a person, knowingly or recklessly, with the intent that it be acted on by another, who as a result suffers damage. Also known as *deceit*. It has been held that while the standard of proof in fraud is that of the balance of probability, where such proof is largely a matter of inference, such inference must not be drawn lightly: Banco Ambrosiano v Ansbacher & Co (1987) ILRM 669.

For the provisions in the BS Act 1989 dealing with fraud, see AUCTIONEERING SERVICE; CONVEYANCING; DERIVATIVE ACTION, BUILDING SOCIETY; DISQUALIFICATION; DISQUALIFICATION ORDER; REGISTRATION, CANCELLATION OF.

freehold. An interest in land being either a fee simple, a fee tail or a life estate (qqv). Interests which are less than freehold are leases and tenancies (qqv).

freeze assets. The colloquial term to describe an order of the court which prevents any dealing in assets to which the order relates eg an order to prevent monies leaving a bank account under powers conferred by the Finance Act 1983 s.18. See also ATTACHMENT OF FUNDS; BANK ACCOUNT OF SOCIETY; BANKER AND CONFIDENTIALITY.

FSIA. [Financial Services Industry Association (qv)].

full age. See AGE OF MAJORITY.

functions. Term used to describe powers and duties eg BS Act 1989 s.2(1). See DIRECTOR..

funds, distribution of. See AMALGAMATION; TRANSFER OF ENGAGEMENTS.

furniture. A building society mortgage usually contains a provision whereby, if the society enters into possession of the mortgaged property which contains *furniture* or *chattels* (qv) of the borrower which he fails to remove, the society is empowered, as agent (qv) of the borrower, to remove store preserve sell or otherwise dispose of the furniture and chattels. Also there is usually provision in such mortgages whereby a society is not required to make any apportionment of rent, of a mortgaged property which is let furnished under a tenancy which is binding on the society, in respect of any furniture or chattels of the borrower comprised in such tenancy. See APPENDIX 5 - TYPICAL MORTGAGE clause 13.

future interest. An interest limited to come into existence at some time in the future. A future interest in land is an interest which confers a right to the enjoyment of the land at a future time eg the right to land after the death of a living person. A future interest may be *vested* or *contingent*. A *vested* future interest is where the persons entitled to the interest are ascertained and the interest in ready to take effect on the determination of all the preceding interests; a *contingent* interest arises where either of these conditions is absent. Future interests can be classified also as reversions, legal remainders, future trusts and legal executory interests.

G

gale. A rent or duty; a periodic payment of rent.

gale day. A rent day. Every tenancy from year to year is presumed to have commenced on the last *gale* *day* of the calendar year on which rent has become due and payable in respect of the premises, unless a contrary intention appears: Deasy's Act 1860 s.6. It has been held that the consistent and regular recognition by parties to a tenancy of a particular day of each month as the gale day, is prima facie evidence of the commencement of the tenancy on that day of some month, and of its being a monthly tenancy: White v Mitchell (1962) IR 348.

garnishee. A debtor in whose hands a debt has been attached by a court. Garnishee proceedings enable a judgment creditor (qv) to have assigned to him the benefit of any debt owed by the garnishee to the judgment debtor (qv). A *garnishee order* is an order, served on the garnishee, attaching a debt in his hands. See RSC O.45 rr.1-8; RCC O.37. See DIRECTION.

gazumping. Popularly understood to describe the situation in which a vendor of a house which is sold *subject to contract*, withdraws from the sale or threatens to do so, in expectation of receiving a higher price elsewhere. See SUBJECT TO CONTRACT.

good title. See MARKETABLE TITLE.

Governor of Central Bank. The person appointed as Governor of the Central Bank of Ireland by the President of Ireland on the advice of the Government: Central Bank Act 1942 s.19. His term of office is for seven years; he is ineligible for election as a director of any bank whatsoever; and he is prohibited from holding shares in any bank. See also Central Bank Act 1989 s.14. For his functions and duties in relation to building societies, see AUTHORISED PERSON; CONFIDENTIALITY. See also CENTRAL BANK.

grace, days of. See DAYS OF GRACE.

grant. See HOUSING BODY, APPROVED; SUBSIDY.

ground rent. A lease may determine by enlargement by *buying out the ground rent*, whereby the lessee can require the ground landlord to transfer the *fee simple* to the lessee. A wide category of lessees are entitled to acquire the fee simple, including persons holding under building (qv) and proprietary (qv) leases, under long leases with low rent, and under certain local authority leases: Landlord and Tenant (Ground Rents) (No 2) Act 1978 ss.9-15 as amended by the Landlord and Tenant (Amendment) Act 1980 ss.70-73. The creation of new ground rents is prohibited. See also Landlord and Tenant (Ground Rents) Acts 1984 and 1987.

The 1984 Act s.7 enacted new provisions regarding the determination of the purchase price by arbitration, particularly to deal with the case of a lease with less than 15 years to run, following the ruling in Gilsenan v Foundary House Investments Ltd and Rathmines Property Ltd (1980) ILRM 273. The 1987 Act extended indefinitely the period of operation of Part III of the 1978 Act; this provides ground rent tenants of domestic dwellinghouses with a cheap and expeditious method of buying out the ground rent.

A building society mortgage usually contains a covenant whereby the borrower undertakes to lodge the documents of title to the fee simple with the society in the event that the borrower enlarges his interest in the mortgaged property to a fee simple eg see APPENDIX 5 - TYPICAL MORTGAGE clause 12(e).

group accounts. The accounts·

which the directors of a building society are required to prepare where the society has subsidiaries at the end of its financial year (qv); such group accounts must deal respectively with the income and expenditure, the state of affairs and the source and application of the funds, of the society and the subsidiaries: BS Act 1989 s.77(2)-(4). The Central Bank may grant a dispensation from this requirement (ibid s.77(5)).

The requirements in relation to the auditors' report in its application to the *group accounts* of a society, must be read as referring to the society and (so far as it concerns the members of the society) the subsidiaries (ibid s.88(7)). See SUBSIDIARY.

guarantee. A collateral promise to answer for the debt, default or miscarriage of another person. It is a contract by which a person (known as the *guarantor*) becomes bound to another (the *creditor*) for the fulfilment or performance of a promise or engagement or other duty of a third party (the *principal*). Although guarantees most often relate to a debt, they can pertain to any type of duty or obligation. Contrast with *warranty* which generally bears no obligations to third parties. See Lombard & Ulster Banking v Murray (1986) HC.

The giving of guarantees by a building society is a *financial service* (qv) which a society may be empowered to provide: BS Act 1989 s.29(2)(b). The Central Bank has power to impose conditions on a society, as regards the exercise of its *adoptable powers*, as to limits on any guarantee, bond, contract of suretyship or indemnity given or entered into by the society (ibid s.36(11)(f)).

A building society mortgage will sometimes contain a guarantee whereby the guarantor becomes bound to the society for the performance by the borrower of all the covenants and obligations in the mortgage eg see APPENDIX 5 - GUARANTEE. See BOND; CONTRACT OF GUARANTEE; DEBT; HOUSING BODY, APPROVED; LOANS; STATUTE OF FRAUDS (IRELAND); SURETY.

guarantee and director. A building society is prohibited from entering into any guarantee or providing any security which is incidental to or connected with any loan or disposal of property made to a director or a *connected person* (qv) or a payment made on behalf of the director or connected person: BS Act 1989 s.57(1)(d). See DISCLOSURE OF LOANS; LEASE TO DIRECTOR; LOAN TO DIRECTOR; PAYMENT ON BEHALF OF DIRECTOR.

guarantor. A person who binds himself by a guarantee; a person who promises to answer for another; a surety (qv).

H

habendum. [To have]. The clause in a conveyance which defines the estate to be taken by the purchaser eg *To have and to hold in fee simple*. See also APPENDIX 5 - TYPICAL MORTGAGE clause 5(a).

head lease. The lease from which lesser interests (ie sub-leases) have been created. See LEASE.

hedge. To reduce by contract the risk of loss arising from changes in interest rates, currency exchange rates or other factors of a similar nature affecting ones business; building societies are empowered to effect such contracts subject to compliance with Central Bank requirements: BS Act 1989 s.34.

hereditament. Real property which on the death intestate of the owner devolved on an heir. *Corporeal* hereditaments are visible and tangible property eg land and structures thereon. *Incorporeal* hereditaments are intangible property eg easements (qv) and profits a prendre (qv).

High Court. The court above the Circuit Court (qv) in the hierarchical system of courts, which is invested with full *original* jurisdiction in and power to determine all matters and questions whether of law or fact, civil or criminal: 1937 Constitution art.34(3)(l). It sits in Dublin and at other locations in the State as required.

In civil matters the High Court can award unlimited damages; in criminal matters it is known as the *Central Criminal Court* and hears only very serious crimes such as treason, murder, attempted murder or conspiracy to murder. The judge sits alone except (a) in criminal cases and in certain civil actions eg defamation, false imprisonment or intentional trespass to the person, when he sits with a jury and (b) in cases of importance at the direction of the President of the High Court, when three judges sit as a *divisional court*, and may give separate judgments, although the decision of the court is the majority.

The High Court exercises considerable supervisory jurisdiction over inferior courts, administrative bodies and individuals by way of *judicial review*. An appeal from the High Court lies to the Supreme Court (qv).

As regards building societies, the High Court has power to prohibit the continuance of a contravention of the BS Act 1989 or the failure to comply with a condition imposed in relation to an authorisation (qv) or certain directions (qv) from the Central Bank eg in relation to an advertisement (qv) or an authorisation to raise funds: BS Act 1989 s.43(1).

In addition the Court may require the cessation of the exercise of an *adoptable* power where there has been a failure to comply with a condition imposed in relation thereto. The Court may make an interim (qv) or interlocutory (qv) order (ibid s.43(2)).

Appeals lie to the court eg in relation to the refusal of the Central Bank to register a society or an alteration to its rules (qv) or its memorandum (qv); or against the revocation by the Bank of an authorisation (qv); or against the cancellation by the Bank of the society's registration; or for an order setting aside a direction (qv). In addition, a petition may be made to the court to cancel a conversion scheme (qv). See Rules of the Superior Courts 1986. See APPEAL; AUTHORISATION, REVOCATION OF; CONVERSION; FORMATION; JUDGMENT CREDITOR; LIQUIDATOR; OFFICER; REGISTRATION, CANCELLATION OF; TERMINATION OF BUSINESS.

hire. Payment for the temporary use of something. As regards hire to a director of a building society, see LEASE TO DIRECTOR.

hire-purchase. An agreement for the bailment of goods under which the bailee may buy the goods or under which the property in the goods will or may pass to the bailee: Hire-Purchase Act 1946 s.1. In practice, the buyer selects goods which the seller sells to a finance house, which then enters into a hire-purchase agreement with the buyer. There is no contract between the seller and the hirer although the hirer may have a cause of action against the seller for breach of an express warranty or condition. The hirer (bailee) has an option to buy the goods on fulfilment of certain conditions, or he may return the goods to the owner on payment of the sum stated in the agreement.

The financing of hire-purchase is a *financial service* (qv) which a building society may be empowered to provide: BS Act 1989 s.29(2)(j). A hire-purchase agreement must meet particular statutory requirements. See also Hire-Purchase (Amendment) Act 1960; SGSS Act 1980.

holder for value. A person who takes a bill of exchange (qv) and who has given, or is deemed to have given, valuable consideration for the bill. Valuable consideration for a bill may be constituted by any consideration sufficient to support a simple contact or any antecedent debt or liability. A holder for value obtains no better title to the bill than the transferor had. See Bills of Exchange Act 1882 s.27.

holder in due course. A person who takes a bill of exchange (qv), complete and regular on the face of it, before it is overdue and without notice of dishonour (qv), in good faith and for value, without notice of any defect of title of the transferor; such a person holds the bill free from any defect of title of prior parties: Bills of Exchange Act 1882 s.29.

holding over. Where a tenant continues in possession of land on termination of his tenancy. See MESNE RATES.

house. Includes any building or part of a building used or suitable for use as a dwelling and any outoffice, yard, garden or other land appurtenant thereto or usually enjoyed therewith and *housing* is to be construed accordingly: BS Act 1989 s.2(1). See CERTIFICATE OF REASONABLE VALUE; FAMILY HOME; HOUSING LOAN; OVERCROWDED HOUSE.

house agent. A person who, as agent for another person and for or in expectation of reward, purchases, sells, lets or offers for sale or letting, or invites offers to purchase or take a letting of, or negotiates for the purchase, sale or letting of a house otherwise than by auction or attempts to effect such purchase, sale or letting: Auctioneers and House Agents Act 1947 s.2. A person may not carry on or hold himself out or represent himself as carrying on the business of house agent except under and in accordance with a *licence* (ibid s.7).

Any agreement in a contract relating to the sale, lease, or letting of property which makes the purchaser, lessee or tenant liable to pay the fees or expense of an auctioneer or house agent is void: Auctioneers and House Agents Act 1973 s.2. See Law v Roberts & Co (1964) IR 292. See AUCTIONEER.

housing. Housing authorities have an express statutory duty imposed on them to assess the adequacy of the supply and condition of housing in their areas and to draw up programmes, known as *building programmes* to meet the needs of the area: Housing Act 1966 ss.53-55. They are empowered to provide dwellings and works, services and building sites and amenities (ibid s.56-57). Housing authorities are also empowered to take account of the needs of persons resident outside their functional area and to build and let houses to such persons: Housing Act 1984; this Act was necessitated by the decision in McNamee v Buncrana UDC (1984) ILRM 77.

A housing authority has a duty to ensure by a proper valuation that a house, offered as a security for a loan, is a good security for that loan and it owes a duty of care in that regard to the person seeking the loan: 1966 Act s.39; Ward v McMaster (1986) ILRM 43 and (1988) SC.

Recent legislation (a) seeks to ensure that the housing needs of categories of persons such as the homeless, the aged, the disabled and travellers obtain due priority and (b) provides a simplified procedure for discharging mortgages in certain cases: Housing Act 1988. See also O'Reilly v Limerick Corporation (1988) HC.

It is usual to have a covenant in a building society mortgage whereby the borrower undertakes not to apply for any grants or loans under the Housing Acts 1966 to 1979 and other specified Acts, without the consent in writing of the society eg see APPENDIX 5 - TYPICAL MORTGAGE clause 8(n). See CERTIFICATE OF REASONABLE VALUE; TENANT PURCHASE SCHEME.

housing body, approved. A body approved of by the Minister for the Environment for the purposes of s.5 of the Housing Act 1988, or a society registered under the Industrial and Provident Societies Acts 1893 to 1978, or under the Friendly Societies Acts 1896 to 1977, or a voluntary group: BS Act 1989 s.28(5). A building society may, subject to the *adoption* of the power and the approval of the Central Bank, support *approved housing bodies* by means of loans, grants, guarantees and the provision of services and property, provided the support is given for the purpose of providing housing (ibid s.28(1)(b)). See also Second Schedule, Part I, para 3. See ADOPTABLE POWERS.

housing loan. A loan on the security of a mortgage (qv) of a freehold or leasehold estate or interest in a *house* (qv) for the purpose of enabling a member of a building society to provide or improve the house or to purchase the said estate or interest: BS Act 1989 s.22. A society is empowered to make *housing loans* to members, including, with the approval of the Central Bank, housing loans in a foreign currency. Otherwise the Bank's approval is not required and *adoption* of the power by the society is not required.

A housing loan must be made on terms that the capital element of the mortgage debt does not exceed the value of the security; however, the amount due to the society on a housing loan may exceed the value of the security where the Bank so approves (ibid s.22(2) and (3)). This latter provision enables societies to introduce, with the approval of the Bank, of a range of different types of mortgages not previously permitted, as the mortgage debt could at some point have exceeded the value of the security, or the capital repaid might not have corresponded to the amount borrowed eg in the case of *index linked* and *equity* mortgages. The rules (qv) of a society must provide for the manner in which housing loans are to be made and repaid (ibid Second Schedule, Part II, para 5(e)).

In the UK, the doubt which existed under the UK BS Act 1962 as to whether *index linked* mortgages were permissable under that Act, was removed in Nationwide Building Society v Registry of Friendly Societies (1983) WLR

1226, where it was held that there was no objection in principle under the general law to index linked mortgages. See BRIDGING LOAN; HOUSING; PRIOR MORTGAGE; LINKING SERVICES; REDEMPTION; SUBSIDY.

housing programme, national. See NATIONAL HOUSING PROGRAMME.

I

ibid, ib, ibidem. [In the same place]. From the same source.

IBSA. [Irish Building Societies Association (qv)].

immunity. The condition of being exempt from some liability to which others may be subject eg the immunity of a judge when performing his judicial functions. In a particular case, the court held that the Registrar of Friendly Societies was entitled to *immunity* from the type of claim being made by a plaintiff depositor: McMahon v Ireland, AG and Registrar of Friendly Societies. The court held that the Registrar was entitled to the protection of the principle stated in Everitt v Griffiths (1921) 1 AC 675 – "If a man is required in the discharge of a public duty to make a decision which affects by its legal consequences the liberty or property of others and he performs that duty honestly and in good faith, it is, in my opinion, a fundamental principal of our law that he is protected. It is not consonant with the principles of our law to require a man to make such a decision in discharge of his duty to the public, and then leave him in peril by reason of the consequence to others of that decision, provided that he acted honestly in making that decision."

improvement notice. The notice which a business tenant (qv) serves on his landlord when he proposes to carry out improvements to the *tenement* (qv). The landlord may within a month serve the tenant with an *improvement consent*, or an *improvement undertaking* where he undertakes to carry out the work himself, or an *improvement objection.* A landlord has only limited grounds upon which he may object to an improvement. A landlord who carries out the improvement himself is entitled to increase the rent; a tenant who carries out improvements may be entitled to compensation when he quits the tenement. See Landlord and Tenant (Amendment) Act 1980. See IMPROVEMENTS, COMPENSATION FOR.

improvements, compensation for. A business tenant (qv) who quits his *tenement* (qv) is entitled to compensation by the landlord for every improvement made which adds to the letting value of the tenement on the termination date, and which is suitable to the character of the tenement: Landlord and Tenant (Amendment) Act 1980 Part IV. A business tenant who quits by surrender or because of non-payment of rent is not so entitled.

The amount of compensation may be agreed upon by the landlord and tenant or in the absence of agreement, it will be an amount determined by the court, as the *capitalised value* of such addition to the letting value of the tenement at the termination as the court determines to be attributable to the improvement (ibid s.47(1)). The maximum capitalised value which the court may determine is 15 times the annual amount of addition to the letting value. See IMPROVEMENT NOTICE.

in alieno solo. On another's land.

See EASEMENT.

in camera. The hearing of a case in private eg in court but with the public excluded or in a judge's chambers. Justice is required to be administered in public, save in such special and limited cases as may be prescribed by law: 1937 Constitution, art.34(1). The law prescribes that justice may be administered otherwise than in public in the case of eg certain proceedings under the BS Act 1989 eg ss.40(6) and 43(4). It has been held in the UK that publication of proceedings in the privacy of chambers was a contempt of court: Alliance Perpetual Building Society v Beltum Investments Ltd and Ors (1957) 1 WLR 720.

in gross. A right which is not appendant, appurtenant, or otherwise annexed to land. See EASEMENT.

inalienability. Not transferable. The general rule of law is that land must not be rendered inalienable; however, no gift for charitable purposes is void merely because it renders land inalienable in *perpetuity*. See also Landlord and Tenant (Amendment) Act 1980 s.66. See In re the Estate of Dunne, decd, (1989) ILT & SJ 22. See CHARITIES; MORTMAIN.

inchoate. Begun, or in an early stage, but not complete. See INCHOATE BILL.

inchoate bill. A bill of exchange (qv) which arises when a person signs a blank stamped paper with the intention that it may be converted into a bill; this operates as an authority to fill it up as a complete bill for any amount the stamp will cover, using the signature already on it: Bills of Exchange Act 1882 s.20. Also, where a bill is wanting in any material particular, the holder of it has authority to fill up the omission in any way he thinks fit (ibid s.20). A promissory note (qv) is inchoate and incomplete until delivery to the payee or bearer (ibid s.84).

income and expenditure account. See ANNUAL ACCOUNTS; AUDITORS' REPORT.

income tax. It is unlawful for a building society to pay a director remuneration (whether as a director or otherwise) free of income tax: BS Act 1989 s.62. See TAXATION ADVICE.

incorporation. Merging together to form a whole; conferring legal personality on an association of persons eg incorporation of a building society: BS Act 1989 s.10(1) and (3). From the date of its incorporation, a building society is a body corporate (with the name contained in its memorandum (qv) and rules (qv)) having perpetual succession and a seal and the power to hold land (ibid s.10(6)). See CERTIFICATE OF INCORPORATION; DEVELOPING LAND.

incorporeal hereditaments. Intangible property eg easements (qv) and profits a prendre (qv). See OWNERSHIP.

indemnify. To make good a loss which one person has suffered in consequence of the act or default of another. Normally an employer will be held to have indemnified an employee against all liabilities and expenses incurred by the employee in the proper performance of his employment.

Any provision in a building society's rules (or in a contract with the society) is void if it exempts or indemnifies an officer or auditor of the society in respect of any liability which attaches to him in respect of his negligence, default, breach of duty or breach of trust: BS Act 1989 s.114(1).

However, the High Court may relieve an officer or auditor from his liability where it appears to the court that the person has acted honestly and reasonably (ibid s.115(1)).

The giving by a building society of indemnities is a *financial service* (qv) which a society may be empowered to provide: BS Act 1989 s.29(2)(b).

Also the Central Bank may indemnify a society against any costs or expenses incurred by it in, or in connection with, any proceedings brought by the Bank in the society's name (ibid s.47(7)).

A contract of insurance usually indemnifies the insured, in consideration of a premium, against loss he has suffered. See Rohan Construction v Insurance Corporation of Ireland (1986) ILRM 419 and (1987) SC. See DERIVATIVE ACTION, BUILDING SOCIETY; GUARANTEE; INSURANCE INTERMEDIARY; LEGAL COSTS; LOAN TO DIRECTOR; PROPERTY TRANSACTION.

indemnity. See INDEMNIFY.

index-linking. See HOUSING LOAN.

indictable offence. An offence which entitles the accused as of right to a trial by jury. If the accused elects for jury trial, the District Court will conduct a *preliminary investigation* to satisfy itself that there is sufficient evidence *to return the accused for trial* to a higher court.

Certain cases of indictable offences can be heard by the District Court if the accused consents (and the Director of Public Prosecutions also consents in particular cases), in which event the maximum punishment is twelve months imprisonment and/or a fine. However, a District Court is now empowered to impose consecutive sentences up to a maximum of two years imprisonment: Criminal Justice Act 1984 s.12. Provision has been made for the transfer of the trial of a person charged with an indictable offence from the Circuit Court before which the person is triable to the Dublin Circuit Court: Courts Act 1981 s.31; The State (Boyle) v Nealon (1987) ILRM 535.

An accused on conviction on indictment (qv) of an offence under the BS Act 1989 is liable to a fine not exceeding £50,000 (£25,000 and £10,000 in certain offences), or, at the discretion of the court, to imprisonment for a term not exceeding 7 years (5 and 3 years in certain offences) or both (ibid ss.119(1)(a)(II) and (3)(a)(ii); 120(2)). See APPENDIX I. See DISQUALIFICATION; INDICTMENT; SUMMARY OFFENCE.

indictment. A written accusation of a crime made against one or more persons and preferred to a jury; formerly it was made by *The People at the suit of the Attorney General*: 1937 Constitution, art.30(3). An indictment is now brought in the name of *The People at the suit of the Director of Public Prosecutions*: Prosecution of Offences Act 1974. For the rules governing the form of an indictment, see Criminal Justice (Administration) Act 1924; Indictment Rules 1924.

It has been held that the inclusion of additional charges in an indictment at the behest of the DPP following the return by a district justice of an accused for trial, pursuant to the Criminal Procedure Act 1967 s.18 is unconstitutional: The State (Walsh) v DPP (1988) HC. See INDICTABLE OFFENCE.

information, disclosure of. See INSPECTION.

inhibition. An entry in the register

of the Land Registry in respect of registered land in the form of a restriction on registration; the restriction will prevent all registrations except those made in compliance with the inhibition. It imposes on a subsequent applicant for registration the onus of ensuring that the registration he applies for complies with the inhibition. Inhibitions are used to protect interests which are not permitted to be registered as *burdens* (qv). See Registration of Title Act 1964 ss.96-98.

injunction. An order of the court directing a party to an action to do, or to refrain from doing, a particular thing. An injunction is enforced by committal for contempt of court in respect of any breach. An injunction is either (a) *prohibitory* (restrictive/preventative) - forbidding continuance of a wrongful act or (b) *mandatory* (compulsive) - directing direct performance of a positive act: Bula Ltd v Tara Mines (1988) ILRM 157.

As regards time, an injunction is either (a) *interim* - restraining the defendant until some specified time; (b) *interlocutory* - a temporary injunction pending trial of the action, only granted where the *balance of convenience* lies in so granting it and where the recoverable damages would be an inadequate remedy: Campus Oil Ltd v Minister for Industry & Energy (No 2) (1983) IR 88; (c) *perpetual* - permanent injunction after hearing of the action.

A *Mareva injunction* (qv) is a particular type of interim injunction granted to restrain a defendant, who is not within the jurisdiction, from removing assets from the jurisdiction, pending trial of an action for a debt due. A *quia timet* (qv) injunction is one to prevent or restrain some act, merely feared or threatened. As regards injunctions and building societies, see HIGH COURT; ULTRA VIRES.

injunction, planning. An order which the High Court has power to make to prohibit the continuation of the development of land or unauthorised use thereof, where such development, being development for which permission is required, *is being carried* out without such permission or an *unauthorised use is being made* of the land: LG(P&D) Act 1976 s.27. An application for such an injunction may be made by a planning authority or any other person, whether or not the person has an interest in the land (ibid s.27(1)).

The order of the court may require any person specified in the order to do or not to do, or cease to do, as the case may be, anything which the court considers necessary to ensure that a development authorised by a permission, is carried out in conformity with that permission (ibid s.27(2)). The court may make an interim or interlocutory order as it deems appropriate. See RSC O.103. See Dublin County Council v Kirby (1984) HC; Morris v Garvey (1982) ILRM 177.

inland bill. A bill of exchange both drawn and payable within Ireland and Britain. A *foreign* bill is any other bill of exchange. See Bills of Exchange Act 1882 s.4. See BILL OF EXCHANGE.

insolvency. See WARRANTY; WINDING UP.

inspection. The inspection or investigation of a building society which an *authorised person* (qv) is empowered to carry out, on the state and conduct of the business of the society or of its subsidiary (qv) or associated body (qv): BS Act 1989 s.41.

The Central Bank or an authorised person, is entitled to require to be furnished such information, documents, or other material or explanations as may be specified, and the authorised person is entitled to enter the premises of a society at all reasonable times and to inspect and take copies of, or extracts from, any document or material (ibid s.41(2) and (3)).

The duty to produce or provide information etc extends to present and past officers, employees and agents of a society and its associated body, and also extends to a liquidator (qv) (ibid s.41(5), (8) and (9)). See ABROAD; ADMISSIBILITY OF EVIDENCE; LIEN; PRIVILEGE, LEGAL PROFESSIONAL. See APPENDIX I.

inspector. A person appointed by the Central Bank to investigate the affairs of a building society: BS Act 1989 s.45(1). He has power, with the approval of the Bank, to investigate and report on a subsidiary or other body corporate associated with the society (ibid s.45(6)). It is an offence for an officer, member or agent of a society to refuse to produce to an inspector any book or document which it is his duty to produce, or to refuse to attend before the inspector or to answer questions put to him by the inspector (ibid s.46(1) and (4)). An inspector is required to make a final report on his investigation to the Bank; he may make an interim report if he so wishes and must make one if so required by the Bank (ibid s.47(1)).

A copy of the inspector's report must be sent by the Bank to the Ministers for Finance and the Environment, and the Bank must, if it thinks fit, send a copy also to the society, its auditors, its members, the applicant for the investigation, or a body corporate dealt with in the report. The Minister for the Environment may lay the report before each House of the Oireachtas and a report not so laid, may be printed and published by the Bank. See DERIVATIVE ACTION, BUILDING SOCIETY; ADMISSIBILITY OF EVIDENCE; DIRECTOR'S BANK ACCOUNT; EXAMINATION; INVESTIGATION; PRIVILEGE; WINDING UP. See APPENDIX I. See also BORD PLEANALA, AN.

insurable interest. An interest giving an insured person a right to enforce a contract of insurance. An insurance contract is void unless the assured has some *insurable interest* in the life or property which is the subject of the insurance at the time the contract is entered into. The interest exists if the insured is liable to sustain some monetary loss, or if he may be claimed against following a loss to another. In life insurance, no contract of insurance may be made by a person on the life of another unless he has an interest in the life of that other: Life Assurance Act 1774 s.1; Life Assurance Act 1886.

A person has an unlimited interest in his own life. A father may not necessarily have an insurable interest in his son's life: Halford v Kymer (1830) 10 B &C 724; a husband may insure his wife and vice versa: Griffiths v Fleming (1909) 1 KB 805; a trustee may insure in respect of an interest of which he is trustee: Tidswell v Ankerstein (1792) Peake 151; tenants-at-will may insure a premises which they occupy and are required to maintain: Church &General Insurance Co v Connolly (1981) HC.

Statutory provisions prevent insurance being used as a means of gaming and wagering: Gaming and Lotteries Act 1956. See also Coen v Employers Liability Assurance Corporation (1962) 104 ILTR 157; P J Carrigan Ltd v Norwich Union Fire Society (1987) HC. See INSURANCE.

insurance. A contract whereby a person called the *insurer* agrees in consideration of money paid to him, called the *premium*, by another person called the *assured*, to indemnify the latter against loss resulting to him on the happening of certain events. The event must constitute an *insurable interest* (qv). The *policy* is the document in which is contained the terms of the contract. Insurance is a contract *uberrimae fidei* (of the utmost good faith) and of indemnity only, except in the case of life and accident insurance, when an agreed sum is often payable.

Insurance is a *financial service* (qv) which a building society may be empowered to provide: BS Act 1989 s.29(2)(g). However, a society must not carry on insurance business otherwise than by a subsidiary (qv) or other associated body (qv) of the society (ibid s.29(4)).

It is normal practice for a building society mortgage to contain a provision whereby the society is entitled, without being obliged to do so, to insure any buildings on the mortgaged property against loss or damage by fire and against other risks as the society thinks fit. Such a provision usually gives full power to the society to settle and adjust with the insurers all questions concerning the amount payable under the policy and the liability of the insurers and to determine how any such moneys received are applied, eg see APPENDIX 5 - TYPICAL MORTGAGE clause 8(e)-(h) and (j).

However, a building society is prohibited from requiring a member to effect insurance on any security for a loan with an insurer directed by the society or through the agency of the society or of any intermediary directed by the society: BS Act 1986 s.6(1)(c); SI No 27 of 1987; SI No 339 of 1987. Notwithstanding the repeal of the 1986 Act, this provision continues in force: BS Act 1989 s.6. Any dispute between a member and the society in relation to this matter is to be determined by the Central Bank.

Also continuing in force is the requirement that a society arrange through an insurer or an intermediary nominated by it for the provision of *mortgage protection insurance* in respect of secured loans, the premium to be payable by the member in monthly instalments; there are exceptions eg in respect of loans in excess of £60,000; and in respect of members who by reason of health would not be acceptable to an insurer. The Central Bank is empowered to prescribe, by regulation, rules (a) removing or restricting the right of a society to require a member to effect or keep effected insurance on the security for a housing loan with an insurer directed by the society or through the agency of the society or of any intermediary directed by the society; and (b) arranging by a society through an insurer or intermediary nominated by it for the provision of mortgage protection insurance: BS Act 1989 s.11(2)(b)(iii) and (v). See APPENDIX 2. See also APPENDIX 5 - TYPICAL MORTGAGE clause 3(a). See BUSINESS ASSOCIATE; INDEMNIFY; INSURANCE BUSINESS; INSURANCE, CONTRACT OF; LINKING SERVICES; PREMIUM; ULTRA VIRES.

insurance, contract of. Insurance policies fall into two broad categories: *life assurance* which insures against an event which must happen and *liability insurance* which insures against events which may happen. A contract of insurance does not come into effect and the insurer put on risk until the precise time specified in the contract or, if not stated, when the parties intended. Often, this is at the time the first premium is paid: Harney v Century Insurance Co Ltd (1983) HC.

Most contracts of insurance provide that disputes between the parties be resolved by arbitration (qv). See Stanbridge v Healy (1985) ILRM 290. See COVER NOTE; UBERRIMAE FIDEI.

insurance, double. See DOUBLE INSURANCE.

insurance agent. Under recent legislation, means any person who holds an appointment in writing from an insurer enabling him to place insurance business with that insurer, but does not include an *insurance broker* or an employee of an insurer when the employee is acting for that insurer: Insurance Act 1989 s.2(1). Certain conditions are specified for insurance agents eg that an agent must hold appointment from not more than four authorised insurers (ibid s.49). An insurance agent is an *insurance intermediary* (qv) and is governed by the provisions in the 1989 Act concerning such intermediaries.

It has been held that where an insurance agent's authority is confined to submitting proposal forms (and not to completing the forms), the insurer is not bound by any statement or representation by the agent: Connors v London & Provincial Assurance Co (1913) 47 ILTR 148. Under the recent legislation, an insurance agent will be deemed to be acting as the agent of the insurer when he completes in his own hand or helps the proposer of an insurance policy to complete a proposal (ibid s.51). See INSURANCE BROKER; INSURANCE INTERMEDIARY; PREMIUM; TIED INSURANCE AGENT.

insurance bond. See INSURANCE COMPANY; INSURANCE INTERMEDIARY.

insurance broker. Under recent legislation, means a person who, acting with freedom of choice (ie being in a position to arrange insurance contracts with at least five insurance undertakings) brings together, with a view to the insurance of risks, persons seeking insurance and insurance undertakings, and carries out work preparatory to the conclusion of contracts of insurance, but does not include an *insurance agent* or an employee of an insurer when the employee is acting for that insurer: Insurance Act 1989 ss.2(1) and 44. Insurance brokers are required to meet certain qualifications eg membership of a recognised body (ibid s.44).

Insurance brokers as *insurance intermediaries* (qv) are governed by the provisions of the 1989 Act regarding such intermediaries. See Chariot Inns Ltd v Assicurazioni Generali SPA (1981) ILRM 173. Contrast with INSURANCE AGENT. See INSURANCE INTERMEDIARY.

insurance business. Insurance business may be carried out by insurance companies which are governed by the Insurance Acts 1909 to 1989, and by registered friendly societies which are governed by the Friendly Societies Act 1896-1977, and by subsidiaries or other associated bodies of building societies which are governed by the BS Act 1989. These Acts and regulations made under the European Communities Act 1972, provide the statutory base for supervision by the State in the interest of policy holders. Insurance companies must hold a *authorisation*, maintain a *bond* with the High Court and make annual returns.

Under recent legislation, the supervising powers of the Minister for Industry and Commerce are updated and clarified, a system of regulation of insurance brokers and agents is introduced, and the Minister is given power to regulate commission payments to insurance intermediaries (qv): Insurance Act 1989. See also European Communities (Non-Life Insurance) Regulations 1976 (SI No 115 of 1976); European Communities (Life Assurance) Regulations 1984 (SI No 57 of 1984). See also RSC O.113. See INSURANCE; INSURANCE AGENT; INSURANCE BROKER; COMMISSION.

insurance compensation fund. The fund established by the Insurance Act 1964. Under recent legislation, the right to compensation via the fund, for refunds of premiums or payment of unsatisfied claims to policyholders or claimants of an insurance company being wound up, is restricted to 65% of unsatisfied claims or £650,000 per claim, whichever is the less: Insurance Act 1989 s.31.

insurance intermediary. An insurance broker or an insurance agent: Insurance Act 1989 s.2(1). Insurance intermediaries are required to keep a separate client bank account (ibid s.48) and to hold a bond in a specified form to a value of not less than £25,000 which, in the event that the intermediary fails to meet his financial obligations, will be available for the benefit of his clients who have thereby suffered loss (ibid s.47).

The Minister for Industry and Commerce may provide by regulation that a person must not act or hold himself out to be an insurance agent or broker unless he effects a policy of *professional indemnity insurance* as the Minister may prescribe (ibid s.45).

Also an insurance intermediary is disqualified from acting as such if adjudged bankrupt (qv); of if convicted of an offence involving fraud (qv) or dishonesty, whether connected with insurance or not; or if he is or was a director in a company involved in insurance which has been wound up (ibid ss.54-55).

Every insurance undertaking is required to keep a register of its appointed insurance intermediaries (ibid s.50). See INSURANCE AGENT, INSURANCE BROKER.

insurance of unnamed persons. See UNNAMED PERSONS, INSURANCE OF.

insured. Includes a person who is indemnified by another (the insurer) against loss resulting to him on the happening of an event.

insurer. The person who indemnifies another (the insured) against loss, in consideration of a premium (qv). The holder of an *authorisation* under the Insurance Acts 1909 to 1989 and SI Nos 115 of 1976 and 57 of 1984: Insurance Act 1989 s.2(1).

An insurer domiciled in a *contracting* state of the EEC may be sued in the courts of the state where he is domiciled, or in another contracting state in the courts for the place where the policy-holder is domiciled: Jurisdiction of Courts and Enforcement of Judgments (European Communities) Act 1988, first schedule, arts.8-12a.

intensification of use. See PLANNING PERMISSION.

interest. (1) A right in property.

(2) Rights, titles, advantages, duties and liabilities connected with a thing, whether present or future, ascertained or potential.

(3) Interest on judgment debts under the Debtors (Ireland) Act 1840 s.26 has been reduced from 11 per cent to 8 per cent as from 23rd January 1989: Courts Act 1981 (Interest on Judgment Debts) Order 1989 (SI No 12 of 1989).

(4) Interest on a dishonoured cheque may be claimed from the time of its presentment for payment: Bills of Exchange Act 1882 s.57(1).

(5) A sum of money payable in respect of the use of another sum of money called the principal. The interest charged by a building society on a mortgage loan provides the cover for the interest paid by the society to its shareholders and depositors. It is usual in the rules (qv) of the society or the mortgage (qv) or both, for provision to be made for adjustments to the rate of interest during the term of the mortgage and for adjustment to the monthly payments in order to ensure that the maturity date originally agreed is maintained, eg see APPENDIX 5 - TYPICAL MORTGAGE clause 4. Any attempt to impose harsh or unconscionable terms are unlikely to be upheld by a court: Kreglinger v New Patagonia Meat & Cold Storage Co Ltd (1914) AC 25; McCoy v Greene & Cole (1984) HC.

It has been held in the UK that interest on a share investment in a building society is to be calculated up to the date of withdrawal where the society has actual use of the money unless there is any stipulation to the contrary in the rules: Morton v Temperance Permanent Building Society (1944) Reg Rep Feb 26. See AUTHORISATION; COMPOUND INTEREST; DEPOSIT WITH CENTRAL BANK; MORTGAGEE, RIGHT OF; RETENTION OF MORTGAGED PROPERTY; SHARE; SHAREHOLDING; SUBSIDY; TIERED INTEREST RATE.

interest, disclosure of. The duty imposed by law on certain persons to disclose their interest in a matter eg the duty of a director of a building society to disclose his interest in any contract between himself and his society. See ARMS LENGTH, AT; DISCLOSURE OF INTEREST.

interest rate. See ANNUAL PERCENTAGE CHARGE; CONVERSION RESOLUTION; HEDGE; INTEREST; REDEMPTION FEE; TIERED INTEREST RATE.

interim injunction. See INJUNCTION.

interim order. An order of the Court, made in the course of proceedings, pending further directions from the Court.

interlocutory. Not final. See INJUNCTION.

internal audit. See ACCOUNTING RECORDS.

interpretation clause. A clause, eg in a statute or deed, which provides that certain specified words and phrases used therein have certain meanings eg *In this Act, unless the context otherwise requires - "commission" includes any gift, bonus fee, payment or other benefit*: BS Act 1989 s.2(1).

investigation. The Central Bank is empowered to appoint an inspector or inspectors to investigate the affairs of a building society or call a *special meeting* of the society where (a) an application is made to the Bank by not less than one-tenth of the members of the society entitled to vote on resolutions or 200 such members, whichever is the lesser, or (b) the Bank is of the opinion that such an investigation should be held or a meeting called: BS Act 1989 s.45(1).

The Central Bank may require the applicants to give security for payment of the costs of the investigation or meeting, to an amount not exceeding £200,000 (ibid s.45(3)(c)), and there are provisions regarding recoupment and apportionment of such costs (ibid s.45(3)(d) and 46(7)).

It is the duty of all officers, members and agents of a society, the affairs of which are being investigated, to produce to the inspector, all books, accounts, deeds, records or other documents, which are in their power, possession or procurement, relating to the society (ibid s.46(1)). *Agents* in this connection include bankers, accountants, solicitors, auditors, and the financial and other advisors of the society (ibid s.46(6)). See INSPECTION; INSPECTOR; PRIVILEGE, LEGAL PROFESSIONAL. In relation to investigations by an auditor, see AUDITOR, DUTY OF.

investigation of complaints. See COMPLAINTS, INVESTIGATION OF.

investment. A building society is empowered, subject to having *adopted* the power, to invest in bodies corporate ie to acquire and hold shares and *corresponding membership rights* in bodies corporate, or form or take part in forming bodies corporate, and to provide them with support eg loans, grants, guarantees, and the use of services or property: BS Act 1989 s.28(1). However, see ASSOCIATED BODY. See also ADOPTABLE POWERS; PASS BOOK; SHARE.

investment, prescribed. See LIQUID ASSETS.

investment service. An investment service is a *financial service* (qv) which a building society may be empowered to provide: BS Act 1989 s.29(2)(d).

inviolability of dwelling. The *dwelling* of every citizen is inviolable and must not be forcibly entered save in accordance with law: 1937 Constitution, art.40(5). In a case where members of a family live together in the family home, the house as a whole is the *dwelling* of each member of the family; however, if a member of a family occupies a clearly defined portion of the house apart from the other members of the family, then it may well be that the part not so occupied is no longer his dwelling and that the part he separately occupies is his dwelling, as would be the case where a person not a member of the family occupied or was in possession of a clearly defined portion of the house: The People (AG) v O'Brien (1965) IR 142. See also DPP v Gaffney (1988) ILRM 39; McCormack v ICS Building Society (1989) HC.

Irish Building Societies Association. The industry association established in the 1950's and currently operating to rules adopted in 1981. Its current members are the Irish Permanent, First National, Educational, and Irish Nationwide building societies, sometimes referred to as the "big four". Its principal object is to maintain a high standard of building society practices. It is a member of the European Federation of Building Societies. [IBSA, Block A, Earlsfort Centre, Earlsfort Terrace, Dublin 2]. See FINANCIAL SERVICES INDUSTRY ASSOCIATION.

irrevocable letter of credit. See LETTER OF CREDIT.

J

joint account. A banking account which can be operated either singly or collectively by the parties to the account, as arranged and agreed.

Money is frequently placed in a bank or other account in the joint names of two persons, often the depositor and another person. If it appears that such a deposit is made with the intention of making a testamentary disposition without complying with the statutory provisions, the court will hold that there is a presumption of a *resulting trust* in favour of the depositor's executors: Owens v Greene, Freely v Greene (1932) IR 225.

Generally, parties to a joint account are entitled to share the funds in the account equally and not in proportion to their contributions to it: Jones v Maynard (1951) Ch 572. Where a joint account is in the name of a husband and wife and the husband only has contributed to it, the doctrine of *advancement* may arise. See also Murray v Murray & Anor (1939) IR 317.

In the UK it has been held that where a person invests money in a building society in the joint names of himself and another, and intends to do so, he thereby confers on the other person a legal joint interest in the shares: Digby v Woolwich Equitable Building Society (1962) Reg Rep 3.

joint and several obligation. An obligation entered into by two or more persons, jointly and severally, so that each is liable separately, and all liable jointly, and an action may be taken against one or more separately or all jointly. The obligation may arise by agreement of the parties or by operation of law. For example, see APPENDIX 5 - TYPICAL MORTGAGE clause 2. See FINANCE HOUSE, LIABILITY OF; LOAN TO DIRECTOR; PROPERTY TRANSACTION.

joint borrower, representative. The person whose name first appears in the records of a building society in relation to a housing loan (qv) made by the society to two or more persons jointly: BS Act 1989 s.16(7). Generally, the *representative joint borrower* exercises the rights of the other joint borrowers on their behalf and notices sent to him are deemed to have been sent to the joint borrowers.

In relation to the conversion (qv) of a society to a public limited company, the rights of joint borrowers as *borrowing members* of the society are treated as the rights of the representative joint borrower alone (ibid s.16(7)(e)). Joint borrowers however are entitled to choose the order in which they are named in the records of the society and to demand a copy of the annual accounts (qv) or summary financial statement (ibid s.16(7)(f) and (g)). See BORROWING MEMBER; FINANCIAL STATEMENT, SUMMARY.

joint holder, representative. The person whose name first appears in the records of a building society in relation to shares jointly held by him and one or more other persons: BS Act 1989 s.16(3) and (6). In general, the *representative joint holder* exercises the rights of the other joint holders on their behalf eg in relation to proposing, circulating and voting on resolutions, appointing proxies, exercising the right to demand a poll (qv) or to appoint an inspector (qv) to the society.

In relation to the amalgamation (qv) of societies, the transfer of engagements, or the conversion (qv) of a society to a public limited company, the representative joint holder is deemed to hold the shares alone, and the other joint holders are not regarded as members of the society (ibid s.16(6)(e)).

The joint holders however are entitled to choose the order in which they are named in the records of the society and any joint holder can demand a copy of the annual accounts (qv) or summary financial statement (ibid s.16(6)(g) and (h)). See FINANCIAL STATEMENT, SUMMARY; MEMBER.

joint tenancy. The ownership of land by two or more persons where there is a *right of survivorship* ie when a joint tenant dies his interest passes to the remaining joint tenants. For this reason it is usual to make trustees joint tenants. The *four unities* of *possession*, *interest*, *title* and *time*, must exist or otherwise the ownership will be a tenancy in common (qv).

The joint tenants must have a unity of possession by which they have equal rights to possession of the whole land; they must have the identical share or interest in the land; they must have the same title by taking it from the same instrument; and their interest must have come into existence at the same time, with some exceptions. See Bodies Corporate (Joint Tenancy) Act 1899. See Maher v Maher (1987) ILRM 582. See PER MY ET PER TOUT; TENANCY IN COMMON.

judgment creditor. One in whose favour a judgment for a sum of money is given against a judgment debtor.

In relation to a company which is being wound up, a creditor who has issued execution against the company's property or attached a debt due to it is not entitled to retain the benefit of the process unless it was completed before the winding up commenced or before the creditor received notice of the meeting at which it was proposed to wind it up: Companies Act 1963 ss.291, 292 and 219. This provision now applies to a building society which is being wound up: BS Act 1989 s.109(1).

Also where judgment is obtained against a building society for the payment of a sum of money due to the judgment creditor, the Central Bank must be notified by the Court, and where all claims under the judgment are not satisfied within 21 days from the date of the judgment, the society is deemed (as regards the provisions dealing with winding up (qv)) to be unable to pay its debts (ibid s.109(2)).

Where an appeal is lodged against the judgment, the court may postpone the presumption that the society is unable to pay its debts, and may make an order requiring lodgment in court of funds or security to meet the amount due under the judgment and for the costs of the appeal (ibid s.109(3)-(5)). See DIRECTION.

judgment debtor. A person against whom a judgment (qv) has been given for a sum of money in favour of a judgment creditor.

judgment mortgage. A mortgage created by the registration as a mortgage, by a judgment creditor against the lands of the judgment debtor, of a judgment of a court for the payment of a sum of money: Judgment Mortgage Acts 1850 and 1858. Judgments which may be registered are such money judgments of the Supreme, High, Circuit and District Courts: Circuit Court (Registration of Judgments) Act 1937; Courts Act 1981 s.24.

A judgment may be registered against all legal and equitable interests of the judgment debtor in freehold and in leasehold property; a judgment mortgage is rarely registered against leaseholds as the judgment mortgagee then becomes liable for rent and convenants therein.

When a judgment is validly registered as a mortgage, the registration has the effect of a mortgage by deed over the debtor's beneficial interest at the time of registration in the lands set out in the *judgment mortgage affidavit* which is sworn by the judgment creditor: Judgment Mortgage Act 1850 s.7. A judgment mortgage does not obtain priority over a prior unregistered mortgage: Eyre v McDowell (1861) 9 HLC 620, unless the judgment mortgage is carried on the back of a subsequent registered mortgage: In re Scott's Estate (1862) 14 Ir Ch R 57.

The remedy of the judgment mortgagee is to seek a sale by the court by instituting a *mortgage suit* (qv). For *priority* of a judgment mortgage in the event of the judgment debtor becoming bankrupt (qv), see Bankruptcy Act 1988 s.51. See Registration of Title Act 1964 s.71. See FAMILY HOME.

just and equitable. The phrase sometimes used in statutes conferring power to a judge to make an order where the court is of opinion that it would be *just and equitable* to do so eg a building society may be wound up if the court is of the opinion that it would be just and equitable: BS Act 1989 s.109(3). See FAMILY HOME; WINDING UP.

K

knock for knock. Phrase used eg to describe an agreement whereby insurance companies pay their own insured on the basis that there will be no action brought by one insured against the other. It also refers to agreements between bodies in relation to their employee pension funds, whereby pension liabilities in respect of an employee moving from one body to the other, are borne by the fund of the receiving body.

L

land. As regards the law of real property or land law, *land* includes things attached to the land, such as buildings and other structures. As regards Acts of the Oireachtas (qv), *land* includes messuages, tenements and hereditaments, houses and buildings of any tenure: Interpretation Act 1937 ss.4 and 12. A general devise of *land* is to be construed as including leasehold land as well as freehold land, unless a contrary intention appears from the will: Succession Act 1965 s.92.

As regards planning permission, *land* includes any structure and any land covered with water, whether inland or coastal: LG(P&D) Act 1963 s.2(1). As regards the Rules of the Superior Courts, *land* includes messuages, tenements, hereditaments, houses and buildings of any tenure: RSC O.125 r.1. In bankruptcy matters, *land* includes any estate or interest in or charge over land: Bankruptcy Act 1988 s.3. In landlord and tenant matters, *land* includes houses, messuages, and tenements of every tenure, whether corporeal or incorporeal: Deasy's Act 1860 s.1. As regards pre 1922 statutes, see Interpretation Act 1889 s.3. See PREMISES.

land, developing. See DEVELOPING LAND.

land, planning and control. See

PLANNING PERMISSION.

land, recovery of. See EJECTMENT.

land, services relating to. See SERVICES RELATING TO LAND.

land certificate. The certificate of title to which the person registered as owner of *registered* land is entitled: Registration of Title Act 1964 s.28. The land certificate must be produced to the Registrar of the Land Registry for alteration, before any subsequent transaction can be noted on the register (ibid s.105). A lien (qv) is created when a land certificate is deposited to secure an advance of money; the depositee protects his rights by refusing to produce the certificate. See LAND REGISTRATION.

land registration. There are two mutually exclusive systems of land registration, the *registration of title* and the *registration of deeds*. Under the registration of deeds, the existence of a deed, will or conveyance may be registered; the document remains itself the evidence of title. Under the registration of title, the document ceases to be evidence of title, being replaced by the register which is conclusive evidence of title of the person whose name appears therein.

The registry of title was established by the Registration of Title Act 1891 and continued by the Registration of Title Act 1964. There are three registers, one each for registering the ownership of freehold land, leasehold land, and subsidiary interests (ibid s.8). The register is kept in *folios*, and each folio is in three parts: the first part has a description of the property; the second part describes the owner of the property, including cautions (qv) and inhibitions (qv) restricting the registration of dispositions of the property; the third part contains burdens (qv) and charges (qv), such as mortgages (qv). The register is prepared and maintained in the Land Registry which is situated in Dublin. Each registered holding is marked on the *registry map* by a plan number corresponding to the register.

Registration is compulsory for (a) all freehold and leasehold property acquired by local authorities and state sponsored bodies; (b) freehold property purchased under the various Land Purchase Acts; (c) acquisition on sale of property in areas designated as compulsory registration areas. Currently the counties of Carlow, Laois, and Meath have been so designated. See Land Registration Rules 1972 to 1986 (SI No 230 of 1972 and SI No 310 of 1986). See DEEDS, REGISTRATION OF; BURDEN; CAUTION; INHIBITION.

landlord. A lessor; the owner or holder of land leased to another called the tenant or lessee. The relationship of landlord and tenant arises *in all cases in which there shall be an agreement by one party to hold land from or under another in consideration of any rent*: Deasy's Act 1860 s.4. A landlord is also defined as the person for the time being entitled to receive (otherwise than as agent for another) the rent paid in respect of premises by the tenant thereof: Landlord and Tenant (Amendment) Act 1980 s.3(1). See COVENANT; GROUND RENT; IMPROVEMENT NOTICE; LEASE.

language, official. The Irish language as the national language is the first official language; the English language is recognised as a second official language: 1937 Constitution, art.8. In the event of conflict between the text of the Constitution, or of a law enrolled in accordance with the Constitution, in both the official languages, the text in Irish will prevail (ibid arts.25(4)(6) and 25(5)(4)). However, in interpreting the Constitution, where there appears to be a conflict between terms used in the two texts, search must first be made for a common meaning before the Irish language text is permitted to prevail: The State (Guilland) v Governor of Mountjoy Prison (1986) ILRM 381 applying O'Donovan v Attorney General (1961) IR 114.

See Tearmaí Dlí, Oifig an tSolathair. See also Irish Legal Terms Act 1945. See RECORDS.

leaflet. See ADVERTISEMENT.

lease. A conveyance or grant by a *lessor* to a *lessee* of possession of property, to last for a certain period of time; it must be for a period less than the estate or interest of the lessor as otherwise it is a conveyance or assignment and not a lease. A lease is usually made in consideration of a *fine* (which is a payment from the lessee to the lessor on the creation of the interest) and on the payment of *rent*. The expression *lease* is usually used to denote an interest for a long period of time, whereas *tenancy* is used to denote a relatively short period. A *sub-lease* or *under-lease* is a lease created by a person who himself is a lessee, for a shorter term then he himself holds.

A letting may be *periodic* eg week to week or month to month; it may be expressly created or arise by reference to the payment by the tenant to the landlord of rent. See Davies v Hilliard (1967) 101 ILTR 50. See PREMISES; TENANCY AT WILL; TENANCY BY SUFFERANCE.

lease, creation of. A lease may be created orally where it is for year certain, from year to year or lesser period: Deasy's Act (qv) 1860; for any other period, writing is required and certain statutes require particular leases to be under seal eg Settled Land Act leases. Also letting, sub-letting or subdividing of agricultural holdings requires the consent of the Land Commission: Land Act 1965 s.12. For the purposes of the Landlord and Tenant (Amendment) Act 1980, a lease is an instrument in writing, whether under or not under seal, containing a contract of tenancy in respect of any land in consideration of a rent or return and includes a *fee farm grant* (qv) (ibid s.3(1)). See MORTGAGOR, RIGHTS OF.

lease, determination of. The ending of a lease or tenancy. It may happen by efflux of time, by surrender, merger, forfeiture or by notice to quit. Where a lease is for a fixed period of time, it automatically expires when the fixed period ends; however certain lessees may have a statutory right to a new lease eg Landlord and Tenant (Amendment) Act 1980 for business leases (qv).

A lease is *surrendered* when the lessee gives up to the lessor the residue of the term still to run; this may arise by express act of the lessee or by operation of law. *Merger* takes place where the lessee acquires the reversion (qv); the lease is absorbed by the reversion. *Forfeiture* can occur for a breach of a condition in a lease, with or without a forfeiture clause, or a breach of a covenant (qv) with a forfeiture clause (sometimes called a *proviso for re-entry*). Forfeiture is strictly construed against the lessor or landlord: Bennett v Kidd (1926) NI 50.

A yearly, monthly, weekly or other periodic tenancy may be determined by a *notice to quit* but not a lease or tenancy for a fixed period of time unless expressly reserved in the lease. See also Deasy's Act (qv) 1860; Conveyancing Act 1881; Landlord and Tenant Act 1967. See GROUND RENT; SURRENDER.

lease for lives renewable for ever. A lease granted for the term of lives, usually three, which contained a provision that when any of the lives dropped out, the grantor would grant a renewal of the lease for a new life on the payment of a sum of money called a renewable fine. A *conversion grant* enabled either party to convert the lease into a fee farm grant (qv); also such a lease, if made for the first time since 1849, operates as a fee farm grant if the lessor is capable of making such a grant: Renewable Leasehold Conversion Act 1849.

Surviving *leases for lives renewable for ever* have been converted into *fee simple* estates: Landlord and Tenant (Amendment) Act 1980 s.74.

lease to director. A building society is prohibited from disposing of property by way of lease or hire to a director or to a *connected person* (qv): BS Act 1989 s.57(1)(b). Certain leases or hiring are exempted however eg where the value when aggregated does not exceed £5000 or where made in the ordinary course of the society's business on not more favourable terms than it is reasonable to expect (ibid s.57(3)).

For provisions dealing with:- prohibited transactions being voidable at the instance of the society, the accountability of directors, and disclosure of transactions which are permitted, see DISCLOSURE OF LOANS; LOAN TO DIRECTORS. See also PROPERTY TRANSACTIONS.

leasehold. The interest created by a lease (qv).

leasehold, mortgage of. In order to prevent the mortgagee (lender) becoming liable to pay the rent and perform the covenants in a lease, it is usual to create a mortgage of a lease, by way of a sub-demise of the residue of the mortgagor's interest in the term, less one day or a number of days, and by way of a declaration by the mortgagor to hold the *nominal reversion* of such day or days as trustee for the mortgagee in order that the mortgagee will be able to sell the whole leasehold interest on exercising his power of sale, should this arise. For example, see APPENDIX 5 - TYPICAL MORTGAGE clause 6. See REVERSION.

leasing. Leasing is a *financial service* (qv) which a building society may be empowered to provide: BS Act 1989 s.29(2)(k).

legal costs. A building society may indemnify (qv) an officer or auditor against any liability incurred by him in defending proceedings, whether civil or criminal, in which judgment is given in his favour or in which he is acquitted, or in connection with an application to the High Court for relief from liability where such relief is granted: BS Act 1989 s.114(2).

legal costs, investigation of title. A building society is precluded from requiring a member to pay its costs of legal investigation of title to any property offered as security for a loan: BS Amendment Act 1986 s.6(1)(d); SI No 27 of 1987, first schedule (iv); SI No 339 of 1987 art.6. Notwithstanding the repeal of the 1986 Act, this provision continues in force as if made by the Central Bank: BS Act 1989 s.6.

The Central Bank is empowered

to prescribe, by regulation, rules precluding or restricting a society from requiring a member to pay its costs of legal investigation of title to the security relating to a housing loan: BS Act 1989 s.11(2)(b)(iv). See APPENDIX 2.

legal mortgage. See MORTGAGE.

legal professional privilege. See PRIVILEGE, LEGAL PROFESSIONAL.

legal tender. Tender or offer of payment in a form which a creditor is bound to accept. A tender of money in coins is legal tender for 20 times the face value of each denomination of coin tendered: Central Bank Act 1989 s.127. Notes issued by the Central Bank are legal tender in the State for the payment of any amount (ibid s.118). In a tender of money, the exact amount must be tendered without any request for change. See MONETARY UNIT; TENDER.

letter. See NAME OF SOCIETY.

letter of credit. An undertaking by a banker (or building society) acting on the instructions of its customer (eg the buyer of goods) to pay or to meet drafts drawn pursuant to it by the beneficiary of the credit (eg the seller of the goods) in accordance with the terms laid down in the undertaking. The issue of letters of credit by a building society is a *financial service* (qv) which a society may be empowered to provide: BS Act 1989 s.29(2)(q).

The sale of goods worldwide is normally arranged by means of *letters of credit* eg the buyer may instruct his bank to open a credit in favour of the seller, which is a promise by the banker to pay money to the seller in return for, say, shipping documents in respect of the goods.

Letters of credit may be revocable or irrevocable. A *revocable* credit may be amended or cancelled at any time without notice to the beneficiary. An *irrevocable* letter of credit constitutes a definite undertaking of the issuing bank, provided that the terms and conditions of the credit are complied with.

liability. Legal obligation or duty; or the amount owed. A person who commits a wrong or breaks a contract or trust is said to be liable or responsible for it. A liability is said to be criminal or civil, depending on whether it is enforced by a criminal or civil court. A *vicarious liability* is one which falls on one person as a result of his relationship with another eg a master is generally liable for the acts of his servant performed in the course of his employment. A *contingent liability* is a future unascertained obligation. See DEPOSIT WITH CENTRAL BANK; LIMITATION OF LIABILITY; LIQUID ASSETS.

liability of member. See MEMBER, LIABILITY OF.

liability of officer or auditor. See INDEMNIFY; LEGAL COSTS; OFFICER; RELIEF.

liabilities outside State. See ASSETS OUTSIDE STATE.

lien. The right to hold the property of another as security for the performance of an obligation. As regards a building society, where a person is required to produce a document over which he claims a lien, the production will be without prejudice to the lien: BS Act 1989 s.41(6). See SOLICITOR.

lien, equitable. See EQUITABLE LIEN.

life assurance. Assurance of a class specified in the European Communities (Life Assurance) Regulations 1984 (SI No 57 of 1984), Schedule 1; Insurance Act 1989 s.2(1). See INSURANCE BUSINESS.

life estate. A freehold estate for the life of a person which arises by grant. The life estate may be for the life of the tenant eg *to A for life*. It may also be for the life of another, *pur autre vie* eg *to A for the life of B*. B is known as the *cestui que vie* and A the *tenant pur autre vie*; the years remaining in the estate on the death of A may be disposed of by his will or, if he dies intestate, the interest devolves on his personal representatives (qv): Statute of Frauds (Ireland) 1695; Succession Act 1965.

life policy. See LIFE ASSURANCE.

limitation, words of. See WORDS OF LIMITATION.

limitation of actions. The provision by which actions to enforce rights are barred if proceedings are not taken within certain periods of time: Statute of Limitations 1957. The time limits prescribed include: (a) simple contract - six years from the date on which the cause of action accrued (ibid s.11(1)(a)); (b) quasi-contract - six years (ibid s.11(1)(b)); (c) specialty contract - 12 years (ibid s.11(5)); (d) tort (other than one causing personal injuries or slander) - six years (ibid s.11(2)); (e) personal injury - 3 years (ibid s.11(2)(b)); (f) slander - 3 years (ibid s.11(2)(c)); (g) recovery of land - 12 years (ibid s.13(2)); (h) recovery of arrears of conventional rent - six years (ibid s.28); (i) redemption of mortgage - 12 years (ibid s.15); (j) judgment of court of record - 12 years (ibid s.11(6)).

There is provision for the extension of the limitation periods in the case of disability, acknowledgement, part payment, fraud, and mistake (ibid ss.47-72).

limitation of liability. The imposition of a ceiling or limit on liability for damage or loss by contract or by statute. See MEMBER, LIABILITY OF; OFFICER; RELIEF.

limited owner. An owner of an interest in land which is less than a fee simple estate eg a life tenant.

linking services. There is a prohibition on a building society making it a condition of a housing loan (qv) that the borrower must take other services from the society eg financial, insurance, conveyancing, auctioneering or other services relating to land, whether provided directly by the society itself or through a subsidiary (qv) or associated body (qv): BS Act 1989 s.35(1).

liquid assets. Assets in readily realisable form or in cash. As regards a building society, liquid assets are assets specified as such by the Central Bank including deposits with the Bank; a society is required to have such a proportion of its total assets in liquid form having such a composition as to enable the society to meet its *liabilities* as they arise: BS Act 1989 s.39(1) and (9).

Pending specification by the Bank, *liquid assets* includes assets held in a form provided for by the BS Act 1976 s.38 eg in cash, on current accounts or on deposit with the Central Bank, a bank, the Post Office Savings Bank, a trustee savings bank, the Agricultural Credit Corporation or the Industrial Credit Company Ltd, or as prescribed by the Minister for Finance under s.38 ie BS (Prescribed Investments) Regulations 1984 (SI No 186 of 1984). *Liabilities* include such *contingent liabilities* as may be specified by the Bank (ibid 1989 Act s.39 (10)(b)).

The Bank is given wide powers to impose prudential ratios ie ratios between assets and liabilities (ibid s.39(4)-(8)). As regards the treatment of premises, see ibid s.21(5). See also ASSETS OUTSIDE THE STATE.

See APPENDIX I.

liquidation. See WINDING UP.

liquidator. A person appointed to carry out the winding up of a body. A building society may, subject to certain modifications, be wound up under the Companies Acts as if it were a company limited by shares: BS Act 1989 s.109.

The principal duties of the liquidator are to get in and realise the assets of the company, to pay or settle its debts, and to distribute to the members the surplus, if any, that may remain. A liquidator appointed by the court is known as an *official liquidator*. The main difference between a liquidator in a winding up by the court and in a voluntary winding up, is that the former must obtain the consent of the court or of the *committee of inspection* in order to exercise many of his powers: Companies Act 1963 s.231.

Where a building society's *authorisation* is revoked and the society is being wound up, the liquidator may continue to carry on the business of the society and hold himself out as a building society to such an extent as the Central Bank (or the Court if the society is being wound up under the supervision of the Court) may consider necessary: BS Act 1989, Fourth Schedule, para 2(8).

A liquidator of a society who proposes to dispose of the society's assets, which are secured by mortgage of freehold estate or interest, must obtain the approval of the High Court, which must be satisfied that the terms are just and equitable and are terms which the borrowers would have been reasonably entitled to expect if the society had not been wound up (ibid s.109(10); Companies Act 1963 s.231(2)(a)).

As regards the *savings protection scheme* (qv), the Minister for the Environment may by regulations, change as necessary, the rights and duties of a liquidator in the winding up of a building society: BS Act 1989 s.94(2)(e). See Irish Savings Building Society (In Liquidation) and Ors v Plunkett and Ors (1987) ILRM 504. See RSC O.74 rr 29-48. See DISQUALIFICATION; INSPECTION; LOANS AND WINDING UP; OFFICER; WINDING UP.

loan. A building society is empowered to make a wide variety of loans, including, with the approval of the Central Bank, loans in a currency other than the currency of the State: BS Act 1989 ss.22 and 23. In addition to *housing loans* (qv), a society is empowered to make (a) loans fully secured by the mortgage of freehold or leasehold estate or interest; (b) bridging loans (qv); (c) loans for the payment of a deposit for the purchase of freehold or leasehold interest which is to be mortgaged to the society up to a maximum of 15 per cent of the purchase price, or such other percentage as may be prescribed by the Central Bank; (d) loans fully secured by securities or guarantees, other than a mortgage of land, as may be specified by the Central Bank; (e) unsecured or partly secured loans to an individual for the purchase or improvement of accommodation for himself or his family; (f) unsecured or partly secured loans to any person for any purpose, on overdraft or other facility accounts.

The power to make unsecured or partly secured loans may be exercised only by a society which has *adopted* the power by special resolution (qv) and recorded the power in its memorandum (qv), and only in accordance with the terms and conditions of the approval from the Central Bank (ibid s.23(2) and s.36)). In addition the amount of a loan under all the categories (a) to (f) above, may be specified by the Central Bank, as may the maximum loan to an individual (ibid s.23(2)(b)).

There are transitional provisions in relation to societies entitled under s.3 of the BS (Amendment) Act 1986 to make unsecured loans to members for the purpose of carrying out improvement works to a dwelling; they continue to be entitled to make such loans until the memorandum of the society takes effect in accordance with s.124(8) of the BS Act 1989 or the date on which the power to make loans under s.23(1)(e) becomes exerciseable (ibid s.6(4)). See AMALGAMATION; BRIDGING LOAN; DISCLOSURE OF LOANS; HOUSING BODY, APPROVED; HOUSING LOAN; MEMBER, LIABILITY OF; REDEMPTION FEE; TRANSFER OF ENGAGEMENTS.

loan, prohibited. It has been held that a loan which is prohibited is illegal and cannot be recovered: Lougher v Molyneux (1916) 1 KB 718. However, the fact that an act is not expressely authorised does not of itself make that act illegal and ultra vires: Sheffield & South Yorkshire Permanent Building Society v Aizlewood & Ors (1889) 44 Ch D 412; Hallifax Building Society v Salisbury (1939) 4 All ER 427.

loan, repayment of. See AUTHORISATION; LOANS AND WINDING UP.

loan to director. A building society is prohibited from making a loan to a director or to a *connected person* (qv): BS Act 1989 s.57(1)(a). Certain loans are exempted eg (a) loans made in the ordinary course of business and not on more favourable terms than is reasonable to expect; (b) loans not exceeding £2,500 in total; (c) loans not exceeding £50,000 in total made for or towards the purchase or improvement of a house used as the director's only main residence, provided such loans on similar terms are ordinarily made to employees of the society; (d) loans not exceeding £10,000 in total to meet expenditure incurred or to be incurred by him as a director, subject to disclosure and approval at an agm of the society (ibid s.57(2) and (5)-(7)).

The director or *connected person* who is a party to a prohibited transaction, or any director who authorised it, is liable to account to the society for any gain made, and, jointly and severally, to indemnify the society for any loss or damage resulting from the transaction (ibid s.58 (2)).

A prohibited transaction is voidable at the instance of the society, except where (a) restitution is no longer possible or (b) the society has been otherwise indemnified for any loss suffered, or (c) any rights acquired *bona fide* (qv) for value and without actual notice by a third party would be adversely affected (ibid s.58(1)). See DISCLOSURE OF LOANS. See APPENDIX I.

loans and winding up. Where a building society is being wound up, a person to whom a loan has been made under a mortgage or other security, must not be required to repay the loan except in accordance with the conditions set out in the mortgage or other security: BS Act 1989 s.109(9).

locus standi. [A place of standing]. The right to be heard in court. It has been held that an established building society had a locus standi as plaintiffs to maintain an action against the defendants (which included a new society) as the plaintiffs had the status of aggrieved persons: Irish Permanent Building Society v Registrar of Building Societies & Irish Life Building Society (1981) ILRM 242.

long possession, title by. The title which a person acquires in land by retaining adverse possession of the land for a certain period without acknowledging the true owner's title. An action to recover land from a person in possession must be brought within 12 years (30 years in the case of a State authority) after the right of action accrued or from the last written acknowledgement signed by the person in possession or his agent.

Time does not run against the true owner in the case of fraud, until he has discovered the fraud or could with reasonable diligence have discovered it. Time does not run also in the case of a person with a disability. See Statute of Limitations 1957. See Registration of Title Act 1964 s.49. See Maher v Maher (1987) ILRM 582. See CARETAKER; LIMITATION OF ACTIONS.

loss of office. See AMALGAMATION; REMUNERATION OF DIRECTOR; TRANSFER OF ENGAGEMENTS.

losses. The rules (qv) of a building society must provide for the manner in which losses are to be ascertained and provided for: BS Act 1989, Second Schedule, Part II, para 5(g). See also WARRANTY.

lost bill. A bill of exchange (qv) which is lost before it is overdue. The person who was the holder of the bill prior to its loss, may apply to the drawer for a duplicate which the drawer must provide, but the drawer can demand security from the applicant against the risk of the original bill being found and the drawer being liable on both bills: Bills of Exchange Act 1882 s.69. If the drawer refuses to give such a duplicate, having been requested, he can be compelled to do so.

lost modern grant. The doctrine by which a court can presume from long user, that at some time in the past an *easement* (qv) was granted by deed but that the deed has been lost and cannot be produced. See PRESCRIPTION.

M

majority. See AGE OF MAJORITY.

management of society. See CHIEF EXECUTIVE; DISQUALIFICATION; DISQUALIFICATION ORDER.

managing director. The director in a corporate body who is given responsibility for managing the everyday business affairs of the corporate body. In a building society, the chief executive (qv) may be referred to as the managing director, where he is also a director (qv) of the society: BS Act 1989 s.49(7).

marketable title. As regards freehold land, a title which goes back 40 years: Vendor and Purchasers Act 1874 s.1; also known as a *good* title. A contract for the sale of land may stipulate that the title may commence at a more recent date. If the vendor shows the title which he is required to prove, he is said to show a *good* title. The conveyance or document with which the title commences is called the *root of title* (qv). See Maconchy v Clayton (1898) 1 IR 291. See CONVEYANCE; OPEN CONTRACT.

marshalling. The equitable doctrine under which if person A has claims against funds X and Y of person B, and person C has a claim only against fund X, A will be required to satisfy himself as far as possible out of fund Y.

The doctrine of marshalling cannot be relied upon as a defence to proceedings instituted by a creditor against one or more of several co-sureties, where they have separately mortgaged different properties as securities for their separate guarantees: Lombard & Ulster Banking Ltd v Murray & Murray (1987) ILRM 522. See also Moxon v Berkeley Benefit Building Society (1890) 59 LJ Ch 524. See SURETY.

matrimonial property. Disputes between husband and wife as to the title to, or possession of, any property, may be resolved by the courts as the courts think proper and just: Married Women's Status Act 1957 s.12. When a wife makes payments towards the purchase of a house which is in the sole name of the husband, or the repayment of the mortgage instalments, he becomes a trustee (qv) for her of a share in the house, the size of the share depending on the size of her contribution of which she becomes the beneficial owner: Conway v Conway (1976) IR 254.

It has been held that the courts are obliged to give effect to the spirit of Article 41 of the Constitution by developing the law in such a manner as to give a woman some reasonable economic security in return for her voluntary sacrifice of being a full-time wife and mother; and having regard for the equal nature of the family relationship, the courts should grant a moiety of not more than a 50 per cent share in the *family home*, not extending to other land, to a wife in such a situation: BL v ML (1989) ILT & SJ 55.

Where an agreement to marry is terminated, the rights of the previously engaged persons to any property, are governed by the rules applicable to matrimonial property: Family Law Act 1981 s.5. See Wall v Wall (1986) HC; DMcC v M McC (1986) ILRM 1. See LRC 1 of 1981. See FAMILY HOME.

maturity. The time when a bill of exchange (qv) becomes due.

meeting. See ANNUAL GENERAL MEETING; SPECIAL MEETING.

meeting, notice of. See NOTICE OF MEETINGS.

meeting, procedure at. The rules (qv) of a building society must provide for the procedure to be observed at meetings of the society: BS Act 1989, Second Schedule, Part II, para 5(p).

meeting, requisition of. The rules (qv) of a building society must provide for the right of members to requisition meetings of the society: BS Act 1989, Second Schedule, Part II, para 5(l). A resigning auditor also has a right to requisition the convening of a general meeting of the society. See AUDITOR, RESIGNATION OF.

member. Every person holding one or more shares (qv) in a building society is a member of that society: BS Act 1989 ss.2(1) and 16(1). A society however, may by its rules, allow a person who does not hold a share to be a member, where that person is an applicant for or a recipient of a *housing loan* (qv). The rules (qv) must provide for the manner in which membership of the society is to cease (ibid Second Schedule, Part II, para 5(t)).

Where two or more persons jointly hold shares in a society, the person whose name first appears in the records is the *representative joint holder* and exercises the membership rights (ibid s.16(6)). There are similar provisions regarding a *representative joint borrower* (ibid s.16 (7)). There are also provisions for *borrowing members* (qv). See JOINT BORROWER, REPRESENTATIVE; JOINT HOLDER, REPRESENTATIVE; MINOR; SHARE.

member and voting. See VOTING.

member, liability of. The liability of a member of a building society is limited to the amount actually paid and in arrear on the shares he holds in the society; however, where a loan has been made on any share, his liability is limited to the amount payable thereon under any mortgage (qv) or other security or under the rules (qv) of the society: BS Act 1989 s.16(4).

Where a society by its rules allows a person to whom a housing loan (qv) has been made to be a member without holding a share, the liability of the member will be no greater than it would be if the rules treated him as being, by reason of the making of the loan, the holder of a share in the society (ibid s.16(2)). See Brownlie & Ors v Russell (1883) 8 App Cas 235.

members, communication with. See COMMUNICATION WITH MEMBERS.

members, register of. See REGISTER OF MEMBERS.

members, number of. Where the number of members of a building society reduces below 10, this is a ground for a petition to the High Court for the winding up of the society: BS Act 1989 s.109(3). See WINDING UP.

memorandum, building society. The persons forming a building society must agree on the objects (qv) of the society and on the extent of its powers in a *memorandum* the provisions of which comply with the requirements for the time being of Part 1 of the Second Schedule of the BS Act 1989 (ibid s.10(2)(a)). The memorandum must specify, inter alia, the name of the society, its objects, the adoptable powers, and restrictions the society has assumed on its powers. The Central Bank may make further provision by regulation, as respects the form and content of the memorandum (ibid s.11(2)) and has power to enforce alteration of the memorandum (ibid s.11(4) and (5)).

A society may alter its memorandum only by *special resolution* (qv), which alteration must be approved and registered by the Central Bank and does not have effect until registered and cannot affect any existing rights, liabilities or legal proceedings (ibid s.14). A refusal by the Central Bank to register the alteration must be notified to the society within 2 months, including its reasons, and an appeal against the decision lies to the High Court.

The memorandum of a society is binding on the society, and on every member and officer of the society (ibid s.11(1)). For transitional provisions on the 1989 Act coming into force, see s.124(5)-(9) and REGISTRATION, CANCELLATION OF. See also DOCUMENTS, PRESUMPTION AS TO; FORMATION; PUBLIC FILE; RULES; SECRETARY.

memorandum, Statute of Frauds. The memorandum required in writing in relation to certain contracts which otherwise are unenforceable eg contracts for the sale of land: Statute of Frauds (Ireland) 1695. In relation to the memorandum (a) it need not be made at the time of the formation of the contract, provided it is made before action is brought; (b) it must contain the names of the parties or a sufficient description of them; (c) the subject matter must be described so that it can be identified and all material terms of the contract must be stated; (d) the consideration must appear, except in contracts of guarantee where by virtue of the Mercantile Law Amendment Act 1856, consideration must be present but need not appear in the memorandum; (e) it must be signed by the party to be charged or his agent. See Casey v Irish Intercontinental Bank (1979) IR 364; Tradax (Ireland) Ltd v Irish Grain Board Ltd (1983) SC; Morris v Barron (1918) AC 1; Hawkins v Price (1947) Ch 645.

If there is no memorandum, the contract cannot be enforced unless there has been *part performance* of the contract by the plaintiff; equity will then decree *specific performance*. For the acts of part performance regarded as supplanting the memorandum required by the Statute of Frauds, see Hope v Lord Cloncurry (1874) IR 8 Eq 555; Lowry v Reid (1927) NI 142; Kennedy v Kennedy (1984) HC. See STATUTE OF FRAUDS.

memorandum of association. A document which regulates a company's external activities and which must be drawn up on the formation of a company. Any seven or more persons associated for any lawful purpose may by subscribing their names to a memorandum of association and otherwise complying with the statutory requirements as to registration, form an incorporated company, with or without *limited liability;* two or more persons are only required where the company to be formed is to be a *private* company: Companies Act 1963 s.5(1).

The memorandum must be delivered to the Registrar of Companies and be accompanied by a statement specifying the situation of the company's registered office and the names of the first secretary and first directors: Companies Amendment Act 1982 s.3. As regards a building society and its conversion into a public limited company, see CONVERSION; REGISTRATION AS COMPANY. See also ARTICLES OF ASSOCIATION; ASSOCIATION CLAUSE.

memorial. An abstract of the material parts of a deed, the enrolment of which is necessary for the registration of a deed in the Registry of Deeds: Registration of Deeds (Ireland) Act 1707 s.7. It must contain: the date of perfection of the deed; the names and addresses of all the parties and witnesses to the deed; and the lands described as in the deed itself. The memorial must be executed by one of the grantors or grantees of the deed, be attested by two witnesses (one of whom was a witness of the grantor's execution of the deed) and be proved by an affidavit made by a witness common to the memorial and the deed (ibid s.6). See also DEEDS, REGISTRATION OF.

merger of societies. See AMALGAMATION; TRANSFER OF ENGAGEMENTS.

mesne rates. The damage for trespass arising in an *ejectment action* for non-payment of rent or for overholding to which a plaintiff is entitled: Deasy's Act 1860 s.77. The measure of the mesne rates is the value of the premises during the period of trespass, usually but not invariably, calculated on the rent; there may also be, if the facts warrant it, damages for deterioration of the premises: Lynham v Butler 67 ILTR 121. See RSC O.41 rr.9-10; RCC O.8 r.2.

minor. A person under the age of eighteen years who is not or has not been married: Age of Majority Act 1985 s.2. This interpretation also applies to the terms *infancy*, *infant* and *minority*.

When a minor acquires an interest in a subject of a permanent nature, which imposes a continuous liability on him, the contract cannot be enforced against him during infancy eg a lease, a partnership, a shareholding in a company or a marriage settlement. After the minor attains full age, it will be binding on him unless he avoids it within a reasonable time eg see Davies v Benyon-Harris (1931) 47 TLR 424. All other contracts are unenforcable against the minor.

A minor may be admitted as a member of a building society provided its rules (qv) do not prohibit such admission and the minor can give all necessary receipts; however a minor cannot hold any *office* in the society or nominate a person for election as a director: BS Act 1989 s.16(5).

Certain contracts entered into by minors are *absolutely void* eg a contract for repayment of money lent or to be lent; goods supplied or to be supplied (other than necessaries) and accounts stated: Infants Relief Act 1874 s.1. It has been held, based on the BS Act 1874, that a mortgage to a minor was void: Nottingham Permanent Benefit Building Society v Thurston (1903) AC 6. See Coutts v Browne- Lecky (1947) KB 104. See also Family Law Act 1981 s.10; Finance Act 1986 s.112; Law Reform Commission Report on Minors' Contracts LRC 15 of 1985. See MEMBER; SHARES, TRANSFER OF.

misfeasance. An improper performance of an otherwise lawful act eg where there is an act of positive negligence. A *misfeasor* is a person who is guilty of a misfeasance. See Kelly v Mayo Co Co (1964) IR 315. As regards proceedings brought in respect of a misfeasance in connection with a building society, see DERIVATIVE ACTION, BUILDING SOCIETY.

misleading statement. It is an offence for an officer or employee of a building society knowingly or recklessly to make a statement to the auditors of the society that is misleading, false or deceptive in a material particular; it is also an offence to fail to provide within two days information or explanations required by the auditors: BS Act 1989 s.90. In this context, an *officer* includes an auditor of a subsidiary or other associated body of a society (ibid s.90(5)). See OFFICER; TIME TO COMPLY.

mistake. See REGISTRATION, CANCELLATION OF.

monetary unit. The monetary unit of the State is the Irish pound which is issued in *legal tender* (qv) form: Central Bank Act 1989 s.24(1). The Minister for Finance is empowered to vary the general exchange rate for the Irish pound in respect of other monetary units (ibid s.24(2)).

money transmission. Money transmission is a *financial service* (qv) which a building society may be empowered to provide: BS Act 1989 s.29(2)(l).

mortgage. A conveyance of an interest in land or other property as security for a loan. A mortgage includes a *charge* (qv): BS Act 1989 s.2(1).

The mortgagor (borrower) normally remains in possession of the land until the debt is repaid. A mortgage may be *legal*, *equitable* or *statutory*. A *legal mortgage* is a transfer of the legal estate or interest in the land or other property; an *equitable mortgage* arises where only an equitable interest is transferred eg by deposit of title deeds (qv); a *statutory mortgage* is one arising by way of judgment mortgage (qv) under the Judgment Mortgage Act 1850.

The mortgagor has a right to redeem his mortgage on repayment of the debt; it is a legal right on the date fixed for redemption and an equitable right thereafter. The mortgagor also has an *equity of redemption*, which is the sum total of the mortgagor's rights in equity, and there must be no *clogs* (qv) on that right.

A mortgage is discharged by redemption (qv), by foreclosure (qv), or by exercise of the mortgagee's right of sale. Mortgages rank in priority according to the date of their registration.

A mortgage on registered land is created by registration of a *charge* as a burden on the land and registration of the chargeant as the owner of the charge. The charge operates as a mortgage by deed within the meaning of the Conveyancing Acts: Registration of Title Act 1964 s.62. See ANNUITY MORTGAGE; CHATTEL MORTGAGE; CHARGE ON LAND; CHARGE, REGISTRATION OF; ENDOWMENT MORTGAGE; PRIOR MORTGAGE; TRUSTEE INVESTMENT.

mortgage, discharge of. See REDEMPTION.

mortgage, equitable. See EQUITABLE MORTGAGE.

mortgage, judgment. See JUDGMENT MORTGAGE.

mortgage, prior. See PRIOR MORTGAGE.

mortgage deed. See TITLE DEEDS.

mortgage of leaseholds. See LEASEHOLDS, MORTGAGE OF.

mortgage protection insurance. See INSURANCE.

mortgage suit. An action in which the plaintiff mortgagee (lender) seeks a sale by the court in lieu of foreclosure (qv). The plaintiff mortgagee usually seeks (a) that his mortgage be declared *well charged* on the lands, (b) an order for payment of the sum due, and (c) an order that in default of payment within the specified time, the lands be sold by the court. A mortgage suit is commenced in the Circuit Court, where the rateable valuation of the land does not exceed £200, or otherwise in the High Court. See RSC O.54 r.3; RCC O.45 r.2. See MORTGAGEE, RIGHTS OF.

mortgagee. The person to whom property is mortgaged; the lender of the mortgage debt.

mortgagee in possession. A mortgagee (lender) who goes into possession of mortgaged property is liable to account strictly; he is not entitled to charge remuneration for the work he does, and having taken possession himself, he cannot charge a receiver's commission: Kavanagh v Workingman's Benefit Building Society (1896) IR 56.

A building society mortgage usually provides that the society may put and keep every building comprised in the security in good and tenantable repair and condition without becoming liable as a *mortgagee in possession*, eg see APPENDIX 5 - TYPICAL MORTGAGE clause 7(a)(ii). See also MORTGAGEE, RIGHTS OF.

mortgagee, rights of. A mortgagee (lender) generally has the following rights where the mortgage is by deed: (a) right to possession, but only in suitable cases eg to aid a sale: Ulster Bank Ltd v Conlon (1957) 91 ILTR 193; (b) power of sale out of court where the redemption date has passed and there is either three months default, after notice, in payment of principal or two months arrears of interest or breach of a covenant:

Holohan v Friends Provident Century Life Office (1966) IR 1; (c) power to appoint a receiver, exercisable under the same conditions as a power of sale; the receiver is deemed to be an agent of the mortgagor and consequently the mortgagee is not liable for the defaults of the receiver; (d) power to insure. See Conveyancing Act 1881 s.19.

A building society mortgage may sometimes provide that the sum advanced is to become due within three or six months after the advance, but that the society will not exercise the power of sale or of entering into possession unless there has been default by the mortgagor in the payment of instalments. The mortgagor may also acknowledge that he is in possession as a tenant of the society. However, an *annuity mortgage* of a building society usually provides that the principal sum advanced becomes due on the expiration of notice to that effect given by the society to the borrower, or forthwith on particular events happening eg when the right of the society to enter into possession of the mortgaged property, or to sell it, becomes enforceable eg see APPENDIX 5 - TYPICAL MORTGAGE clause 3(b), 3(c), and 7(d).

It has been held that in the case of a default, the mortgagor should be ordered to give up possession as the property, when sold with vacant possession, would realise more: Irish Permanent Building Society v Ryan (1950) IR 12. See also Irish Civil Service (Permanent) Building Society v Ingram's Representative (1959) IR 181.

However, in the absence of a court order to repossess a *family home*, a building society may be restrained from exercising a right to possession pursuant to a clause in a mortgage deed and be ordered, by way of interlocutory relief, to deliver up possession of the house so repossessed: McCormack v ICS Building Society (1989) HC (ITLR 17 Apr 1989).

A mortgagee may obtain an order for sale by the court of the mortgaged property by way of *mortgage suit* (qv). He also has the usual creditors' remedy against a debtor for repayment of the principal and interest due. He is entitled to retain possession of the title deeds until the mortgage is redeemed.

The court has power to adjourn proceedings by a mortgagee for possession or sale of a *family home* (qv) where it appears that the other spouse is desirous and capable of paying the arrears: Family Home Protection Act 1976 s.7. Also, the court can give permission to a mortgagee to bid and purchase at the sale of the property of a bankrupt (qv) or arranging debtor (qv): Bankruptcy Act 1988 s.53. However, it has been held that a building society may not dispose of a mortgaged property to one of its own officers or agents: Martinson v Clowes (1882) 21 Ch D 857.

Where mortgaged property is sold by a building society in exercise of a power of sale, the society must ensure that the property is sold at the best price reasonably obtainable and must notify the mortgagor and any other mortgagee, with particulars of the sale within 21 days thereof: BS Act 1989 s.26(1) and (5).

It has been held that a society is not bound to retain a property indefinitely until a higher price could be reached: Reliance Permanent Building Society v Harwood-Stamper (1944) 2 All ER 75. See RECEIVER OF MORTGAGED PROPERTY; RETENTION OF MORTGAGED PROPERTY; VOID AGREEMENT.

mortgaged property, sale of. See MORTGAGEE, RIGHT OF.

mortgages, consolidation of. See CONSOLIDATION OF MORTGAGES.

mortgages, sale of. The typical building society mortgage usually has a provision which empowers the society, at any time after its power of sale of the mortgaged property has become exercisable, to transfer the benefit of the mortgage to any person eg see APPENDIX 5 - TYPICAL MORTGAGE clause 11.

However, the Minister for the Environment may now make regulations (qv) in relation to the transfer, sale or assignment of mortgages held by a building society: BS Act 1989 s.18(6). Subject to any such regulations, and the approval of the Central Bank, a society may give security for money borrowed, including the security of mortgages held by the society (ibid s.18(5)).

mortgagor. The person who mortgages his property as security for the mortgage debt; the borrower. A mortgagor is also the person to whom a loan is made by a building society, and includes the successor in title of that person in relation to the sale or retention of mortgaged property: BS Act 1989 s.26(7).

mortgagor, rights of. A mortgagor (borrower) has the following rights: (a) *equity of redemption* which he can assign, devise or mortgage again; (b) possession - he can keep all rents and profits without rendering an account; he is not liable for *waste* unless it would render the property an inadequate security; he can sue for rent or injury done to the land without joining the mortgagee; (c) leases - a mortgagor in possession may make leases which bind the mortgagor and the mortgagee; however this right is to be exercised by the mortgagee after a receiver has been appointed; Conveyancing Act 1881 s.18; Conveyancing Act 1911 s.3.

It is usual in a building society mortgage to have a provision which restricts the power of the mortgagor in possession to grant leases or tenancies without the consent in writing of the society eg see APPENDIX 5 - TYPICAL MORTGAGE clause 9.

A mortgagor may also enforce his right to redeem his mortgage by a *redemption suit*. The mortgagor is entitled to possession of the title deeds on redemption of the mortgage. It has been held that the rights of a building society mortgagor in respect of the mortgage were affected by the contract of membership with the society: Rosenberg v Northumberland Building Society (1889) 22 QBD 373. See EQUITY OF REDEMPTION; REDEMPTION; WASTE.

mortmain. [Dead hand]. Land which is inalienable. Alienation in mortmain was prohibited eg land could not be conveyed originally to a corporation except by statutory authority or by licence. There was a *mortmain* restriction on gifts of land to charities: Charitable Donations and Bequests (Ireland) Act 1844. Mortmain restrictions were repealed by the Mortmain (Repeal of Enactments) Act 1954.

multi-storey buildings. Buildings of five storeys or more, built since 1950 or to be built. New provisions to improve and ensure the safety standards of such buildings are contained in the Local Government (Multi-Storey Buildings) Act 1988 and SI Nos 285 and 286 of 1988.

mutilation. See FALSIFICATION.

mutual society. A society which is owned and controlled generally by the persons who consume the product or service which the society provides eg a credit union, a building society. The term *mutual* (which does not appear in the BS Act 1989 or in previous legislation) "is used to indicate an organisation the ownership and ultimate control of which is vested in the members broadly on the basis of equality rather than in proportion to financial interest": Report of Registrar of Building Societies (1981) p.8. See DEPOSIT.

N

name of director. See DIRECTOR'S NAME.

name of society. The name specified in the memorandum (qv) and rules (qv) of a building society, registered by the Central Bank; a society is not permitted to use any name or title other than its registered name, although it may in addition use any abbreviated version of that name: BS Act 1989 s.13(3) and (5); and Second Schedule, Part II, para 5(a). The words *building society* or *cumann foirgniochta* must be included in the name of a society, and these words are restricted to a building society (ibid s.13(1) and (2)).

A society may change its name by special resolution (qv); however, the change cannot take effect until the Central Bank is satisfied that the changed name is not undesirable (ibid s.14(3)). A society may be directed by the Central Bank to change its registered name and is given considerable powers in the event of a failure of the society to comply (ibid s.13(6) and (7)).

Where the winding up of a society commences within one year after the society has changed its name, the former name as well as the existing name must appear on all notices and advertisements relating to the winding up (ibid s.109(13)).

A society is required to paint or affix its name on the outside of its offices; have its name in legible characters on its seal; mention its name in all its notices, letters, cheques and receipts; and include in all its letters, the number with which it is registered and the address of its chief office (qv) (ibid s.13(4)).

national housing programme. Every building society must submit to the Minister for the Environment such information as he requires for the purposes of his functions in relation to the national housing programme: BS Act 1989 s.38(3).

negligence. A tort (qv) involving the breach of a legal duty of care whereby damage is caused to the party to whom the duty is owed. It is the doing by a person of some act which a reasonable and prudent man would not have done in the circumstances of the case in question, or the omission to do something which would be expected of such a man under such circumstances.

For actionable negligence there must be: (a) a duty of care between the parties; (b) a failure to observe the required duty of care; and (c) reasonably foreseeable damage suffered. The law recognises that many persons owe a duty of care to others.

In a particular case, it has been held that there was not such close and direct relations between the

Registrar of Friendly Societies and a plaintiff depositor as to give rise to any duty of care on behalf of the Registrar towards the plaintiff: McMahon v Ireland, AG, Registrar of Friendly Societies (1987) HC.

An indemnity may not be given to exempt an officer or auditor of a building society from liability for negligence; however relief may be given to such a person by the court and a proceedings may be withdrawn by a judge from a jury. In addition, there are provisions to provide by regulations for compensation to be paid to persons arising from negligence in the provision by societies of auctioneering and conveyancing services. See AUCTIONEERING SERVICE; CONVEYANCING; INDEMNIFY; RELIEF; WITHDRAWAL FROM JURY.

negotiable instrument. An instrument, the transfer of which to the transferee (who takes it in good faith and for value) passes a good title, free from any defects affecting the title of the transferor. Notice is not required to be given to the person liable on the instrument and the transferee may sue in his own name.

The most important negotiable instruments are bills of exchange, promissory notes, cheques, share and dividend warrants and debentures payable to bearer. Negotiability may be conferred by custom or statute and restricted or destroyed by the holder of the instrument. See Bechaunaland Exploration Company v London Trading Bank Ltd (1898) 2 QB 658. See Bills of Exchange Act 1882 ss.31-32.

A negotiable instrument which is drawn on or given to a building society before the *conversion* of the society into a public limited company, has the same effect as if it had been drawn on or given to the company: BS Act 1989 s.107(2)(f).

negotiation of a bill. The transferring of a bill of exchange (qv) from one person to another so that the transferee becomes the holder of the bill: Bills of Exchange Act 1882 s.31(1).

newspaper. There are provisions in the BS Act 1989 which require notice in newspapers of a proposed amalgamation of a building society with another, or the transfer of engagements to another. Notice in newspapers is also required in relation to the election of directors and may suffice as notice, if the Central Bank consents, in the case of general meetings of a society. See AMALGAMATION; DIRECTOR, NOMINATION OF; NOTICE OF MEETINGS; TRANSFER OF ENGAGEMENTS.

nominal reversion. See LEASEHOLD, MORTGAGE OF.

nomination of director. See DIRECTOR, NOMINATION OF; DIRECTOR, RETIREMENT OF.

nominee. See SUCCESSOR COMPANY.

non-associated societies. See FINANCIAL SERVICES INDUSTRY ASSOCIATION.

non-cash asset. See PROPERTY TRANSACTION.

non-life insurance. Insurance of a class specified in Schedule 1 to the European Communities (Non-Life Insurance) Regulations 1976 (SI No 115 of 1976); Insurance Act 1989 s.2(1). A person generally may not carry on the business of non-life insurance in the State unless he is the holder of an authorisation granted by the Minister (ibid 1976 Regulations art.4). There is a requirement to establish and maintain *technical reserves* in respect of underwriting liabilities assumed (ibid arts.14 and 27) and to establish an adequate *solvency* *margin* (ibid art.16(1) and 28). See INSURANCE.

non-receipt. See ACCIDENTAL OMISSION.

non-resident account. See DEPOSIT INTEREST RETENTION TAX.

not negotiable. The words marked on a cheque which gives the holder no better title than the previous holder: Bills of Exchange Act 1882 s.81. See Great Western Railway Co v London & County Banking Co (1900) 2 QB 464. See CHEQUE.

notice. Knowledge or cognisance. To give *notice* is to bring matters to a person's knowledge or attention. Members and officers of a building society are deemed to have notice of the provisions of the memorandum (qv) and rules (qv) of the society: BS Act 1989 s.11(1). See Hudson v Irish Permanent Building Society (1982) - Report of Registrar of Building Societies (1981) p.28.

It has been held that a claim by a person to be registered as the owner of shares in a building society must fail as the society had, without notice of this claim, already made payment to the person legally entitled: Nolloth v Simplified Permanent Benefit Building Society (1885) 53 LT 859.

The *doctrine of notice* is often crucial in deciding a contest for priority between competing equitable interests or between equitable and legal interests. Notice can be *actual* where a person is aware by his own knowledge of a previous claim: In re Fuller & Co Ltd (in liquidation) (1982) IR 161; or it can be *constructive*, where the person is not himself aware but could have been, had he made proper enquiries: Northern Bank Ltd v Henry (1981) IR 1; or it may be *imputed*, eg where an agent of the person has either actual or constructive notice of a previous claim: In re Burmester (1858) 9 Ir Ch R 41. See also Conveyancing Act 1882 s.3(1).

In the case of registered land, the register generally governs priorities, except that certain interests and rights may affect registered land without registration: Registration of Title Act 1964 s.31(1); Tench v Molyneux (1914) 48 ILTR 48. In relation to notice and personalty, see Deale v Hall (1823) 3 Russ 1; Molloy v French (1849) 13 Ir Eq R 216. See also APPENDIX 5 - TYPICAL MORTGAGE clause 7(c). See ADVERTISEMENT; PRIORITY; PROPERTY TRANSACTION.

notice for receipt of nominations. See DIRECTOR, NOMINATION OF.

notice of dishonour. The notice which must be given to those whom the holder of a bill of exchange (qv) wishes to hold liable. See DISHONOUR OF BILL.

notice of interest. See DISCLOSURE OF INTEREST.

notice of meetings. Notice of a meeting of a society (including the agm) must be given to the Central Bank and to every member eligible to vote on the day of the notice; it is given by sending it to every member or, with the consent of the Bank, by publishing it in at least two daily newspapers: BS Act s.68(3) and (5). Notice must be given not less than 21 or more than 42 days before the date of the meeting or before the latest date for the receipt of proxy instruments, whichever is the earlier, unless the Central Bank permits shorter notice to be given (ibid s.68(1) and (2)).

The notice must contain a statement, appearing with reasonable prominence, that a member entitled to attend and vote may appoint a *proxy* (qv) to attend, speak and vote instead of him, that the proxy need not be a member of the society, and, that the member may direct the proxy how to vote at the meeting (ibid s.72(3)). The notice must have annexed to it one instrument for appointing a proxy (ibid s.72(4)).

If the notice is by newspaper publication, then the proxy instrument must be published along with the notice, or the notice must state that the proxy instrument may be obtained at all offices of the society during normal office hours (ibid s.68(4)).

The rules (qv) of a society must provide for the form of notice for the convening of a meeting and the manner of service of the notice (ibid Second Schedule, Part II, para 5(m)).

Under previous legislation, the Registrar of Building Societies refused permission to a society to give notice of a meeting by publishing it in a newspaper: Report of Registrar (1984) p.12. See ANNUAL GENERAL MEETING; JOINT BORROWER, REPRESENTATIVE.

notice of postal ballots. See POSTAL BALLOT.

notice of resolutions. The rules (qv) of a building society must provide for the manner in which notice of any resolution (including a *special resolution* (qv) or *conversion resolution* (qv)) to be moved at a meeting is to be given to members: BS Act 1989, Second Schedule, Part II, para 5(o). See also ADOPTABLE POWERS; AUDITOR, APPOINTMENT OF; AUDITOR, REMOVAL OF; CONVERSION RESOLUTION; RESOLUTION, PROPOSAL OF; SPECIAL RESOLUTION.

notice re mortgage. It is usual for a building society mortgage to provide that a notice required to be served on the borrower is sufficiently served if sent by ordinary pre-paid post in a letter addressed to the borrower at the mortgaged property and is deemed to be served at the time at which the letter would in the ordinary course of post have been delivered eg see APPENDIX 5 - TYPICAL MORTGAGE clause 15.

notice re transfers. See TRANSFER OF ENGAGEMENTS.

notice to quit. A yearly, monthly, weekly or other periodic tenancy may be determined by a *notice to quit* but not a lease or tenancy for a fixed period of time unless expressly reserved in the lease. See EJECTMENT; LEASE, DETERMINATION OF.

noting a bill. A brief note or memorandum made by a *notary public* as an interim measure, recording that a bill of exchange has been dishonoured, as a first step to a protest (qv). The note must be made at the time of dishonour and is written into the notary's *protest register*. See Bills of Exchange Act 1882 s.51. See NOTING AND PROTESTING.

noting and protesting. The process by which formal *notice of dishonour* of a foreign bill of exchange is made: Bills of Exchange Act 1882 s.51. If a foreign bill is not so protested, the drawers and endorsers are discharged (ibid s.51(2)). A notary public must present the bill for acceptance or payment, must note the reply made on the bill, and issue a formal *certificate of dishonour* called a *protest*.

nuisance. A tort (qv) which involves an act or omission which amounts to an unreasonable interference with, disturbance to, or annoyance to another person in the exercise of his rights; if the rights so interfered with belong to the person as a member of the public, the act or omission is a *public nuisance*; if these rights relate to the ownership or occupation of land, or some easement (qv), profit (qv) or some other right enjoyed in connection with land, then the act or omission amounts to a *private nuisance*: Connolly v South of Ireland Asphalt Co (1977) IR 99.

O

oath. A solemn declaration by which a party calls his God to witness that what he says is true, or that what he promises to do he will do. An *affirmation* may be made instead of an oath. See Oaths Act 1888; Interpretation Act 1937 s.12 sch; BS Act 1989 s.46(2). See AFFIRMATION; EXAMINATION.

objects of building society. A building society may have as its *objects* the undertaking of any of the activities permitted by or under the BS Act 1989; it must have as one of its objects the raising of funds for making *housing loans* (qv): 1989 Act s.9(1). The objects of a society must be agreed by those forming a society (ibid s.10(2)(a)). See FORMATION; MEMORANDUM.

offences. A building society or a person who contravenes a requirement of or under the BS Act 1989 is guilty of an offence (ibid s.119(2)). In addition, specific offences are defined eg s.119(1). There is provision for fines or imprisonment on summary conviction or on conviction on indictment (qv); there is also provision for penalties in the case of the continuation of an offence after conviction.

Where an offence is proved to have been committed with the consent of, or connivance of, or to be attributable to, or to have been facilitated by, any neglect on the part of any officer or employee of a society, that person is guilty of an offence (ibid s.119(6)). See also ibid s.124(3). For list of offences and applicable penalties, see APPENDIX I. See INDICTABLE OFFENCE; OFFICER. See also SUMMARY PROCEEDINGS.

office, loss of. See AMALGAMATION; TRANSFER OF ENGAGEMENTS.

officer. In relation to a building society or other body corporate, means a director, chief executive or secretary, by whatever name called, and, in relation to any offence, also includes any person who purports to act as an officer of the body: BS Act 1989 s.2(1).

Officers and former officers of a society which is being wound up and is unable to pay all of its debts, may be held personally liable, without any limitation in liability, for the debts and other liabilities of the society where the High Court considers that the society has failed to comply with the statutory requirement to maintain proper accounting records etc, and that this failure contributed to the society's inability to pay its debts, or has resulted in substantial uncertainty as to its assets and liabilities, or has substantially impeded its orderly winding up (ibid s.112). An application in this regard may be brought by the liquidator, the Central Bank, or any creditor or contributory of the society. See Cross & Ors v Fisher & Ors (1892) 1 QB 467. See ACCOUNTING RECORDS; ASSESSMENT OF SECURITY; AUDITOR, QUALIFICATIONS OF; DISQUALIFICATION; EXAMINATION; FALSIFICATION; INDEMNITY; MINOR;

MISLEADING STATEMENT; OFFENCES; TIME TO COMPLY. See APPENDIX I.

official language. See LANGUAGE, OFFICIAL.

official search. See DEEDS, REGISTRATION OF; SEARCHES.

Oireachtas. The national parliament consisting of the President (qv) and two houses, a house of representatives called Dail Eireann (qv) and a senate called Seanad Eireann (qv); the sole and exclusive power of making laws for the State is vested in the Oireachtas: 1937 Constitution, art.15. As regards the Oireachtas and building societies, see INSPECTOR; PRIVILEGE; REGULATIONS; SUBSIDY.

omission. A failure to do something. It may amount to the tort of negligence (qv) where a duty existed to do that something. See ACCIDENTAL OMISSION; AUDITOR, DUTY OF.

open space. Land which is required to be provided or maintained as *open space* as part of a condition to the grant of planning permission (qv) for the development of land; a planning authority (qv) has the power to serve a notice on the owner of such land, requiring him to take such steps, in the nature of levelling or planting the land, as are necessary to make it suitable for open space purposes: LG(PD) Act 1976 s.25. If the owner fails to comply with such a request, the planning authority may acquire the land compulsorily by means of a *vesting order*. See SI No 226 of 1976.

operative part. The part of a deed which carries out the main object as opposed to the recitals (qv). The operative part in a conveyence consists of the testatum, the consideration, the receipt clause, and the operative words.

operative words. The words which in a deed, create or transfer an estate. See WORDS OF LIMITATION.

opinion. The opinions of witnesses are generally irrelevant and inadmissable; a witness is required to give evidence of facts which he observed, it being left to the court to draw inferences from the facts, to form opinions and to come to conclusions. There are exceptions, including the opinion of an inspector appointed to investigate a building society; see ADMISSIBILITY OF EVIDENCE.

order bill. A bill of exchange payable to order, or which is expressed to be payable to a particular person, or does not contain words prohibiting transfer. An *order* bill is negotiated by an endorsement coupled with delivery, whereas a *bearer* bill is negotiated by delivery alone. See Bills of Exchange Act 1882 s.8(4) and 34. See BEARER BILL; BILL OF EXCHANGE; ENDORSEMENT.

ordinary resolution. See RESOLUTION.

outgoings. The necessary expenses and charges which the *receiver* of mortgaged property is required to discharge: Conveyancing Act 1881 s.24(8). See RECEIVER OF MORTGAGED PROPERTY.

outside the State. See ABROAD; ASSETS OUTSIDE THE STATE.

outstanding loan. See AMALGAMATION; TRANSFER OF ENGAGEMENTS.

overcrowded house. A house is deemed to be *over-crowded* at any time when the number of persons ordinarily sleeping in the house and the number of rooms therein either (a) are such that any two of those persons, being persons of ten years of age or more of opposite sexes and not being persons living together as husband and wife, must sleep in the same room, or (b) are such that the free air space in any room used as a sleeping apartment for any person is less than four hundred cubic feet (disregarding any height over eight feet): Housing Act 1966 s.63.

It is an offence for the owner of such a house to fail to comply with a notice served on him by the housing authority requiring him to desist from causing or permitting the overcrowding (ibid s.65).

overdraft. A loan from a bank to a customer effected by permitting the customer's current account to go into debit. A building society is empowered to make unsecured or partly secured loans on overdraft or other facility accounts to any person for any purpose: BS Act 1989 s.23(1)(f). The power may be exercised by the society only where it has *adopted* the power and recorded it in its memorandum (qv) and may be exercised only in accordance with the terms and conditions of Central Bank approval (ibid s.36(2) and (4)). See CHEQUE, DRAWING OF.

overdue bill. A bill of exchange (qv) which remains in circulation when the time for its payment has passed or, if it is payable on demand, when it appears to have been in circulation for an unreasonable length of time: Bills of Exchange Act 1882 s.36(3). A person who takes an overdue bill takes it subject to the equities of prior holders (ibid s.36(2)).

overdue cheque. See CHEQUE, OVERDUE.

overreaching conveyance. A conveyance which enables the owner of an estate to transfer it free from equitable interests or charges to which it is otherwise subject, such interests being shifted from the land to the purchase money eg on the sale of land held on trust, the equitable interest is transferred from the land to the money in the trustee's hands. Overreaching also occurs in settled land when the tenant for life transfers the *fee simple* freed and discharged from all the various estates attaching to the land by or under the settlement. See Connolly v Keating (No 1) (1903) 1 IR 353.

overriding interests. The burdens which affect registered land whether they are registered or not eg rights of the public; rights acquired under the Statute of Limitations, rights of persons in actual occupation of the land. See Registration of Title Act 1964 s.72.

ownership. Right to the exclusive enjoyment of something; it does not necessarily depend on possession. Ownership may be *absolute* where it is without conditions and is complete, or it may be *restricted* where it is subject to some limitation. It may be *corporeal* where it is visible or tangible, or *incorporeal* eg a right to recover a debt, or an easement (qv). It may be *legal* or *equitable* depending on the title eg in a fee simple subject to a trust, the legal fee simple is vested in the trustee, whereas the equitable fee simple resides in the beneficiary. Ownership may also be *vested* where there is a present right to the ownership, or *contingent* where ownership awaits or depends on the happening of an event. Ownership may also be *concurrent* (qv). See POSSESSION.

P

pamphlet. See ADVERTISEMENT.

panel of arbitrators. See ARBITRATOR.

parcels. (1) Parts or plots of land. (2) The part of a conveyance of land, following the operative words (qv), which describes the property and often refers to a plan drawn on the deed.

particular estate. An estate less than the fee simple (qv) ie given for a particular length of time. It is a term used to refer to an estate granted out of a larger estate.

particulars, land. The precise physical description of a property to be sold by auction (qv) and a short statement of the nature of the title; these are usually fixed by the auctioneer (qv) following instructions by the vendor's solicitor (qv). See CONDITIONS OF SALE; SALE OF LAND.

partition. The division of land owned by persons jointly among the owners in severalty (qv). Co-owners may partition by consent of the other co-owners by deed: Real Property Act 1845. A co-owner may without the consent of his co-owners apply to the court for partition: Partition Acts 1868 and 1876. The court has power to order a sale with division of the proceeds as an alternative to partition (ibid 1868 Act ss.3 and 4 as amended). See FF v CF (1987) ILRM 1. See RSC O.51 r.3; RCC O.6 r.14; O.45.

partnership. The relationship existing between two or more persons carrying on business in common with a view of profit: Partnership Act 1890 s.1. *Business* means a series of acts which, if successful, will produce profit or gain; it includes every trade, occupation or profession; *person* means a legal person and includes human and artificial or corporate persons. There are rules in s.2 for determining if a partnership exists.

There are two types of partnership: the *ordinary partnership* which is governed by the Partnership Act 1890 and the *limited partnership* formed under the Limited Partnership Act 1907. A formal document is not necessary to create a partnership; there may be an implied partnership from the acts of the parties thereto: see Greenham v Gray (1855) 4 ICLR 501. The receipt by a person of a share in the profits of a business is prima facie evidence that he is a partner in the business, but the receipt of a share or payment contingent or varying with the profits does not of itself make someone a partner in a business: O'Kelly v Darragh (1988) ILRM 309. See RSC O.46 rr 3-4.

As regards partnerships and building societies, see AUDITOR, QUALIFICATIONS OF; DISCLOSURE RE BUSINESS ASSOCIATE; FIRM; UNINCORPORATED ASSOCIATION.

party wall. The wall between adjoining properties. The general presumption at common law is that adjoining property owners are *tenants-in-common* (qv) of the party wall: Jones v Read (1876) IR 10 CL 315; Miley v Hutchinson (1940) Ir Jur Rep 37. This presumption can be rebutted eg by evidence that the wall was built entirely on one owner's land: Barry v Dowling (1968) HC. An owner is entitled to build a party wall (or banks, trenches, or fences) between adjoining lands and charge half the cost to his neighbour: Boundaries Act (Ireland) 1721. See also Dublin Corporation Act 1890 ss.3-5 and 9-12.

pass book. The book which records the amount invested in a building society by a member and also subsequent investments and withdrawals. Originally, a building society would issue share certificates to members in respect of their investments, but these have now all been replaced by pass books. Generally the production of a pass book is essential to obtain a withdrawal of funds or to gain access to a general meeting of a society.

It has been decided that a mere entry in a pass book is not conclusive evidence that a particular lodgement has in fact been made; a pass book entry does not on its own, give a investor a legal entitlement to the sum entered: Leen v Irish Permanent Building Society (1976) - Report of Registrar of Friendly Societies (1976) p.10 and Report of Registrar of Building Societies (1981) p.12. "The fact that an unsupported passbook entry is insufficient evidence of a lodgment does not mean that a Building Society can delete a particular entry without first having evidence that the entry is not backed by a lodgment" (ibid 1976 Report p.10).

pasturage. The right to graze animals on the lands of another. See PROFIT A PRENDRE; RUNDALE SYSTEM..

payee. The person to whom a cheque (qv) or negotiable instrument (qv) is payable.

payment. The passing of money from payer to payee in satisfaction of some debt or obligation. An unindorsed cheque which appears to have been paid by the banker on whom it is drawn is evidence of the receipt by the payee of the sum payable by the cheque: Cheques Act 1959 s.3.

payment in due course. Discharge of a bill of exchange (qv) by payment made at or after the maturity of the bill to the holder thereof in good faith and without notice that his title to the bill is defective: Bills of Exchange Act 1882 s.59(1). See DISCHARGE OF A BILL.

payment into court. See SECURITY FOR COSTS.

payment on behalf of director. A building society is prohibited from making a payment on behalf of a director or a *connected person* (qv) in connection with the provision of any services under Part III of the BS Act 1989 (ibid s.57(1)(c)). Part III deals with the power of building societies and contains the provisions under which societies are empowered to provide a wide range of services (eg, financial, conveyancing, auctioneering, insurance) and to invest in residential and commercial property.

For provisions dealing with:- prohibited transactions being voidable at the instance of the society, the accountability of directors, and disclosure of the transactions which are permitted, see DISCLOSURE OF LOANS; LOAN TO DIRECTORS.

pensions. See REMUNERATION OF DIRECTORS.

peppercorn rent. See RENT.

permanent society. Originally was a building society which had not by its rules any fixed date or specified result at which it would terminate: BS Act 1874 s.5, since repealed and only of historical importance now. See TERMINATING SOCIETY.

per my et per tout. [By the half and by the whole]. Joint tenants are said to be seised *per my et per tout,* in that they have an equal right to the possession of the whole property and no one is entitled to exclusive possession of any part. See JOINT TENANCY.

perpetuities, rule against. A *limitation* of any interest in land is void if it is capable of vesting outside the perpetuity period, which consists of a life or lives in being at the time of the gift and 21 years thereafter. A *life in being* includes everyone who is alive at the time of the gift and mentioned in it either expressly or by implication. Lives must be human lives and not animals: In re Kelly (1932) IR 255. If there is no reference to lives in being, the period is 21 years.

The rule does not apply to (a) a limitation following an estate tail or (b) a gift over from one charity to another. The perpetuity period may be extended for a *gestation period*. See also Cadell v Palmer (1833) 1 Cl & Fin 372. See CHARITIES; FEE TAIL; REMOTENESS; WORDS OF LIMITATION.

personal liability. See OFFICER; VALUABLE CONSIDERATION.

personal representative. An executor or administrator of the estate of a deceased person. The real and personal estate of a deceased person devolve on his death and become vested in his personal representatives, notwithstanding any testamentary disposition. The personal representatives are deemed in law to be his heirs and assigns within the meaning of all trusts and powers. See Succession Act 1965 s.10.

It has been held that a personal representative of a member of a building society is not a member of the society unless he takes steps to become so: In re Bowling & Welby's Contract (1895) 1 Ch 663. See ADMINISTRATOR; DEATH OF SHAREHOLDER; EXECUTOR.

personalty. Personal property; includes leaseholds.

petition. A written application to the court for relief or remedy which is used in particular cases to commence proceedings eg in relation to the cancellation of a *conversion scheme* in a building society. Unless the court gives leave to the contrary, there must be at least two clear days between the service of a petition and the day for hearing it: RSC O.5 r.17. See also RSC O.5 r.15-16; O.40 r.1. See CONVERSION SCHEME, CANCELLATION OF.

photograph. See ADVERTISEMENT.

planning authority. In the case of a county or other borough, the corporation; in the case of a county exclusive of any borough or urban district, the county council (qv); and in the case of an urban district, the urban district council (qv): LG(P&D) Act 1963 s.2(2).

planning injunction. See INJUNCTION, PLANNING.

planning law. The body of law dealing with: (a) the permission which is required for every form of development of land, save in the case of *exempted developments* (qv); (b) the statutory duty of local planning authorities to prepare a *development plan*; (c) the appeal mechanisms which exist where there is an adverse decision of the planning authority; (d) the *compensation* which is payable in respect of a refusal to grant permission or in respect of the conditions imposed; and (e) the enforcement powers of the planning authorities to ensure compliance with the terms of planning permission and to restrain unauthorised development. See LG(P&D) Acts 1963, 1976, 1982 and 1983.

The 1963 Act established the basic framework; the 1976 Act sought to remedy the more serious deficiencies by providing new and more extensive enforcement machinery and establishing a planning appeal board (An Bord Pleanala); the 1982 Act provided more stringent penalties for breaches; and the 1983 Act altered the method of appointing the chairman and members of the planning appeal board. See BORD PLEANALA, AN.

planning permission. The permission which is required in respect of any *development* of land other than *exempted* development and development commenced before 1st October 1964; LG(P&D) Act 1963 s.24. *Development* means the carrying out of any *works* on, in or under land or the making of any *material change* in the *use* of any structures or other land (ibid s.3(1)). *Land* includes any structure and any land covered with water, whether inland or coastal; *work* includes any act or operation of construction, excavation, demolition, extension, alteration, repair or renewal (ibid s.2(1)). *Use*, in relation to land, does not include the use of the land by the carrying out of any works thereon (ibid s.2(1): Viscount Securities Ltd v Dublin County Council 112 ILTR 17).

The duration of planning permission is normally five years (ibid 1982 Act s.2). However, a planning authority has the power to grant permission for a longer period (ibid s.3). There is also provision for an extension of the time limit where *substantial* works were carried out during the relevant period or for a further extension where failure to carry out the works during the extended period was due to circumstances outside the control of the developer (ibid s.4).

It is usual in a building society mortgage to have a covenant (qv) whereby the borrower undertakes to comply with all enactments relating to planning and development and not to make any alteration or change of user for which permission is required without the written consent of the society, eg see APPENDIX 5 - TYPICAL MORTGAGE clause 8(k) and (l). See EXEMPTED DEVELOPMENT; INJUNCTION, PLANNING; PURCHASE NOTICE; WARNING NOTICE.

policy. See INSURANCE.

poll. Taking a vote on a motion or at an election. The rules (qv) of a building society must provide for the right of a member to demand a poll and the manner in which a poll is to be taken: BS Act 1989, Second Schedule, Part II, para 5(q). The rules must not have the effect (a) of excluding the right of members to demand a poll or (b) of making ineffective a demand for a poll by 10 or more members having the right to vote (ibid s.73(1)). A proxy may demand or join in demanding a poll.

The election of directors to a building society at the agm must be by poll where the number of candidates exceeds the number of vacancies (ibid s.50(2)). The papers issued by the society where there is a poll, whether conducted at a meeting or by way of postal ballot, must show with equal prominence the name of each candidate, alphabetically in the order of the surnames (ibid s.50(13)).

possession. Physical detention with the intention to hold the thing detained as one's own; continuing exercise of a claim to the exclusive use of some material object. Possession is prima facie evidence of ownership and may be good against all claims except that of the true owner. Possession may develop into ownership with the efflux of time eg adverse possession (qv) of land. The holder of a negotiable instrument (qv) can give a better title than he himself has, provided the buyer takes in good faith and for value. See ENTRY, RIGHT OF; OWNERSHIP.

possession, order for. The order which a court may give to a mortgagee to aid a sale out of court, or a sale by the court in lieu of foreclosure (qv): Irish Permanent Building Society v Ryan (1950) IR 12; Irish Civil Service (Permanent) Building Society v Ingram's Representative (1959) IR 181; Ulster Bank Ltd v Conlon (1957) 91 ILTR 193. See MORTGAGEE, RIGHTS OF.

postal ballot. The rules (qv) of a building society may provide for the voting in an election of directors or on any resolution (qv) of the society to be conducted in all or in any particular circumstances by *postal ballot*: BS Act 1989 s.75(1). Notice of a postal ballot must be given:- (a) not less than 21 and not more than 42 days before the date specified as the final date for receipt of completed ballot papers (the *voting date*); (b) to every member who would be entitled to vote if the voting date fell on the date of the notice (ibid s.75(3) and (4)).

The notice must be accompanied by such other documents which would have been required if the voting had been at the meeting rather than by postal ballot, except those documents in relation to proxy voting (s.75(5)).

post-date. To insert a date on a document subsequent to the date of execution thereof eg to post-date a cheque. See CHEQUE, POST-DATED.

power of attorney. A formal instrument under seal by which one person authorises another person to act for him, in relation to certain specified matters. The donor of the power is the *principal* and the donee is the *attorney*. The authorisation must be under seal in order for the attorney to execute a deed on behalf of the principal. A power of attorney given for value and expressed to be irrevocable, cannot (in favour of a purchaser) be revoked without the agreement of the agent; a power of attorney, given for value or not, expressed to be irrevocable for a fixed period not exceeding one year is similarly irrevocable: Conveyancing Act 1882 ss.8 and 9.

It is usual in a building society mortgage to have a provision whereby the borrower appoints the society (or the secretary thereof) irrevocably to be his attorney in respect of the mortgaged property and: (a) claims for compensation as regards planning permission or compulsory purchase; (b) the assignment of the nominal *reversion* in the lease of the property; and (c) in respect of certain landlord and tenant proceedings pursuant to the Landlord and Tenant Acts 1967 to 1980 eg see APPENDIX 5 - TYPICAL MORTGAGE clause 5(d), 6, 12, and 13(a).

power of sale. See CONCESSIONS; MORTGAGEE, RIGHTS OF; SETTLEMENT; TRUSTEE, POWER OF.

powers, adoptable. See ADOPTABLE POWERS.

powers of society. A building society has such powers as are necessary for the achievement of its objects (qv) subject to compliance with any requirement that, for a power to be exercisable by the society, it must be *adopted* by the society: BS Act 1989 s.9(2)(a).

The powers of a society as regards a mortgage of property, as security for an advance from the society, are usually specified in the mortgage instrument, eg see APPENDIX 5 - TYPICAL MORTGAGE clause 7. See ADOPTABLE POWERS; ULTRA VIRES.

preference shares. Shares in a building society which carry prior or preferential rights over other shares. The rules of a building society must state whether any preferential shares are to be issued and, if so, within what limits and on what terms: BS Act 1989 s.10 and Second Schedule, Part II, para 5(d).

It has been held in the UK that preference shares must have the right to a fixed rate of interest; to preferential repayment on dissolution; to priority on withdrawal; and the right to insist upon losses being borne by the ordinary shareholders in priority to holders of preference shares: Alliance Perpetual Building Society v Clifton (1962) 1 WLR 1270. See SHARES.

preliminary view. The view which the Central Bank is empowered to give to a building society, before a special resolution (qv) for the *adoption* of a power by the society is proposed, and following consultation by the society with the Bank; the *preliminary view* may be as to whether and to what extend the Bank would approve the exercise of the power, if adopted, and is without prejudice to any decision the Bank might subsequently make on the application being made: BS Act 1989 s.36(6). See ADOPTABLE POWERS.

premises. [That which went before]. The operative parts of a conveyance (qv) which precede the *habendum* (qv) and come after the *recitals* (qv). (2) Popularly, land and buildings. A building society is empowered to provide, whether by lease, rent, purchase or construction, premises for the conduct of its business and that of a subsidiary (qv) or associated body (qv) of the society: BS Act 1989 s.20. This power applies even if part only of the premises is or will be required.

A society may dispose of the whole or part of any such premises; however, it must sell its estate or interest in the premises, as soon as is practicable to do so without undue loss, if no part of the premises is occupied for its business, unless it resolves by its board of directors to hold the premises for residential or commercial purposes under s.21 of the 1989 Act. See DEVELOPING LAND; HOUSE; LIQUID ASSETS.

premium. (1) The consideration in a contract of insurance. It is often a periodical payment; an insurer is not bound to accept a *renewal premium* except in the case of a life insurance policy. Policies usually provide that the insurer is not on risk until the premium is paid. There is a duty on the insured to disclose material facts which could affect the renewal or the renewal premium. In marine insurance, where an insurance is effected at a premium to be arranged, and no arrangement is made, a reasonable premium is payable: Marine Insurance Act 1906 s.31. See also ibid ss.52-54.

Under recent legislation, a premium paid to an insurance intermediary (qv) is treated as having been paid to the insurer when it is paid to the insurance intermediary in respect of a renewal of a policy which has been invited by the insurer, or in respect of an accepted proposal: Insurance Act 1989 s.53.

Additionally, an insurance intermediary must not accept money from a client (a) in respect of a proposal unless it is accompanied by the completed proposal or the proposal has been accepted by the insurer, or (b) in respect of a renewal unless it has been invited by the insurer (ibid s.52).

It is usual in a building society mortgage to have a covenant whereby the borrower undertakes that nothing will be done on the mortgaged property which may prejudicially affect any insurance thereof or which may increase the *premium* payable eg see APPENDIX 5 - TYPICAL MORTGAGE clause 8(j).

prescribe. To lay down with authority; to set out under a regulation. *Prescribed*, in relation to the BS Act 1989, means prescribed by regulations (qv) made under that Act (ibid s.2(1)).

prescribed investments. See LIQUID ASSETS.

prescription. The vesting of a right by reason of the lapse of time eg an easement (qv). Prescription at common law required proof of user since time immemorial, *nec vi, nec dam, nec precario,* ie without force, without secrecy, without permission. The doctrine of the *lost modern grant* (qv) overcame some difficulties in establishing this proof. The Prescription Act 1832, extended to Ireland in 1859, lays down the periods of enjoyment required to establish title to an easement and a *profit a prendre* (qv). See Scott v Goulding Properties Ltd (1973) IR 200.

price for mortgaged property. See MORTGAGEE, RIGHT OF; VOID AGREEMENT.

prior mortgage. A building society is prohibited from making a *housing loan* (qv) on the security of any freehold or leasehold estate or interest which is subject to a *prior mortgage* unless the prior mortgage is in favour of the society: BS Act 1989 s.22(4). However, the Central Bank may, by regulations, specify charges or descriptions of charges which would not materially affect the security, and a *prior mortgage* will not include any charge so specified (ibid s.22(5)).

Pending such regulations, a *prior mortgage* does not include charges specified in the BS (Amendment) Act 1983 or in the Land Act 1984 s.4(2), notwithstanding their repeal eg a charge on land to secure payment of the whole or part of a conventional rent, a fee farm rent or a crown rent or to secure payment of a purchase annuity, a land reclamation annuity or any other annual payment to the Land Commission. The 1983 Act was necessitated by the decision in Rafferty v Crowley (1984) ILRM 350.

It has been held in the UK that the statutory prohibition on making an advance on land subject to a prior mortgage does not make void a second mortgage where the society has taken a first mortgage already as security for the same debt; it was further held that the society was entitled to refuse to allow redemption of the collateral charges until the total debt outstanding was repaid: Hayes Bridge Estate v Portman Building Society (1936) 2 All ER 1400.

It was further held in the UK that the statutory prohibition was to protect a building society's property for the benefit of the society and its members and accordingly, even where the advance of money by a society was an illegal transaction, the society was entitled to recover the money and enforce the security of the advance: Nash v Halifax Building Society and Anor (1979) 2 All ER 19.

priority. Precedence; the right to enforce a claim in preference to others. As regards *registered land,* the register is conclusive evidence of the title of the owner of the land as appearing on the register and of any right or burden, and such title, in the absence of fraud, is not affected by the owner having notice of any deed relating to the land: Registration of Title Act 1964 s.31. Registered burdens on registered land rank *inter se* according to the order in which they are registered, not according to the order in which they are created (ibid s.75).

As regards *unregistered land,* registered deeds rank inter se according to their date of registration, irrespective of whether the deed passes the legal or equitable estate: Registry of Deeds (Ireland) Act 1707 s.4. As between registered and unregistered deeds, the unregistered deed is deemed fraudulent and void as against the registered one; however a party claiming through a registered deed who has actual *notice* of a prior unregistered deed, cannot rely on the priority given by the 1707 Act (ibid s.5). Registration gives priority but it does not amount to notice.

In the absence of registration, priority as between equitable interests or between legal and equitable interests is determined by the equitable maxims *where the equities are equal, the first in time prevails; where the equities are equal, the law prevails.*

As regards securities for a debt held by a building society prior to the conversion of the society into a public limited company, the company is entitled to such *priority* as if the society had not become so converted: BS Act s.107(2)(d). See DEEDS, REGISTRATION OF; JUDGMENT MORTGAGE; LAND REGISTRATION; NOTICE; WINDING UP, COMPULSORY.

private property, right to. The State acknowledges that man, in virtue of his rational being, has the natural right, antecedent to positive law, to the private ownership of external goods; the State accordingly guarantees to pass no law attempting to abolish the right of private ownership or the general right to transfer, bequeath and inherit property: 1937 Constitution, art.43(1).

However, the Constitution recognises that the exercise of the rights to private property ought, in civil society, be regulated by the principles of social justice, and consequently provides that the State may delimit by law the exercise of these rights with a view to reconciling their exercise with the exigencies of the common good (ibid art.43(2)).

The right to property is delimited by many statutes eg compulsory purchase of land; planning permission; succession law. Many State agencies have considerable powers to enter, use and acquire land to fulfil their statutory function. Where property is taken by the State, compensation must generally be paid. See Dreker v Irish Land Commission (1984) ILRM 94.

private treaty. A sale of land by agreement between vendor and purchaser, as distinct from a sale by auction (qv). See SALE OF LAND.

privilege. A special right or immunity. Privilege is given by statute to the report of an inspector appointed by the Central Bank to investigate the affairs of a building society, which is laid by the Minister for the Environment before each House of the Oireachtas: BS Act 1989 s.47(3).

Also any communication between a building society and a client in conjunction with providing *conveyancing services* for him are privileged from disclosure in like manner as if the society had at all material times been acting as the client's solicitor (ibid s.31(5)). See CONVEYANCING.

privilege, legal professional. The right whereby evidence of communications between counsel or solicitor and a client may not be given without the client's consent. As regards building societies and their requirement to produce documents to the Central Bank or to an *authorised* (qv) person, there is no requirement on a barrister or solicitor to produce a document or material containing a privileged communication made by him or to him: BS Act 1989 s.41(7). Similar provisions apply to disclosure in connection with an investigation (qv) of a society (ibid s.46(5)). See Tromso Sparebank v Beirne & Ors (1989) ILT & SJ 83. See INSPECTION; PRIVILEGE.

privy. A person who is a party to, or has a share or interest in something. An officer of building society who is *privy* to the destruction, mutilation or falsification of any record or documents affecting or relating to the property or affairs of the society, or is privy to the making of a false entry therein, is guilty of an offence, unless he proves that he had no intention to defeat the law: BS Act 1989 s.120(3).

procedure at meetings. See MEETING, PROCEDURE AT.

professional qualifications. See CHARTERED BUILDING SOCIETIES INSTITUTE.

professional indemnity insurance. See INSURANCE INTERMEDIARY.

promissory note. An unconditional promise in writing, made by one person to another, signed by the maker, engaging to pay, on demand or at a fixed or determinable future time, a sum certain in money to, or to the order of, a specified person or to bearer: Bills of Exchange Act 1882 s.83.

Most of the rules applicable to bills of exchange (qv) also apply to promissory notes; the main distinction between them being that a note is a *promise* to pay, whereas a bill is an *order* to pay; a promissory note must be presented for payment (ibid s.87) although it need not be presented for acceptance as must a bill. See Creation Press Ltd v Harman (1973) IR 313.

promoter. A person who undertakes to form a company with reference to a given project, and to set it going, and who takes the necessary steps to accomplish that purpose: Twycross v Grant (1877) 36 LT 812. For disqualification of a person being a promoter of a building society, see DISQUALIFICATION.

property. That which can be owned; *real* property (realty) and *personal* property (personalty).

property, removal and storage. See SERVICES RELATING TO LAND.

property, matrimonial. See MATRIMONIAL PROPERTY.

property, right to. See PRIVATE PROPERTY, RIGHT TO.

property, taxation of. It has been held that a taxation based on the occupation of property does not infringe any personal rights to equality: Madigan v AG & Ors (1986) ILRM 136.

property transactions. Substantial property transactions between a building society and a director of the society or a *connected person* (qv) must be approved by a resolution of the society in general meeting, otherwise the transaction is voidable at the instance of the society: BS Act 1989 s.56. The transactions include arrangements involving a *non-cash asset* of not less than £50,000 (or of not less than 10 per cent of the reserves of a society where the reserves are less than £500,000). A *non-cash asset* means any property or interest in property other than cash (ibid s.56(3)).

The director or connected person who enters into such a transaction, or any director who authorised it, is liable to account to the society for any gain made, and, jointly and severally with any other person liable, to indemnify the society for any loss or damage resulting from the transaction (ibid s.56(5)).

A transaction is not voidable where (a) restitution is no longer possible, or (b) the society has been otherwise indemnified for any loss suffered, or (c) any rights acquired *bona fide* (qv) for value and without actual notice by a third party would be adversely affected; or (d) the arrangement is, within a reasonable period, affirmed by the society in general meeting (ibid s.56(4)). See also LEASE TO DIRECTOR; LOAN TO DIRECTOR.

proposal form. A form completed by or for a person seeking insurance (qv). Until it is accepted by the insurer there is no contract and generally the insurer does not come on risk in respect of the event insured until the first premium has been paid. See however INSURANCE, CONTRACT OF; INSURANCE AGENT; PREMIUM.

proprietary lease. A sub-lease, mediate or immediate, under a building lease (qv), where the term of the former was either not less than 99 years or, if less, was equal to or greater than 20 years, or, if this was the lesser period, two thirds of the term of the building lease, and which expired at the same time as, or not more than 15 years before, the expiration of the building lease: Landlord and Tenant (Reversionary Leases) Act 1958. A proprietary lease (although not now referred to as such), entitled to acquire the fee simple, is entitled to a reversionary lease (qv): Landlord and Tenant (Amendment) Act 1980 s.30.

protection of deposits. See CENTRAL BANK; SAVINGS PROTECTION SCHEME.

protection of shares. See CENTRAL BANK; SAVINGS PROTECTION SCHEME.

protector of the settlement. The person without whose consent a tenant in tail cannot *bar* the entail except as against his own issue. The consent of the *protector* is also required by the tenant in base fee who wishes to enlarge his estate into a fee simple. The office of protector was established by the Fines and Recoveries Act 1833. See BARRING THE ENTAIL.

protest. (1) Payment *under protest* is a payment of money made by a person who denies that the money is due from him, with a view to its later recovery. (2) A certificate under seal made by a notary public attesting the dishonour of a bill of exchange (qv) ie a formal written statement made and signed by the notary public that the bill was duly presented for acceptance or payment, as the case may be, and that it was refused. Such a certificate is accepted as proof that a bill has been dishonoured. See Bills of Exchange Act 1882 s.51. See NOTING AND PROTESTING.

proxy. A person deputed to vote for another; the instrument appointing such a person. A member of a building society who is entitled to attend and vote at a meeting of the society may appoint another person as his proxy to attend, speak and to vote at the meeting instead of him, and may direct the proxy how to vote at the meeting: BS Act 1989 s.72(1). The proxy appointed need not be a member of the society and the entitlement to vote is limited to a vote on a poll (qv) or to demand a poll, unless the rules of the society allow him also to vote on a show of hands (ibid s.72(1) and (2) and 73(2)).

The rules (qv) of the society must provide for the right of a member to appoint a proxy (ibid Second Schedule, Part II, para 5(r)).

An instrument for appointing a proxy must be in such form as the Central Bank directs; one such instrument must be annexed to the notice calling a meeting for completion by the member; and no such instrument may be issued by the society or at the society's expense other than the instrument annexed to the notice, except at the written request of the member (ibid s.72(4), (6) and (7)).

A society may require that the instrument appointing the proxy be received by the society up to 10 days before a meeting in order to be effective (ibid s.72(5)). Also a society is required to keep in a safe place for one year all instruments appointing proxies and written requests from members (ibid s.72(8)). See Report of Registrar of Building Societies (1984) p.10-11, Appendix II. See CANVASSING; NOTICE OF MEETINGS; POLL; SUPERVISOR OF ELECTION.

public confidence. A building society is not required to circulate material to members of the society if it is likely to diminish substantially *public confidence* in the society, eg see AUDITOR, REMOVAL OF; AUDITOR, RESIGNATION OF; ELECTION ADDRESS; RESOLUTION, PROPOSAL OF.

public file. The file relating to each building society prepared by and maintained by the Central Bank at its head office: BS Act 1989 s.122. The file must contain various documents as required by the various provisions of the Act; members of the public are entitled to inspect the public file and to obtain copies of documents from it on payment of such fee, if any, as determined by the Bank. Examples of documents required to be kept in the public file are: copies of the memorandum (qv), rules (qv) and the certificate of incorporation (qv) (ibid s.10(5)); the name and address of the chief executive (qv) (ibid s.49(4) and (5)). See DISCLOSURE OF LOANS.

public holiday. See BANK HOLIDAY.

public interest. The Central Bank is required to have regard for the *public interest* in carrying out some of its functions under the BS Act 1989, eg see AMALGAMATION; AUTHORISATION, REVOCATION OF; CONVERSION SCHEME, CONFIRMATION OF; DERIVATIVE ACTION, BUILDING SOCIETY; TRANSFER OF ENGAGEMENTS.

public limited company. See COMPANY, PUBLIC LIMITED.

public relations. See BUSINESS ASSOCIATE.

puisne mortgage. An equitable mortgage created out of the mortgagor's equity of redemption (qv): Antrim County Land, Building and Investment Co Ltd v Stewart (1904) 2 IR 357. Where a redemption suit is brought by a puisne mortgagee, the costs of each prior mortgage are added to his security, and the total is paid, with interest, according to the respective priority of each mortgage. See Hilliard v Moriarty (1894) 1 IR 316. See REDEMPTION.

pur autre vie. [For the life of another]. See LIFE ESTATE.

purchase. To acquire land by a lawful act eg by a conveyance, as opposed to a title acquired by act of law.

purchase, words of. See WORDS OF PURCHASE.

purchase notice. The notice whereby the owner of land may require the planning authority to purchase his interest in the land; it arises only where planning permission is refused on an appeal to An Bord Pleanala (qv) and where as a result of that decision, the land has become *incapable of reasonably beneficial use in its existing state*: LG(P&D) Act 1963 s.29. It has been held in England that this does not mean merely that the land has become less valuable: R v Minister of Housing and Local Government, ex parte Chicester RDC (1960) 2 All ER 407. An appeal to confirm or annul a purchase notice lies to An Bord Pleanala. See also Portland Estates Ltd v Limerick Corporation (1980) SC.

purchaser. (1) A person who acquires land by purchase (qv). (2) In a transaction of sale, the opposite party to the vendor.

purchaser for value without notice. A person who purchases property bona fides for valuable consideration without notice of any prior right or title; he is generally entitled to priority. See NOTICE; VALUABLE CONSIDERATION.

pyramid of titles. The series of titles which may exist, particularly in respect of urban land, where a particular piece of land may have been the subject of a series of successive fee farm grants (qv), long leases and sub-leases. See TITLE.

Q

qualifications of auditor. See AUDITOR, QUALIFICATIONS OF.

qualifications of personnel. See AUCTIONEERING SERVICE.

qualifications to report. See AUDITOR, DUTY OF.

qualified title. The registration of an interest in land in the Land Registry where the title can be established only for a limited period or only subject to specified reservations: Registration of Title Act 1964 ss.33, 39, 40, 48. Registration with a *qualified title* has the same effect as if the registration were absolute, save that it will not prejudice the enforcement of any right appearing on the register as excepted.

qualifying capital. In relation to a building society applying for *authorisation* (qv), means: (a) the aggregate of the nominal value of the deferred shares (qv) issued and paid up at the date of the application and the amount of the reserves as shown in the last balance sheet of the society less any accumulated deficit as so shown; or (b) where there is no such balance sheet, the aggregate of the nominal value of the deferred shares issued and paid up at the date of the application, such shares being held by not less than 10 members of whose number at least 10 each hold shares to the value of £10,000 or more: BS Act 1989 s.17(10).

The Central Bank must be satisfied that a society has a *qualifying capital* that is not less than the *prescribed minimum* before it grants an *authorisation* to the society; the *prescribed minimum* is £250,000 or such other sum as may be prescribed by the Bank by regulation (ibid s.17(4) and (10)).

quasi-tail. An estate *pur autre vie* which is limited to a person and the heirs of his body eg *to B and the heirs of his body for the life of A*. See Ex p Sterne (1801) 6 Ves 156. See FEE TAIL; LIFE ESTATE.

quiet enjoyment, covenant for.

The usual covenant (qv) in a lease (qv) that the lessee will have quiet enjoyment eg *And the Lessor doth hereby covenant with the Lessee that the Lessee performing and observing his covenants may quietly hold and enjoy the said premises during the said term without interruption by the Lessor or any person claiming through him.* A covenant for quiet enjoyment is implied in every lease on behalf of the landlord: Deasy's Act 1860 s.41.

quit, notice to. See NOTICE TO QUIT.

quit rent. Perpetual rents on land reserved to the Crown (now the State) under the Settlement of Ireland Acts 1662 and 1665. They have largely disappeared as the Land Purchase Acts provided that if land was subject to a quit rent, the rent could be redeemed by the tenant purchasing the land. Where not redeemed and where the land is registered, a quit rent remains a burden which affects the land without registration: Registration of Title Act 1964 s.72(1)(a). See also Statute of Limitations 1957 s.2(1).

R

rate of interest. See ANNUAL PERCENTAGE CHARGE; INTEREST.

rates. A form of taxation on property based on a valuation (qv) which is used to finance expenditure by local authorities: Poor Relief (Ireland) Act 1838. The making and levying of such rates as may be necessary is provided for (ibid s.61) and must be paid *by the person in the actual occupation of the rateable property at the time of the rate made* (ibid s.71). An occupier includes every person in the immediate use of any hereditament rateable under the Act, whether corporeal or incorporeal. Where a hereditament is unoccupied at the making of the rate, the rate is made on the owner, who is defined as the person for the time being entitled to occupy the hereditament: Local Government Act 1946 ss.14 and 23. Rates levied by county councils are known as the *county* rate and by urban authorities as the *municipal* rate. See URBAN RENEWAL.

rates, mesne. See MESNE RATES.

ratios. See LIQUID ASSETS.

real estate. Real property; realty; land, tenements, and hereditaments.

real security. A security charged on land.

realty. Real property; generally freehold interest in land.

reasonable value, certificate of. See CERTIFICATE OF REASONABLE VALUE.

receipt. See ACCIDENTAL OMISSION; NAME OF SOCIETY; REDEMPTION.

receiver. A person appointed by a court or by creditors of a corporate body to manage the body until satisfaction of a debt. Often a debenture will authorise the appointment of a receiver on certain conditions being satisfied. The appointment of a receiver operates to *crystallise* floating charges which then become fixed; it also operates to suspend the corporate body's powers and the directors' authority in relation to the assets covered by the receivership.

A receiver over the property or over any part of the property or the undertaking of a building society may not be appointed when a *direction* (qv) under s.40 of the BS Act 1989 is in force, except with the prior sanction of the High Court (ibid s.40(5)). See Grange Properties v Dublin County Council (1989) SC.

receiver of mortgaged property. A receiver appointed by the mortgagee (lender) under an express power in the mortgage deed or under statutory power given by the Conveyancing Act 1881 s.19. The statutory power arises when the mortgage is by deed and after the redemption date has passed; it becomes exercisable where there is default of three months after notice is given to the mortgagor demanding payment of the principal outstanding, or interest is in arrears for two months, or there has been a breach of covenant, other than for payment of money.

The receiver is deemed in law to be the *agent of the mortgagor* and consequently the mortgagee is not liable to the mortgagor for the receiver's default. Monies received by the receiver must be applied: to discharge the outgoings; to meet annual payments which have priority to the mortgage; to discharge his commission, insurance and repairs; to discharge interest on the mortgage and, if directed by the mortgagee in writing, to discharge the principal; and to pay the residue to the mortgagor.

It has been held that the powers of s.24(3) of the 1881 Act do not entitle the receiver to apprioriate any part of the proceeds of sale of the dairy produce or the cattle on land subject to a mortgage: Donohue v Agricultural Credit Corporation (1986) IR 165.

A building society mortgage usually specifies the right of the society to appoint a receiver over the mortgaged property, to provide for his commission or remuneration, and to provide for his removal by the society, eg see APPENDIX 5 - TYPICAL MORTGAGE clause 7(b), (c) and (e). Sec FURNITURE; MORTGAGEE, RIGHTS OF.

recitals. Statements in an instrument, commencing *whereas...*, which explain or lead up to the operative part of the instrument. In a conveyance (qv), they may be *narrative recitals* which set out the facts and instruments necessary to show title, or *introductory recitals* which explain the motive for the execution of the deed. They are not necessary to the validity of the deed (qv), but they are useful from the purchaser's standpoint because: they may act as an estoppel against the vendor; they explain the operative part of the deed; they are evidence of their truth after 20 years: Vendor & Purchaser Act 1874 s.2(2).

reconversion. The notional restoration of previously notionally converted property to its original character in contemplation of equity. Reconversion may take place by act of the party for whose benefit the conversion was directed or by operation of law. An absolute owner who is *sui juris* may elect to take the property in whatever form he chooses; if he wishes to take it in its unconverted form, a reconversion takes place. Reconversion also takes place by law in certain conditions where property, though subject to an inoperative trust for conversion, has not actually been converted, and the property is *at home*. See McDonagh v Nolan (1882) 9 LR IR 262.

reconveyance. The revesting in the mortgagor of the legal estate on redemption of the mortgage. A reconveyance is not necessary in specified circumstances. See APPENDIX 5 - TYPICAL MORTGAGE clause 5. See REDEMPTION.

records. Any register or record, required to be maintained by a building society, may be kept by making entries in bound books or by recording the matter in question in any other manner (eg in computer or fiche form), provided such recording is readily accessible and readily convertible into written form in an *official language* of the State: BS Act 1989 s.117(2). Apart from accounting records (qv), a society is required to keep such other records as may be specified by the Central Bank (ibid s.117(1)). See FALSIFICATION; LANGUAGE, OFFICIAL.

records, accounting. See ACCOUNTING RECORDS.

recovery of land. See EJECTMENT; MORTGAGEE, RIGHTS OF.

reddendum. That which is to be paid; the clause in a lease which specifies the rent which is payable and the time when payable eg *Yielding therefor during the said term, the yearly rent of £... clear of all deductions by equal half yearly payments on..., the first payment to be made on... .*

redeem. See REDEMPTION.

redemption. The repayment of a mortgage debt whereby the equitable and legal estates merge in the mortgagor (qv). A mortgage cannot be expressed to be irredeemable. A mortgagor may bring a *redemption suit* to compel the mortgagee to reconvey the land on payment of debt and interest and to return his title deeds: RSC O.18 r.2; O.54 r.3; RCC O.8 r.2.

The rules (qv) of a building society must provide for the conditions on which a borrower of a housing loan (qv) can redeem the amount due from him before the end of the period for which such a loan was made: BS Act 1989, Second Schedule, Part II, para 5(e).

Where all moneys secured by a mortgage have been fully paid or discharged, a building society may issue a receipt under the seal of the society; this receipt operates to vacate the mortgage and, without any reconveyance or re-surrender, vests the estate or interest in the property in the person for the time being entitled to the *equity of redemption* (qv) (ibid s.27).

It has been held in the UK that when a mortgagee has contracted to sell a mortgaged property under a power of sale, the contract extinguishes the mortgagor's right to redeem, in the absence of any evidence of lack of good faith on the part of the mortgagee: Waring (Lord) v London & Manchester Assurance Co Ltd (1935) Ch 310.

A simplified procedure for discharging mortgages of housing authorities and other specified cases is provided for in the Housing Act 1988 s.18. See APPENDIX 5 - TYPICAL MORTGAGE clause 3(a) and 5. See also PRIOR MORTGAGE; REDEMPTION FEE.

redemption, equity of. See EQUITY OF REDEMPTION.

redemption fee. In relation to a loan, any sum in addition to principal and any interest due on such principal (without regard to the fact of the redemption of the loan) at the time of redemption of the whole or part of the loan: Building Societies Act 1986 s.6; SI No 27 of 1987, first schedule; SI No 339 of 1987. A member of a building society may at any time before the time agreed, repay the society the whole or any part of a loan, and is not liable to pay any redemption fee in relation to the loan or any part of the loan.

Notwithstanding the repeal of the 1986 Act, this provision is continued in force as regards existing and future housing loans as if made by the Central Bank; however the ban on redemption fees will not apply to fixed rate interest loans as it restricts the making of such loans: BS Act 1989 s.6. The 1989 Act provides that the ban will not apply to a *housing loan* (qv) in respect of which the mortgage or loan agreement provides that the rate of interest may not be changed or may only be changed at intervals of not less than one year (ibid s.6(3)).

The Central Bank is empowered to prescribe, by regulation, rules prohibiting or restricting the charging of redemption fees (ibid s.11(2)(b)(i)). See APPENDIX 2; APPENDIX 5 - TYPICAL MORTGAGE clause 3(a). See RULES.

refer to drawer. It has been held that the return of cheques by a bank marked *refer to drawer - present again* and *return to drawer* are reasonably capable of a defamatory meaning: Pyke v Hibernian Bank (1950) IR 105. See also Grealy v Bank of Nova Scotia (1975) HC. See DEFAMATION.

reference. (1) The submission of a matter to an arbitrator for his decision. (2) The submission to the Central Bank of a refusal by a building society to circulate (a) an election address of a candidate in a director election or (b) a notice or statement regarding a resolution which is proposed. See ELECTION ADDRESS; RESOLUTION, PROPOSAL OF.

register. A building society is required under the BS Act 1989 to maintain a variety of registers, containing information which generally must be made available for inspection by members of the society, eg see ARBITRATOR; CONTRACT OF SERVICE; DISCLOSURE OF INTEREST; DISCLOSURE OF LOANS; DISCLOSURE RE BUSINESS ASSOCIATE.

register of directors. See DIRECTORS, REGISTER OF.

register of members, building society. Every building society must keep a register of the names and addresses of its members at its chief office (qv), or with the consent of the Central Bank, at one or more of its offices other than its chief office: BS Act 1989 s.65(1) and (2).

A member of a society does not have a right of access to information on the register, except in the case of a society which has had its *authorisation* (qv) revoked, when any 10 members have the right to obtain the names and addresses of members for the purpose of communicating with them on a subject relating to the affairs of the society (ibid s.65(8)). In other instances, there is a procedure for a member to communicate with other members. See COMMUNICATIONS WITH MEMBERS; JOINT BORROWER, REPRESENTATIVE; JOINT HOLDER, REPRESENTATIVE.

register of members, company. Every company must keep a register of its members, which must not be kept outside the State: Companies Act 1963 s.116. It must be open to the inspection of any member (ibid s.119). The maintenance of a company's register of members is a *financial service* (qv) which a building society may be empowered to provide: BS Act 1989 s.29(2)(h).

There is no requirement on a company into which a building society has become converted, to enter in the register of members of the company, the occupation of the person who immediately before the conversion date (qv) was a member of the society, if the register of members of the society did not contain this information (ibid s.106(7)). This exception applies for 5 years from the conversion date.

registered name. See NAME OF SOCIETY.

Registrar of Building Societies. The Registrar of Friendly Societies who as Registrar of Building Societies had statutory responsibility for the regulation and control of building societies under the BS Acts 1976-1986. It has been held that the duty of the Registrar in his examination of alterations to the rules (qv) of a building society was to ensure that the rules made were not in conflict with the provisions of the 1976 Act: Irish Civil Service Building Society v Registrar of Friendly Societies (1985) IR 167.

Under the BS Act 1989, statutory responsibility for the regulation and supervision of building societies is transferred to the Central Bank. Also, proceedings in relation to building societies pending before the Registrar under the BS Acts 1976-1986 are to be transferred to and dealt with by the Central Bank as from the date of commencement of s.125 of the BS Act 1989. Documents and records relative to societies are likewise to be transferred. See also 1989 Act s.6. See AUTHORISATION; NEGLIGENCE.

Registrar of Companies. The officer, appointed by the Minister for Industry & Commerce, with responsibility for administering the registry of companies, which is located at Dublin Castle: Companies Act 1963 s.368. The Registrar must be satisfied that all statutory prerequisites have been met before he issues the certificate of incorporation (ibid s.17-20 and Companies Amendment Act 1983 Part 11). The Registrar may refuse to register a company where the objects are unlawful: R v Registrar of Companies (1931) 2 KB 197. See ALLOTMENT, SHARES; BANK; MEMORANDUM OF ASSOCIATION; REGISTRATION AS COMPANY.

registration, cancellation of. The Central Bank must cancel the registration of a building society where (a) the society has been dissolved arising from the *amalgamation* of societies or the *transfer of engagements*; (b) the society has been wound up and dissolved; or (c) the society has been converted into a plc: BS Act 1989 s.110(1).

The Bank may cancel the registration where it is satisfied that (a) a *certificate of incorporation* has been obtained for the society by fraud or mistake; (b) the society has ceased to function: or (c) the society incorporated under the *repealed enactments*, has failed to adopt a memorandum and rules in accordance with the 1989 Act eg within 2 years from the commencement of s.124(5) (ibid s.110(2)).

The Bank must give a society at least 2 months' notice of and specify the grounds of proposed cancellation; an appeal lies to the High Court within 1 month of the actual cancellation (ibid s.110(4)-(5)). From the time of cancellation, the society ceases to be a building society but without prejudice to any liability actually incurred by the society (ibid s.110(6)-(7)). See Middle Age Pension Friendly Society (1915) 1 KB 432.

registration certificate. See TRANSFER OF ENGAGEMENTS. See also CERTIFICATE OF REGISTRATION.

registration as company. The Registrar of Companies (qv) is required to register a building society as a public company limited by shares, on having delivered to him a copy of the conversion resolution (qv) certified by the Central Bank, a copy of the conversion scheme (qv) confirmed and registered by the Bank, the certificate of incorporation of the society as a building society, any court order as regards the conversion scheme, the memorandum and articles of association (qv) and such other documents and fee as are required under the Companies Acts to register as a company: BS Act 1989 s.106(1)-(2).

On being satisfied that the documents are in order, the Registrar retains and registers the memorandum and articles and issues a *certificate of incorporation* for the company (ibid s.106(2)). On the date shown in the certificate, the society ceases to be incorporated as a society under the Building Societies Act 1989 and is then a company incorporated under the Companies Acts (ibid s.106(4)).

On becoming a company, every shareholding in and deposit with the society become a deposit of the same amount with the successor company; also the business, property, rights and liabilities of the society, vest in the company (ibid s.107(1)).

registration of charge. See CHARGE, REGISTRATION OF.

registration of conversion scheme. See CERTIFICATE OF REGISTRATION.

registration of deeds. See DEEDS, REGISTRATION OF.

registration of land. See LAND REGISTRATION.

registration of society. See CERTIFICATE OF INCORPORATION; FORMATION.

registration of title. See LAND REGISTRATION.

regulations. The Minister for the Environment, the Minister for Finance, the Minister for Justice, or the Central Bank as the case may be, are empowered to make *regulations* (a) for the general purposes or for any particular purpose of the BS Act 1989, or (b) prescribing any matter referred to in the Act as prescribed or to be prescribed, or in relation to any matter referred to as the subject of regulations (ibid s.3(1)).

If any difficulty arises in bringing any provision of the Act into operation or in relation to any such provision, the Minister for the Environment is given significant power to modify by regulation the relevant provision to such an extent as may be necessary to bring the provision into effect (ibid s.4). This power lapses after 3 years from the day on which the relevant provision of the Act came into operation.

Also the Minister for the Environment is empowered to modify the Act by *regulation* for the purpose of assimilating the law relating to building societies to the law relating to companies and banks (ibid s.5). This will enable relevant changes in company and banking law to be applied to building societies, as many of the provisions in the 1989 Act have their origin in company and banking law.

Every regulation made under the Act must be laid before each House of the *Oireachtas* as soon as may be after it is made and may be annulled by either House (ibid s.3(4)). See DIRECTIONS; SPECIFICATIONS. See also APPENDIX 2.

re-instatement clause. Replacement or repair of damaged property under an insurance policy; many such policies have a re-instatement clause therein giving the insurer the right to re-instate the property, at the option of the insurer, rather than paying an amount in respect of damage to the property. If the insurer chooses this option, he has a duty to replace it substantially to the same condition prior to the damage and may be liable in negligence if he fails to do so properly. See St Alban's Investments Co v Sun Alliance & London Insurance Co Ltd (1984) ILRM 501.

re-insurance. The act of an insurer in relieving himself of part or of the whole of the liability he has undertaken, by insuring the subject matter himself with other insurers. Re-insurance was formerly illegal. Re-insurance can take the form of *facultative re-insurance* ie re-insurance against liability on a stated policy, or *treaty re-insurance* ie re-insurance against liabilities on policies in general.

Under recent legislation, direct insurers authorised in the State are not allowed to carry on re-insurance business in classes of insurance for which they do not hold a direct *authorisation*: Insurance Act 1989 s.22. See Winterthur Swiss Insurance v Insurance Corporation of Ireland (1986) HC.

relevant services. See BUSINESS ASSOCIATE.

relief. Generally, the remedy which a plaintiff seeks or obtains in an action. An officer or auditor to a building society may apply to the High Court for relief, where he has reason to apprehend that a claim will or might be made against him in respect of any negligence, default, breach of duty or breach of trust: BS Act 1989 s.115(2). See also INDEMNIFY; LEGAL COSTS; WITHDRAWAL FROM JURY.

remainder. A grant to take effect in possession on the natural determination of a *particular* (qv) estate of freehold created by the same instrument eg *to A for life, remainder to B for life, remainder to C in tail*; B and C take remainders and the grantor retains the reversion (qv) in fee simple. See CONTINGENT REMAINDER.

removal of auditor. See AUDITOR, REMOVAL OF.

removal of director. See DIRECTOR, REMOVAL OF.

remuneration of auditor. The rules (qv) of a building society must provide for the manner of remunerating auditors: BS Act 1989, Second Schedule, Part II, para 5(j).

remuneration of director. The rules (qv) of a building society must provide for the manner of remunerating directors (including pensions), and where it is not fixed by resolution at the agm, the maximum amount of remuneration to be paid to directors: BS Act 1989, Second Schedule, Part II, para 5(i). There must be disclosed in the annual accounts (qv) of a society on an aggregate basis the emoluments, pensions and compensation for loss of office paid to directors (ibid 1989 Act s.61 applying the Companies Act 1963 s.191, subject to any necessary modification). See also INCOME TAX.

remuneration of trustees. Generally, a trustee is not entitled to remuneration for his work as a trustee no matter how onerous it may be: In re Ormsby (1809) 1 Ball & B 189. This is based on the principle that a trustee should not obtain a material benefit from his position. There are exceptions eg where remuneration is provided for expressely in the trust instrument; or where so ordered by the court; or where the trustee's work has generated a profit for the beneficiary which the trustee is not allowed to retain. See Boardman v Phipps (1967) 2 AC 46.

rent. A periodic payment payable by a tenant to the landlord for the possession and use of land. It includes any *sum or return* and consequently may include money or services and goods: Deasy's Act 1860 s.1. A *peppercorn* rent is a nominal rent which serves as an acknowledgement of the tenancy. A landlord may bring an action for *ejectment* for non-payment of rent. See McQuaid v Lynam (1965) IR 564. See PREMISES.

rent, collection of. See SERVICES RELATING TO LAND.

rent control. The control of rents in respect of *controlled dwellings*: Housing (Private Rented Dwellings) Act 1982. The terms of the tenancy of a controlled dwelling are fixed by a Rent Tribunal: Housing (Private Rented Dwellings) (Amendment) Act 1983. See CONTROLLED DWELLING.

rent review clause. A clause in a lease which provides for a periodic review of the rent payable under the lease, provided the property is not subject to some statutory rent control. The clause may provide for a pre-determined increase, or an increase based on an escalator clause, or it may be subject to agreement or arbitration. For review of rents payable under sporting leases and reversionary leases (qv), see Landlord and Tenant (Amendment) Act 1984 ss.3 and 5. See also Landlord and Tenant (Amendment) Act 1980 s.24. See DISREGARD CLAUSE.

rent seck. [Dry rent] A rent payable in respect of land to a person who has no reversion in it (eg a fee farm grant) and with no power of distress. Distress and other remedies however are provided by Deasy's Act 1860 and the Conveyancing Act 1881 s.44. See FEE FARM GRANT.

rentcharges. Charges relating to land which do not arise from the relationship of landlord and tenant eg tithe rentcharges (qv); perpetual rentcharges sometimes created by a fee farm grant (qv); payment of advances under the Landed Property Improvement (Ireland) Act 1847; and an annuity charged on land: Revenue Commissioners v Malone (1951) IR 269. See also the definition of rentcharges in the Statute of Limitations 1957 s.2(1).

rented residential accommodation relief. See SECTION 23 RELIEF.

repairs. It is usual in a building society mortgage to have a covenant (qv) whereby the borrower undertakes to keep the mortgaged property in good and tenantable repair to the satisfaction of the society and, in default thereof, to permit the society to effect the repairs, eg see APPENDIX 5 - TYPICAL MORTGAGE clause 8(d).

repayment of loans. See AUTHORISATION; HOUSING LOAN; LOANS AND WINDING UP.

repealed enactments. The enactments repealed, in whole or in part by the BS Act 1989 (First Schedule). The Acts repealed in whole are the BS Act 1976 and the BS (Amendment) Acts 1980, 1983 and 1986. The partial repeals are the Housing (Miscellaneous Provisions) Act 1979 s.20 and the Land Act 1984 s.4(2). However, continuing in force are those parts of the BS Regulations 1987 (SI No 27 of 1987 as amended by SI No 339 of 1987) relating to redemption fees (partly), valuation reports, property insurance, legal charges and mortgage protection insurance in so far as existing and future housing loans are concerned: BS Act 1989 s.6. The complete ban on redemption fees (qv) is removed (ibid s.6(3)).

The repeals do not affect the registration or incorporation of any building society registered or incorporated under an enactment so repealed, and any such registration and incorporation is to be deemed to be a registration or incorporation under the 1989 Act (ibid s.124(2)).

Pending the making of regulations under the 1989 Act, the repeals do not affect the operation of the 1983 and 1984 Acts regarding *charges* which do not constitute a *prior mortgage*. Also pending specification by the Central Bank, *liquid assets* include assets held in a form provided for by the 1976 Act s.38. See LIQUID ASSETS; PRIOR MORTGAGE; TIERED INTEREST RATE. See APPENDIX 1.

report of auditor. See AUDITORS' REPORT; DISCLOSURE OF LOANS.

report of directors. See DIRECTORS' REPORT.

report of inspector. See INSPECTOR.

report on election. See SUPERVISOR OF ELECTION.

report on security. See VALUATION OF SECURITY.

repossession of home. See MORTGAGEE, RIGHTS OF.

representations. See AMALGAMATION; AUDITOR, REMOVAL OF; AUTHORISATION, REVOCATION OF.

requisition of meeting. See MEETING, REQUISITION OF.

requisitions on title. The questions in writing which are put by the purchaser to the vendor of real property, having received from the vendor the *abstract of title* (qv). The vendor is bound to answer all relevant questions put to him. Compliance with the questions usually requires the production of originals of documents, the furnishing of searches (qv) and statutory declarations (qv), the proving of performance of covenants (qv) and of compliance with planning permission (qv).

reservation. A clause in a deed whereby the donor, lessor or grantor reserves to himself some new thing out of that which he has granted eg a rent in a lease, a wayleave (qv).

reserves. The Registrar of Building Societies has expressed his view that the level of reserves equivalent to 4% of the total assets of a building society is the minimum that should be considered adequate: Report of Registrar (1984) p.13. This was also the minimum level established to enable a building society under the repealed enactments to make unsecured loans for bridging finance and for improvement works: BS Regulations 1987 (SIs No 27 and 339 of 1987). For statistical information on reserves, see APPENDIX 4, Table 1. See also QUALIFYING CAPITAL.

residential property tax. The tax charged in respect of all *relevant residential property* owned by an assessable person where the *market value* exceeds an exemption limit and the income of the assessable person exceeds an income limit: Finance Act 1983 s.96. *Relevant residential property* is any residential property to which the assessable person is the owner and which is occupied by him as a dwelling or dwellings (ibid s.97). *Market value* is the price which the unencumbered fee simple (qv) of the property would fetch on the open market (ibid s.98). There is inflation relief in respect of the income limit and exemption limit (ibid ss.100-101). An assessable peson who does not lodge a return or fails to comply with a notice is liable to penalty (ibid s.112). See Madigan v Attorney General Ors (1986) ILRM 136.

residential purposes. A building society is empowered, subject to having *adopted* the power by special resolution (qv) and recorded in its memorandum, to acquire, hold, dispose of and develop or participate in the development of land where the land is to be used for residential purposes and purposes ancillary or incidental thereto: BS Act 1989 ss.21(1) and 36. However, see DEVELOPING LAND.

resignation of auditor. See AUDITOR, RESIGNATION OF.

resolution. A specific proposal formally advanced by persons entitled to do so and voted upon at duly convened meetings; the major decisions of a building society are made by way of *resolutions*. The rules (qv) of a building society must provide for the right of members to move resolutions at meetings: BS Act 1989, Second Schedule, Part II, para 5(n). A resolution is (a) an *ordinary resolution*, or (b) a *special resolution*, or (c) a particular type of resolution, namely a *conversion resolution*, in the case of a proposal to convert a society into a public limited company. An *ordinary resolution* is one which is neither a *special* or *conversion* resolution (ibid s.50(17)). See CONVERSION RESOLUTION; DIRECTOR'S EMPLOYMENT CONTRACT; PROPERTY TRANSACTIONS; NOTICE OF RESOLUTIONS; RESOLUTION, PROPOSAL OF; SPECIAL RESOLUTION.

resolution, amendment of. See SPECIAL RESOLUTION.

resolution, proposal of. A resolution may be proposed by 25 members of a building society, who are entitled to vote thereon, by giving notice in writing to the society of their intention to move the resolution at the agm: BS Act 1989 s.74. The notice must be given not later than the last day of the financial year (qv) preceding the agm (ibid s.74(6)) and the text of the resolution must be included in the notice (ibid s.74(1)). A lesser number of members may be specified in the rules (qv) of the society (ibid s.74(1)). There are separate provisions governing *conversion resolutions* (qv).

A society has a duty (a) to include in the notice of the agm a notice specifying the intention to move the resolution at the meeting; and (b) to send, at the request of the proposers, to each member a copy of a statement of not more than 300 words with respect to the matter referred to in the resolution (ibid s.74(1)(a)). The statement must be given to the society also not later than the last day of the financial year preceding the agm.

The rules of a society may provide that a resolution must not be in substantially the same terms as any resolution which was defeated in the previous 3 years (ibid s.74(3)). The society may also refuse to send notices of a resolution or copies of the statement to members on certain specified grounds eg that the contents would be likely to diminish substantially public confidence in the society; that there is an abuse to seek needless publicity for defamatory matter or for frivolous or vexatious purposes; or that the society would be involved in activities likely to be ultra vires if the resolution were passed; or that the resolution or statement does not relate directly to the affairs of the society (ibid s.74(2)).

Notice of a refusal, and the grounds therefor, must be given by the society to the proposers within 14 days of receipt of the resolution; an appeal (by way of reference) lies to the Central Bank within 7 days of the refusal (ibid s.74(4)). See POSTAL BALLOTS; SHARE; VOTING; VOTING RIGHTS.

restitution. See LOAN TO DIRECTOR; PROPERTY TRANSACTION.

retail funds. See DEPOSIT; WHOLESALE FUNDS.

retention of mortgaged property. A building society may retain a mortgaged property on the default of the mortgagor (borrower), in exercise of a power given by the mortgage and in exercise of an *adopted* power to develop land which it may also have: BS Act 1989 ss.26(2) and 21.

The *value* of the mortgaged property must be determined by an independent competent person, appointed by the society and agreed to by the mortgagor, and any other mortgagee and the value so determined is to be treated as if it were money received by a mortgagee arising from a sale (ibid s.26(2)). Particulars of the value must be sent by registered post to the mortgagor and any other mortgagee (ibid s.26(5)). In the event of failure to agree a valuer, there is provision for the court to appoint a valuer (ibid s.26(3)). See DEVELOPMENT LAND; VOID AGREEMENT.

retention tax. See DEPOSIT INTEREST RETENTION TAX.

retirement of director. See DIRECTOR, RETIREMENT OF.

retours sans protêt. [Return without protest]. A direction by the drawer that a bill of exchange (qv) should not be protested. See PROTEST.

reversion. The residue of ownership which continues in the person who makes a grant of an estate eg when a fee simple owner makes a grant of a life estate, the fee simple which he retains is a reversion. See LEASEHOLD, MORTGAGE OF.

reversionary lease. The lease to which *building lessees* and *proprietary lessees* were entitled to on termination of their leases: Landlord and Tenant (Reversionary Leases) Act 1958. The right to a reversionary lease is now linked to the right to purchase the fee simple under the Landlord and Tenant (Ground Rents) (No 2) Act 1978: Landlord and Tenant (Amendment) Act 1980 s.30.

In the absence of agreement, the court will fix the terms of the reversionary lease according to the provisions of the 1980 Act s.34 ie for a term of 99 years at a rent not lower than the old rent, unless a new covenant or condition is included, with the rent being calculated at one-eighth of the open market value of the land. The reversionary lease is deemed to be a *graft* on the previous lease.

It is usual in a building society mortgage to have a provision whereby the borrower irrevocably appoints the secretary (qv) of the society as his attorney (qv) in respect of proceedings for obtaining a reversionary lease in respect of the mortgaged property eg see APPENDIX 5 - TYPICAL MORTGAGE clause 12(c).

revesting. The vesting of property again in its original owner. See REDEMPTION.

revocation of authorisation. See AUTHORISATION, REVOCATION OF.

right of way. See WAY, RIGHT OF.

right to demand a poll. See POLL.

right to emblements. See EMBLEMENTS.

right to light. See LIGHT, RIGHT TO.

right to private property. See PRIVATE PROPERTY, RIGHT TO.

right to support. See SUPPORT, RIGHT TO.

right to vote. See VOTING.

rights of auditor. See AUDITOR, RIGHTS OF.

root of title. The conveyance or other document with which the title to land commences. A *good root* of title is some instrument dealing with the ownership of the whole legal and equitable estate, containing a description by which the property can be identified and showing nothing to cast any doubt on the title eg a conveyance for value, a settlement for value, a legal mortgage of a fee simple.

The conditions of sale of land may provide for any document to be a satisfactory root of title; in the absence of such a provision the purchaser can ask for: (a) 40 years title where the freehold is being sold; (b) in the case of the sale of leasehold, the lease itself, however old, in addition to assignments during the forty years prior to the purchase date; (c) in the sale of a reversionary interest, the document creating the reversionary interest, however old, in addition to the 40 years prior to the purchase date. See Vendor and Purchasers Act 1874 ss.1-2; Conveyancing Act 1881 s.13. See ABSTRACT OF TITLE; MARKETABLE TITLE.

rules. The persons forming a building society must agree on *rules* for the regulation of the society which comply with the requirements of Part II of the Second Schedule of the BS Act 1989 and any regulations made by the Central Bank (ibid s.10(2)(b)). The rules must provide for specified matters eg the name of the society, the manner of determination of the terms on which shares are issued and repaid, the powers and duties of the board of directors, the procedure to be observed at meetings etc (ibid Second Schedule, Part II).

The Central Bank may by regulation prescribe rules in respect of matters in that schedule or in respect of specified matters as respects *housing loans* (qv) regarding eg redemption fees, valuation report, costs of legal investigation of title, insurance with an insurer directed by the society, provision of mortgage protection insurance (qqv) (ibid s.11(2)). Rules so prescribed become part of the rules of the society with effect from one month after commencement of the regulations (ibid s.11(3)).

The rules of a society are binding on the society and every member and officer (qv) of the society (ibid s.11(1)). A society is required to supply to any person a copy of its rules for such fee as may be fixed by the Central Bank (ibid s.11(6)).

A society may alter its rules only by *special resolution* (qv), which alteration must be approved and registered by the Central Bank and does not have effect until registered and cannot affect any existing rights, liabilities or legal proceedings (ibid s.14). A refusal by the Central Bank to register an alteration must be notified to the society within 2 months, including its reasons, and an appeal against the decision lies to the High Court.

It has been held that rules of a building society which have been duly certified can be ultra vires (qv): Cullerne v London & Suburban General Permanent Building Society (1890) 25 QBD 485. However, see 1989 Act s.10(7). It has also been held that the previous legislation governing building societies should be regarded as setting out a general framework but not as legislating in detail for the government of each society, so that a society was free, within the general framework, to make such rules as were thought best for the administration and management of the society: Irish Civil Service

Building Society v Registrar of Friendly Societies (1985) IR 167; Report of Registrar of Building Societies (1984) p.9-10.

It is usual for a building society mortgage to have a covenant (qv) whereby the borrower agrees to observe and be bound by the rules of the society and that the rules are incorporated in the mortgage, except in so far as there is a difference or discrepancy between the provision of the rules and the mortgage, in which case the provision of the mortgage prevails, eg see APPENDIX 5 - TYPICAL MORTGAGE clause 8(a) and (m).

For transitional provisions on the 1989 Act coming into force, see s.124(5)-(10) and REGISTRATION, CANCELLATION OF. See ARBITRATION AGREEMENT; DISPUTES; DOCUMENTS, PRESUMPTIONS AS TO; REGISTRAR OF BUILDING SOCIETIES; SECRETARY; SHARE; SPECIAL RESOLUTION; SUBSIDIARY; SUPERVISOR OF ELECTION.

run with the land. See COVENANT.

rundale system. A system of frequent redistribution of land, prevalent in the western counties of Ireland, whereby rights of pasturage continue to be owned in common by many landowners, particularly of mountain land, and whereby rights to arable land are periodically redistributed amongst the farmers of a neighbourhood. The Land Commission is empowered to purchase land where it requires it to facilitate re-arrangement of lands held in rundale or intermixed plots: Land Act 1950 s.27(1)(c).

S

sale of land. The usual practice in the sale of land by *private treaty* (qv) is for the purchaser to sign the contract for the sale of land which is then returned to the vendor for his acceptance and signing, whereupon a binding agreement is in force. There is no provision, as in the UK, for an exchange of contracts with the contract being binding only on such exchange.

In a sale by *auction* (qv) of land, an agreement is in force when the property is knocked down to the highest bidder, the necessary memorandum to that agreement being signed by the bidder while still in the auctioneer's premises and signed by the auctioneer on behalf of the vendor. See CONVEYANCE; CONDITIONS OF SALE; EJECTMENT; MORTGAGEE, RIGHT OF; SETTLEMENT; STATUTE OF FRAUDS; TRUSTEE, POWER OF; VOID AGREEMENT.

sale of mortgaged property. It is usual for a building society mortgage to specify the right of the society to sell the mortgaged property eg see APPENDIX 5 - TYPICAL MORTGAGE clause 7(b) and (c). However, see also MORTGAGEE, RIGHT OF; VOID AGREEMENT.

sale of mortgages. See MORTGAGES, SALE OF.

sans frais. [Without expense]. An endorsement of a bill of exchange *sans frais* indicates that the endorser accepts liability for the value of the bill but not for the expenses involved in enforcing it. See Bills of Exchange Act 1882 s.16. See ENDORSEMENT.

sans recours. [Without recourse (to me)]. An endorsement on a bill of exchange such that the endorser (eg an agent endorsing for his principal) is not personally liable: Bills of Exchange Act 1882 s.16.

satisfaction, certificate of. The certificate which issues from the judgments office of the courts to authenticate that a judgment has been paid. Lodgement of this certificate (a) in the Registry of Deeds will operate as a reconveyance of the land so as to vacate a judgment mortgage in the case of unregistered land or (b) to cancel a judgment mortgage as a burden on registered land: Judgment Mortgage Act 1850 s.9; Judgment Mortgage Act 1858; Registration of Title Act 1964. See JUDGMENT MORTGAGE.

savings protection scheme. The Minister for the Environment is empowered to provide, by regulations, for the application to shareholdings in and deposits with building societies of the provision of any enactment for the protection of deposits with banks (*the savings protection scheme*): BS Act 1989 s.94. The intention is to apply, with modification, the savings protection scheme contained in the Central Bank Act 1989.

Although a shareholding ranks behind a deposit in a winding up, the regulations may provide for the treatment of shareholdings as deposits for the purpose of the scheme or for the exclusion of certain shareholders and depositors eg these could be persons involved in the management of the society (ibid s.94(2)(b) and (2)(c)). The regulations may also provide for the transfer of deposits maintained by societies with the Bank to an account maintained by the Bank for the purposes of the savings protection scheme (ibid s.94(2)(a)).

Under the savings protection scheme contained in the Central Bank Act 1989, a depositor may be compensated for 80 per cent of a deposit up to £5,000 (or the first £5,000 of a larger deposit), 70 per cent in respect of the next £5,000 of a deposit and 50 per cent in respect of the next £5,000, thereby providing maximum compensation of £10,000 for a qualifying deposit of £15,000 or more: Central Bank Act 1989, Chapter V, ss.53-73. See DEPOSIT WITH CENTRAL BANK; LIQUIDATOR; APPENDIX2, P.177.

seal. Wax impressed and attached to a document so as to authenticate it. Every building society must have a seal with its name engraved on it: BS Act 1989 ss.10(6) and 13(4). The rules (qv) of a building society must provide for the form, and arrangements for custody and use, of the seal of the society (ibid Second Schedule, Part II, para 5(k)). See also BUILDING SOCIETY; NAME OF SOCIETY; REDEMPTION.

searches. Investigations made by or on behalf of a purchaser for the purpose of finding any incumbrances affecting the title to property. Searches in the Registry of Deeds comprise: (a) *hand search* which may be made by any member of the public; (b) *official search* with the issue of an official certificate of the result.

Official searches comprise a *common search* and a *negative search*, the latter rendering the officials, signing the certificate issued therein, liable to damages to the party aggrieved by any fraud, collusion or neglect in making the search. The search is directed at ascertaining whether any acts are disclosed by the Registry which are inconsistent with the title as disclosed by the *abstract of title* (qv). See CHARGE, REGISTRATION OF; LAND REGISTRATION.

second mortgage. A mortgage subsequent to a prior mortgage. A building society is not permitted to make a loan on the security of any freehold or leasehold estate which is subject to a prior mortgage unless the prior mortgage is in favour of the society making the loan. See PRIOR MORTGAGE.

secrecy. See CONFIDENTIALITY.

secretary. The officer in a building society whose principal function is regarded as being to ensure that the society's affairs are conducted in accordance with the law and with its own rules. Every building society must have a secretary, who is appointed by the board of directors: BS Act 1989 s.49. The board of directors must ensure that the person appointed has the knowledge and experience to discharge the functions of the office (ibid s.49(3)). The offices of secretary and chief executive (qv) must not be held by the same person except with the consent of the Central Bank (ibid s.49(2)).

The secretary must, along with three members, sign 3 copies of the *alteration* (qv) of a society's memorandum (qv) or rules (qv) which is submitted to the Bank, following the passing of a special resolution (qv) approving the alteration; he must also sign a letter confirming the passing of the special resolution (ibid s.14(2)). See BUSINESS TENANT; DIRECTORS, REGISTER OF; DISQUALIFICATION; OFFICER; POWER OF ATTORNEY; REVERSIONARY LEASE; SERVICE.

section 23 relief. Generally understood to mean the tax relief obtained by a person incurring expenditure on the construction of certain residential premises for letting, whereby he can deduct the qualifying expenditure from the resulting rental income: Finance Act 1981 s.23 and 24. The qualifying period of this scheme was originally extended to 31st March 1987: Finance Act 1983 s.29-30. The qualifying period of the restored scheme is now 27th January 1988 to 31st March 1991: Finance Act 1988 s.27. There is also a scheme of tax relief applicable to expenditure incurred on the *refurbishment* of *specified buildings*: Finance Act 1985 s.21 which has been similarly restored: Finance Act 1988 s.28.

securities. (1) Things deposited or pledged to ensure the fulfilling of an obligation. (2) Written evidence of ownership eg certificates. (3) *Securities* are also defined as shares in the share capital of any body corporate or stock of any body corporate, or debentures, debenture stock or bonds of any body corporate: Central Bank Act 1971 s.2.

The sale and purchase of financial obligations, debts and securities is a *financial service* (qv) which a building society may be empowered to provide: BS Act 1989 s.29(2)(c). The rules (qv) of a society must provide for the arrangements for the custody of mortgage deeds and other securities belonging to the society (ibid Second Schedule, Part II, para 5(f)). As regards a security held by a society on conversion by the society to a public limited company, see s.107(2)(d) and (2)(g)(v).

Provision has recently been made for the transfer of ownership of certain designated securities to be effected by electronic means: Central Bank Act 1989 s.139. See ASSESSMENT OF SECURITY; DEBENTURE; DEPRECIATION OF SECURITY; GUARANTEE AND DIRECTOR; VALUATION OF SECURITY; LOAN.

security, assessment of. See ASSESSMENT OF SECURITY.

security, valuation of. See VALUATION OF SECURITY.

security for costs. The security, by way of lodgment into court of money or by a bond, which the court may order the plaintiff in an action to provide, on the application of the defendant: RSC O.29. Security may be ordered eg (a) where the plaintiff resides outside the jurisdiction and the defendant has a defence upon the merits; (b) where an insolvent person sues as nominal plaintiff for another; (c) where the plaintiff is a corporate body without realisable assets.

The Court may require security for all or some of the costs of an application for a *disqualification order* (qv) where the application is made by any member or creditor of a building society: BS Act 1989 s.64(6). It may also require security from a building society in an appeal against a judgment; see JUDGMENT CREDITOR. For other circumstances where the Central Bank or a building society may require security to be given, see also COMMUNICATION WITH MEMBERS; INVESTIGATION; JUDGMENT CREDITOR. See Irish Savings Building Society (In Liquidation) & Ors v Plunkett & Ors (1987) ILRM 504.

security of tenure. See TENURE, SECURITY OF.

security of mortgage. See MORTGAGES, SALE OF.

sequestration. The legal process whereby a person is temporarily deprived of his property until he clears his contempt, arising from his refusal or his neglect to obey a direction to pay money into court in a limited time, after due service of such judgment or order. The property of a building society may not be sequestered while a *direction* (qv) under s.40 of the BS Act 1989 is in force, except with the prior sanction of the High Court (ibid s.40(5)).

service. Where a notice, direction or other document is authorised or required by or under the BS Act 1989 or the regulations made thereunder to be served on a person, it must, unless otherwise specified by the Act, be addressed to him and be served on or given to him in one of a number of specified ways eg by sending it by ordinary prepaid post: 1989 Act s.7. In the case of a building society, a document may be served on the secretary (qv) of the society (ibid s.7(2)(a)). See APPENDIX 5 - TYPICAL MORTGAGE Clause 15; NOTICE OF MEETINGS; UNINCORPORATED ASSOCIATION.

services, linking. See LINKING SERVICES.

services relating to land. Any service relating to the acquisition, disposition, management or development of land (including valuation, surveying, the collection of rent and the removal and storage of moveable property) or other services of a similar nature (including advisory services) that appear to the Central Bank to be services relating to such matters: BS Act 1989 s.32(6)(b). A building society is empowered to provide such services relating to land, subject to the *adoption* of the power and the approval of the Central Bank (ibid s.32(1)(b)). See AUCTIONEERING SERVICES; BELOW COST SELLING; LINKING SERVICES.

servient tenement. A tenement subject to a servitude or easement (qv).

settlement. A deed, will or other instrument under which any land stands for the time being limited to, or in trust for, any persons by way of succession: Settled Land Acts 1882 and 1890. Extensive powers are given by these Acts to the *tenant for life* or other limited owner in possession of the settled land, including the power of sale at the best price; the power to lease the land, or to exchange settled land for other land and take money for equality of exchange; the power to concur in partition of the land and to raise money by mortgage of the land. See also Conveyancing Act 1881 s.60; Landlord and Tenant (Reversionary Leases) Act 1958. See TRUST FOR SALE.

several. Separate, in contrast to *joint*. See JOINT AND SEVERAL OBLIGATION

severalty. Separate and exclusive possession. Property is said to belong to persons in *severalty* when the share of each is sole and exclusive, as contrasted with concurrent or co-ownership. See JOINT TENANCY; PARTITION

severance, words of. Words in a grant which denote that tenants are to take a distinct share in a property eg *in equal shares* or *equally*. See JOINT TENANCY; TENANCY IN COMMON.

share. A share in a building society is entirely different from a share in a limited liability company. "A share in a limited liability company is part of the capital and is something which cannot be got rid of. It may be transferred to someone else, but it cannot be put out of existence. A share in this building society represented no proportionate quota of the company's capital. There might be as many shares in this society as people like to apply for ...": Irvine & Fullarton Building Society v Cuthbertson (1905) 45 SLR 17.

A building society with an *authorisation* (qv) may raise funds to be used for the objects (qv) of the society, by the issue of shares of one or more than one denomination, either with or without accumulating interest, and may repay such funds: BS Act 1989 s.18(1). A repayment of such funds to a shareholder however is not permitted, other than at the shareholder's request, at particular times eg between the date the member indicated his intention to propose a resolution at a meeting and the date of the meeting (ibid s.18(2)). Also shares must not be issued without voting rights (ibid s.18(4)).

A society is required to keep at least 50 per cent of its funding liabilities in the form of members' shareholdings, although the Central Bank may grant a dispensation from this requirement (ibid s.18(3)).

The rules (qv) of a society must state the manner of determination of the terms on which shares are to be issued and repaid, and the manner in which shareholders are to be informed of changes in the terms on which their shares are held: BS Act 1989 s.10(2)(b) and Second Schedule, Part II, para 5(c). The rules must also state whether any preferential or deferred shares (qv) are to be issued and, if so, within what limits and on what terms.

Every person holding one or more shares in a society is a *member* (qv) of the society (ibid s.16(1)) and two or more persons may jointly hold shares in a society (ibid s.16(3)). The Central Bank may impose as a condition to an *authorisation* (qv) granted to a society, limitations on the issue of shares or debt instruments (ibid s.17(6)(a)). See AUTHORISATION, REVOCATION OF; DEFERRED SHARES; DEPOSIT; DIRECTOR; DIRECTOR, NOMINATION OF; FOREIGN CURRENCY; JOINT HOLDER, REPRESENTATIVE; MEMBER; MEMBER, LIABILITY OF; PASS BOOK; RULES; STAMP DUTIES; ULTRA VIRES; VOTING RIGHTS; WITHDRAWALS.

share, transfer of. A share in a building society may be transferred from the member to another person, unless there is a contrary provision in the rules (qv) of the society. It has been held that a minor cannot effect such a transfer: Swears v Mayfair Mutual Benefit Building Society (1881) Reg Rep 39.

shareholder, death of. See DEATH OF SHAREHOLDER.

shareholding. The value of a person's shares in a building society is taken as the amount standing to his credit in respect of the payments made by him on the shares and interest credited to the shares by way of capitalisation: BS Act 1989 s.2(2). Where a society becomes converted into a public limited company, every shareholding in the society becomes a deposit of the same amount with the successor company (ibid s.107(1)(a)). See REGISTRATION AS COMPANY; SAVINGS PROTECTION SCHEME.

Shelley's case, rule in. It is a rule of law that when a person by any deed or will takes an estate of freehold (qv) and by the same deed or will an estate is limited either mediately or immediately *to his heirs* or *to the heirs of his body,* these words are words of limitation and confer no estate to his heirs: Shelley's Case 1581. See Finch v Foley (1949) Ir Jur Rep 30. See WORDS OF LIMITATION.

short title. The title by which an Act may be cited eg "Building Societies Act 1989".

society. In the BS Act 1989, means a *building society* (ibid s.2(1)). See PERMANENT SOCIETY; TERMINATING SOCIETY.

soliciting. See CANVASSING.

solicitor. A person who advises on legal matters and conducts legal proceedings. He has a right of audience before all courts: Courts Act 1971 s.17. A person may not practice as a solicitor unless (a) he has been admitted as a solicitor, (b) he has his name on the roll of solicitors, and (c) he has a current *practising certificate* issued by the Incorporated Law Society of Ireland (qv). A solicitor is an officer of the court.

A solicitor owes a duty of care to his client and he also is in a fiduciary relationship to him. He has a lien (qv) on documents in his possession for his costs; this arises by operation of law and not by unilateral act of the solicitor: In re Gandon Properties Ltd (1988) SC. See Solicitors Acts 1954 to 1960.

As regards a solicitor and building societies, see CONVEYANCING SERVICES; LEGAL COSTS, INVESTIGATION; INVESTIGATION OF TITLE; PRIVILEGE; PRIVILEGE, LEGAL PROFESSIONAL.

solvency. Being in a position to pay debts as they fall due. See WARRANTY; WINDING UP.

sound broadcasting. See ADVERTISEMENT.

special meeting. The meeting of a building society which the Central Bank is empowered to call where it is of the opinion that the affairs of the society call for consideration by a meeting of the members: BS Act 1989 s.45(1). The Bank may give such directions (qv) as it thinks fit in relation to the meeting, including the time and place of the meeting and the matters to be discussed and determined by the meeting; the Bank must appoint the chairman of the meeting (ibid s.45(4)).

Under the repealed enactments, the Registrar of Building Societies refused an application from members of a society for permission for the convening of a special meeting: Healy & Ors v Irish Mutual Building Society (1982) - Report of Registrar (1981) p.10 and 29. See INVESTIGATION.

special resolution. A resolution (qv) of a building society which is required to be passed as a special resolution by this Act or by the rules (qv) of the society: BS Act 1989 s.70(1). Under the Act, only resolutions relating to certain limited matters are required to be special resolutions eg involving the *adoption* of powers and the alteration of its memorandum (qv) or its rules (ibid s.14), the amalgamation (qv) of societies (ibid s.95(2)(c)), and the change in name of a society (ibid s.14(3)).

Notice of intention to move a resolution as a special resolution must be given (ibid s.70(2)). The terms of a special resolution before a general meeting may be amended by ordinary resolution moved at the meeting if the chairman of the meeting is satisfied that adequate notice can be deemed to have been given (ibid s.70(3)).

Exceptional provision is made for special resolutions in the case of the ICS Building Society, which was entitled to issue shares under the repealed enactments (qv) to which voting rights did not attach; provision is made for arbitration to determine whether the resolution, if passed, is unreasonable having regard to particular shareholders (ibid s.74(9)). See ADOPTABLE POWERS; NOTICE OF RESOLUTIONS; PRELIMINARY VIEW; RESOLUTION, PROPOSAL OF; TRANSFER OF ENGAGEMENTS; VOTING; WINDING UP.

specific performance. The equitable discretionary remedy by which a party to an agreement is compelled by order of the court to perform his obligations according to the terms of that agreement eg in contracts for the sale, purchase or lease of land, or the sale of unique chattels not readily available on the market.

sporting lease. See RENT REVIEW CLAUSE.

squatter. A person who wrongfully enters upon land; he may acquire a title to it by *adverse* or *long possession.* Where a squatter bars the right of action and title of the dispossessed owner of land, he acquires a title good against anyone other than a person with a better title to the land. See O'Connor v Foley (1906) 1 IR 20; Perry v Woodfarm Homes Ltd (1975) IR 104. See LONG POSSESSION, TITLE BY.

stale cheque. See CHEQUE, STALE.

stamp duties. Revenue raised by means of stamps affixed to written instruments eg to conveyances, leases etc: Stamp Duty Act 1891 as amended. Stamp duties are either fixed in amount or *ad valorem* ie proportionate to the value of the property on which the instrument is based. The government is empowered to impose, vary or terminate stamp duties by order, provided the order is validated by confirmation by the Oireachtas (qv): Imposition of Duties Act 1957; McDaid v Judge Sheehy (1989) HC - ITLR (13 Feb 1989).

Stamp duty is not chargeable on any instrument effecting the transfer of a share in a building society; it is not chargeable also on any transfer, conveyance or other instrument executed for the purpose of effecting the amalgamation (qv) of societies, or a transfer of engagements (qv), or the *conversion* of a society into a plc: BS Act 1989 s.118. See CERTIFICATE OF REASONABLE VALUE.

statement, display of. The statement in relation to the business of a building society which the society is required to display in a conspicuous place in every office, branch or other place of business of the society; it must be in such form as the Central Bank directs: BS Act 1989 s.80.

statute-barred. Term used to indicate that proceedings in a cause of action have not been commenced within the time allowed by statute. See LIMITATION OF ACTIONS.

Statute of Frauds (Ireland). The Statute passed in 1695 to prevent fraud and perjury. It required certain contracts to be *evidenced* by some memorandum in writing signed by the party to be charged or his agent. These contracts are: (a) any special promise by an executor to answer damages out of his own estate; (b) any special promise to answer for the debt, default or miscarriage of another person (a *contract of guarantee*): Dunville Co v Quinn (1908) 42 ILTR 49; (c) an agreement in consideration of marriage; (d) any contract for the sale of land or any interest in land; (e) any agreement not to be performed within the space of one year from the making thereof: Naughton v Limestone Land Co Ltd (1952) Ir Jur Rep 19; Hynes v Hynes (1984) HC. See also Guardian Builders Ltd v Sleecon Ltd and Berville Ltd (1989) ILT & SJ 22. See MEMORANDUM, STATUTE OF FRAUDS.

statutory declaration. A written statement of facts which the person making it, the *declarant*, signs and solemnly declares conscientiously believing it to be true, before a notary public, a commissioner of oaths, or a peace commissioner: Statutory Declarations Act 1938. It is an offence for a person to make a statutory declaration knowing it to be false or misleading in any material respect (ibid s.6). Declarations were substituted for oaths in many cases by the Statutory Declarations Act 1835 and are now required by many statutes eg a building society must in certain circumstance satisfy itself as to the death of a shareholder, by evidence contained in a statutory declaration: BS Act 1989 s.19. See also Interpretation Act 1937 s.12 sch. See DEATH OF SHAREHOLDER.

statutory instrument. An order, regulation, rule, scheme or bye-law made in exercise of a power conferred by statute: Statutory Instruments Act 1947. Statutory instruments may be cited by number and year and also by their title eg "SI No 339 of 1987; Building Societies (Amendment) Regulations 1987". See DISPUTES; REGULATIONS. See also APPENDIX 2.

step in proceedings. Delivery of pleadings or taking any other steps in court proceedings is fatal to an application by a party to an arbitration agreement to have the court proceedings stayed in respect of any matter agreed to be referred to arbitration: Arbitration Act 1980 s.5.

The court will only refuse to stay proceedings if satisfied that the party seeking such order has instituted some process in the action which involves costs which are lost when the matter is referred to arbitration; seeking an extension of time from the other party within which to lodge a defence is not a step in the proceedings: O'Flynn v An Bord Gais Eireann (1982) ILRM 324. See also MacCormack Products Ltd v Town of Monaghan Co-op Ltd (1989) ILT & SJ 21. See ARBITRATION.

stolen pass book. See WITHDRAWALS, UNAUTHORISED.

subject to contract. Generally, an offer or acceptance made *subject to contract* means that no legally binding agreement or contract will exist until the formal contract has been completed by the parties. There may be a binding contract if the court can conclude that all the terms of a bargain have been agreed and set down in writing and signed. See Lowis v Wilson (1949) IR 347; O'Flaherty v Arran Property (1976) SC; Kelly v Park Hall Schools (1979) 113 ILTR 9 ; Casey v Irish Intercontinental Bank (1979) IR 364; Irish Mainport Holdings Ltd v Crosshaven Sailing Centre Ltd (1980) HC. See GAZUMPING.

sub-letting. A grant to another by a *lessee* of a letting for a period less than the period held by the lessee under his lease. The lessee retains a reversion (qv) on the sub-letting or sub-lease and remains subject to all the rights and liabilities under the lease. See Deasy's Act 1860 ss.9,12,13; Landlord and Tenant (Amendment) Act 1980 s.66. See LEASE; LEASE, CREATION OF.

subrogation. Substitution eg the right of an insurer to enforce a remedy which the insured could have enforced against a third party. In subrogation, a person or thing is substituted for an other, so that the same rights and duties which attach to the original person or thing, attach to the substituted one. If one person is substituted for another, he is said *to stand in the other's shoes.*

In insurance, the insurer can be subrogated to the rights of the insured and can maintain an action against a third party who caused the loss suffered by the insured, but only when the insured has been paid. Also, a person paying the premium on a policy of insurance belonging to another may be subrogated to that other. See Driscoll v Driscoll (1918) 1 IR 152; Orakpo v Manson Investments (1978) AC 95; Hibernian Insurance v Eagle Star Insurance (1987) HC; Zurich Insurance v Shield Insurance (1987) SC.

subsidiary. A company is a subsidiary of another company if (a) the other company is a member of it and controls the composition of its board of directors; or (b) the other company owns more than half in nominal value of its equity share capital or of its shares carrying voting rights: Companies Act 1963 s.155. Also where a company is a subsidiary of another company which is itself a subsidiary of a third company, the first named company is also a subsidiary of the third named company.

A *subsidiary* to a building society has the same meaning as it has in the Companies Act 1963 (and every enactment which is to be construed with that Act as one Act): BS Act 1989 s.2(1). A society is empowered to set up subsidiaries or to take a majority or minority stake in a body corporate and to support such bodies corporate or *approved housing bodies* by means of loans, grants, guarantees and the provision of services and property (ibid s.28).

However, this power is subject to *adoption* by the society, and the approval of the Central Bank (ibid s.36), which may specify the minimum share capital which the society must hold in order to exercise the power (ibid s.28(3)). See also s.36(16). See ADOPTABLE POWERS; ASSOCIATED BODY; CONVERSION RESOLUTION; GROUP ACCOUNTS; HOLDING COMPANY.

subsidy. A subvention. The Minister for the Environment is empowered to pay, out of moneys provided by the Oireachtas (qv), a subsidy to a building society in respect of interest payable to the society by a member in respect of a housing loan: BS Act 1989 s.123. In this context, a housing loan includes an outstanding loan secured by a mortgage of freehold or leasehold estate or interest in a house under the *repealed enactments* (qv) (ibid s.123(3)).

succession, law of. The branch of law governing the devolution of property on the death of its owner. Property devolves on death to *personal representatives*, known as *executors* where the deceased left a will (testate succession) and *administrators* where there is no will (intestate succession). Executors are usually appointed by the will and administrators by the court. The personal representatives transfer the property to the *beneficiaries*.

The State guarantees to pass no law attempting to abolish the general right to bequeath or inherit property, subject to regulation of that right by the principles of social justice: 1937 Constitution, art.43. The Succession Act 1965 changed the previous law significantly; inter alia, it gives the surviving spouse a *legal right* to a share in the estate and provides protection for the interest of children. See EXECUTORSHIP.

successor company. The public company, limited by shares, into which a building society converts itself: BS Act 1989 s.100. Such a company's independence is protected for a period of 5 years after conversion against any one person gaining control.

The successor company is not permitted for 5 years after the conversion date to offer or allot or register a transfer of any shares or debentures (qv) in the company if the effect would be that 15 per cent or more of the shares or debentures or of the voting rights would be held by any one person (ibid s.102). In the case of voting rights, this includes persons or their nominees acting in concert. The Central Bank may waive this requirement if it considers it necessary to do so in the interest of depositors with the successor company (ibid s.102(4)). Also an exception is made in respect of the transfer of shares or debentures which occur by operation of law (ibid s.102(5)).

The successor company has vested in it, the business, property, rights and liabilities of the society on the conversion date (qv) (ibid s.107(1)(b)). All contracts, agreements, conveyances, and mortgages entered into by the society are binding and enforceable against the company to the extent that they were previously binding and enforceable against the society eg the provisions of the conversion scheme (qv) will be enforceable against the company (ibid s.107(2) and (3)). See also CONVERSION; CONVERSION SCHEME; REGISTRATION AS COMPANY.

successor society. See AMALGAMATION; AUTHORISATION.

sum assured. Often refers to the maximum sum which is payable under a policy of insurance. The sum payable may be less if there is an average clause (qv). Where a fixed sum is payable irrespective of loss the policy is called a *valued policy*. The sum payable may also be affected by the operation of a *reinstatement clause* (qv).

summary financial statement. See FINANCIAL STATEMENT, SUMMARY.

summary offence. An offence heard by the District Court (qv), without a jury and for which the maximum punishment is generally six months imprisonment and/or a fine. An accused is not entitled to trial by jury in such cases either because the offence is *minor* or because the accused has waived his right to a jury trial, which he can do in certain cases.

Generally, an accused on summary conviction of an offence under the BS Act 1989 is liable to a fine not exceeding £1,000 or, at the discretion of the court, to imprisonment for a term not exceeding 12 months or both (ibid s.119 (1)(a)(I) and (3)(a)(i)). See INDICTABLE OFFENCE; SUMMARY PROCEEDINGS. See also APPENDIX I.

summary proceedings. Proceedings, without a jury, in the District Court of summary offences (qv) and those indictable offences (qv) which may be heard by the District Court on the consent of the accused and, in certain instances, the agreement of the Director of Public Prosecutions (qv). Summary proceedings in relation to an offence under the BS Act 1989 may be brought and prosecuted by the Director of Public Prosecutions or the Central Bank, and, notwithstanding s.10(4) of the Petty Sessions (Ireland) Act 1851, may be instituted within 3 years from the date of the offence (ibid 1989 Act s.119(4) and (5)).

supervisor of election. The rules (qv) of a building society must provide for the manner of appointing an independent person or persons, not being an officer or employee of the society, to supervise the conduct of a poll for the election of a director: BS Act 1989, Second Schedule, Part II, para 5(v).

The supervisor must prepare and submit to the Central Bank a report on the conduct of the election (a) stating whether the election was conducted in accordance with the statutory provisions, the rules of the society and otherwise with fairness and integrity; (b) containing details of the number of proxy instruments received, the number declared invalid categorised by cause of invalidation, and the number of votes attributable to valid instruments; and (c) containing such other information as may be required by the Bank (ibid s.51(5)(a)).

The Bank may disclose some or all of the contents of the supervisor's report to a duly nominated candidate (ibid s.51(5)(b)). See CANVASSING; DIRECTOR, ELECTION OF.

support, right to. The natural right of support is a right not to have support removed by a neighbour, and is confined to support for land in its natural state: Latimer v Official Co-operative Society (1885) 16 LR Ir 305. No natural right to support exists in respect of buildings on land although such a right may be acquired by easement (qv): Gatelly v Martin (1900) 2 IR 269. See FLAT.

supra protest. See ACCEPTANCE OF BILL.

surety. A guarantor; a person who binds himself, usually by deed, to satisfy the obligations of another person, if the latter fails to do so. As regards a building society and a surety where the society becomes converted into a public limited company, see BS Act 1989 s.107(2)(g)(iv). See BOND; GUARANTEE; MARSHALLING; STATUTE OF FRAUDS.

surplus assets. A building society is permitted to keep a proportion of its assets in liquid form as specified by the Central Bank. See LIQUID ASSETS.

surrender. The yielding up of the residue of a term of interest in land. It is usual in a building society mortgage to restrict the powers to accept surrenders of leases, conferred on a *mortgagor in possession* by the Conveyancing Acts 1881 to 1911, eg see APPENDIX 5 - TYPICAL MORTGAGE clause 9. See also LEASE, DETERMINATION OF.

surrender value. The amount which an insurer will pay to an insured on termination before the maturity date of a policy of insurance.

surveying. See BUSINESS ASSOCIATE; SERVICES RELATING TO LAND.

surveyor. It is usual in a building society mortgage to have a provision requiring the completion of unfinished buildings (or the execution of repairs prescribed by the society), to the satisfaction of the surveyor of the society, eg see APPENDIX 5 - TYPICAL MORTGAGE clause 8(c).

surveyor's report. See ASSESSMENT OF SECURITY; ASSESSOR'S REPORT; VALUATION REPORT.

T

tacking. The equitable doctrine by which a third mortgagee, with no notice of a second mortgage at the time his mortgage was made, can squeeze out the second mortgage, by acquiring the first mortgage and the legal estate therein. He could tack on his third mortgage to the legal estate; the doctrine is based on the maxim of *where the equities are equal, the law prevails.* However the doctrine of tacking has no application to registered instruments, where the priority of mortgages is based on their time of registration: Registration of Deeds (Ireland) Act 1707 and Registration of Title Act 1964.

tail. See FEE TAIL.

taxation advice. The provision of advice in relation to taxation is a *financial service* (qv) which a building society may be empowered to provide: BS Act 1989 s.29(2)(i).

television. See ADVERTISEMENT.

temporary dwellings. A sanitary authority is empowered to make bye-laws regulating the use of *temporary dwellings* and to prohibit the erection or retention of such dwellings on any land or water of their district if they are of opinion that such erection or retention would be prejudicial to public health or the amenities of the locality or would interfere to an unreasonable extent with traffic on any road: Local Government (Sanitary Services) Act 1948 ss.30-31. See Listowel UDC v McDonagh 105 ILTR 99; Gammell v Dublin Co Council (1983) ILRM 413.

tenancy, controlled. See CONTROLLED DWELLING.

tenancy at will. A lease where the lessor lets land to another to hold at the will of the lessor; the lessee is known as a *tenant at will.* Either party may terminate the tenancy at any time. See LEASE.

tenancy by sufference. Arises where a tenant holds on after the lawful title under which he previously held the tenancy has expired; he has no estate in the land and is just not a trespasser. See LEASE.

tenancy in common. The ownership of land by two or more persons where they have undivided possession but where there is no *right of survivorship*; the interest of a tenant in common passes on death as part of his estate. Tenants in common need not have an equal share; they need not claim under the same interest, and their interests need not have been created at the same time. Equity favoured tenancy in common as it regarded the right of survivorship of *joint tenancies* to be unfair. See JOINT TENANCY.

tenant. Lessee; a person who holds land. A tenant is obliged to pay the rent as it becomes due, and not to damage the premises over and above normal wear and tear. He must permit the landlord to enter the premises from time to time to inspect them. He must observe the covenants in the lease. See LEASE; COVENANT.

tenant, business. See BUSINESS TENANT.

tenant, statutory. A tenant who is given statutory protection eg security of tenure is given in business leases by providing for a renewal of such a lease at a marketable rent: Landlord and Tenant (Amendment) Act 1980. The statutory protection given to certain tenants by the Rent Restrictions Act 1960 was declared unconstitutional as an unjust attack on the landlord's property rights: Blake v Attorney General (1982) IR 117. See CONTROLLED DWELLING.

tenant for life. See SETTLEMENT.

tenant in tail. See FEE TAIL.

tenant pur autre vie. [Tenant for the life of another]. See LIFE ESTATE.

tenant purchase scheme. A scheme whereby the tenant of a dwelling may purchase the dwelling from a local authority; the sale is effected by a *transfer order*, which may be subject to *special conditions*, and since 1978 must vest in the tenant the fee simple: Housing Act 1966 s.60; Landlord and Tenant (Ground Rents) Acts 1978 s.4 and 1987.

A *transfer order* normally provides for payment of the purchase money by instalments and may be secured by way of mortgage (qv) or charge (qv). The *special conditions* may include (a) a requirement that the dwelling be occupied as a normal place of residence by the purchaser and (b) a prohibition on the sale of the dwelling without the consent of the housing authority (ibid 1966 Act s.89). Before giving their consent, the housing authority may require the payment to them of an amount approved by the Minister for the Environment (ibid 1966 Act s.90(6)). Future tenant purchase schemes will not require a housing authority to put the dwelling into good structural condition before selling it to a tenant: Housing Act 1988 s.23.

tenement. A thing which could be held by common law tenure, ie land. For the purposes of statutory protection of business tenants (qv), a *tenement* means a premises consisting of a defined portion of a building, or of land covered wholly or partly by buildings where the land not covered by buildings is subsidiary and ancillary to the buildings; such premises must be held by the occupier on a tenancy and the letting must not have been made either for the temporary convenience of either party or be dependent on the continuance in any office, or employment, or appointment of the tenant: Landlord and Tenant (Amendment) Act 1980 s.5. A tenement in this context, excludes agricultural lettings.

tenure. The relationship between a tenant and his reversioner or landlord.

tenure, security of. A landlord cannot recover possession of a *controlled dwelling* without a court order; such an order will not be made unless the court considers it reasonable and one of the specified grounds for such an order is proved by the landlord: Housing

(Private Rented Dwellings) Act 1982 s.16. These restrictions do not apply to service or employment lettings, or to lettings bona fide for the temporary convenience or to meet a temporary necessity of the landlord or the tenant, or to recovery by a local authority in exercise of their statutory powers (ibid ss.9 and 16; Housing Act 1966 ss.62(6), 66(17) and 118(1)). See also BUSINESS TENANT; CONTROLLED DWELLING; MORTGAGEE, RIGHTS OF.

terminating society. Originally was a building society which by its rules was to terminate at a fixed date or when a result specified in its rules was attained: BS Act 1874 s.5; since repealed and only of historical importance now. For list of terminating societies operating in the State in 1927, see APPENDIX 4, Table 4. See also PERMANENT SOCIETY.

termination of business. The High Court is empowered to grant an order, on the application of the Central Bank, directing a building society to prepare in consultation with the Bank, a scheme for the orderly termination of its business and the discharge of its liabilities to its shareholders and depositors under the supervision of the Bank: BS Act 1989, Fifth Schedule, para 6.

The Bank is required to apply to the court where the Bank forms the opinion that a society, to whom a *direction* (qv) has been given under s.40(2), is able to meet its obligations but the circumstances which gave rise to the direction are unlikely to be rectified.

testimonium. The concluding clause in a deed or will by which the parties have signed their names *in witness* of what it contains eg *In witness whereof the parties hereto have hereunto set their respective hands and seals the day and year first above written.*

tied insurance agent. Under recent legislation, means a person who enters into an agreement or arrangement with an insurer, whereby he undertakes to refer all proposals of insurance to such insurer, or which restricts his freedom to refer proposals of insurance to other insurers: Insurance Act 1989 s.51(3). An insurer is responsible for any act or omission of its tied insurance agent in respect of contracts of insurance offered or issued by the insurer, as if the tied insurance agent was an employee of the insurer (ibid s.51(2)).

tiered interest rate. The rate of interest on a loan where the rate (a) is determined by reference to the amount of the loan made, or to the amount outstanding at any time on foot of the loan, or to the income of the member to whom the loan is made, as the case may be, and (b) is greater than the lowest rate of interest applicable at the time to loans of the same type made by a building society to members generally: BS Act 1989 s.24(2).

Under the BS (Amendment) Act 1986 it was prohibited to charge tiered interest rates on loans made by a society on or after 23rd October 1986 or on loans made before 1st August 1986 on which a tiered rate was not being charged on that date (ibid ss.4(1) and 4(2)). Notwithstanding the repeal of the 1986 Act by the 1989 Act, a society must not charge a tiered interest rate on a loan made under the *repealed enactments* (qv) in respect of a *house* (qv), unless a tiered rate was lawfully charged on the date of the repeal: 1989 Act ss.24(1)(a) and 24(2)(b). Furthermore, a society must not charge a tiered interest rate on a *housing loan*(qv), unless the tiered rate is charged from the day on which the mortgage securing the loan is created, and the charging of a tiered rate is specifically mentioned in the mortgage, and is acknowledged in writing by the member (qv) in a form to be specified by the Central Bank (ibid s.24(1)(b)).

A member who is wrongly charged a tiered interest rate is not in breach of his mortgage agreement if he does not pay the additional sum involved (ibid 1986 Act s.5).

time to comply. In relation to the two day period (excluding Saturday, Sunday or a public holiday) within which an officer or an employee of a building society must provide information or explanations to the auditor of the society, it is a good defence for the defendant to show that it was not reasonably possible for him to comply but that he did comply as soon as reasonably possible: BS Act 1989 s.90(4).

title. The right to ownership of property or evidence of such right. Such a title may be (a) *original,* where the person entitled does not take from any predecessor eg in the case of copyright, and (b) *derivative,* where the person takes the place of a predecessor, by act of parties or by operation of law. See ABSTRACT OF TITLE; MARKETABLE TITLE; ROOT OF TITLE.

title by long possession. See LONG POSSESSION, TITLE BY.

title deeds. The documents and instruments conferring or evidencing the title to land. In the case of *unregistered* land, they consist of deeds and conveyances, eg conveyances of freehold, fee farm grants and sub-grants, leases and sub-leases and mortgages. In the case of *registered* land, they consist of the entries in the Land Registry on the folio relating to the land, the charges registered thereon, the land certificate and charge certificates.

Every building society must establish and maintain a system to ensure the safe custody of all documents of title belonging to the society and of deeds relating to property mortgaged to the society: BS Act 1989 s.76(11). The rules (qv) of a society must provide for the arrangements for the custody of mortgage deeds and other securities belonging to the society (ibid Second Schedule, Part II, para 5(f)).

It is usual to have a covenant (qv) in a building society mortgage whereby the borrower undertakes to hand over to the society to be kept with the title deeds affecting the mortgaged property, all permissions consents or licences relating to bye-laws or planning and development eg see APPENDIX 5 - TYPICAL MORTGAGE clause 8(1). See also APPENDIX 1; DEPOSIT OF TITLE DEEDS.

tort. [Crooked; twisted; distorted; a wrong]. A civil wrong, independent of contract, which arises from a breach of a duty imposed by law, the main remedy for which is an action for unliquidated damages ie unascertained damages to be determined by a court. The principal torts are trespass, nuisance, defamation and negligence (qqv).

Exemption from being guilty of a civil wrong is given to a building society which is converted into a public limited company and to the company in respect of their compliance with the statutory requirements: BS Act 1989 s.107(2)(g)(i).

See DATA PROTECTION.

training. See CHARTERED BUILDING SOCIETIES INSTITUTE.

transfer of engagements. A building society may transfer its engagements to another society to any extent, and that other society may undertake to fulfil the engagements, provided each resolves to do so by *special resolution* (qv), or, if the Central Bank consents, by resolution of the board of directors: BS Act 1989 ss.96(1)-(2) and 99(2).

A transfer of engagements between societies has no effect unless the transfer is confirmed by the Bank upon application and a *registration certificate* issued (ibid s.96(4)). A notice giving particulars of the application and indicating that objections and representations relating to it may be made to the Bank, must be published in at least 2 newspapers; the societies have a right to comment on any representations received (ibid s.98).

Where a special resolution (qv) is required, a statement, the contents of which have been approved by the Bank, must be sent by each society to its members entitled to notice of a meeting of the society, showing specified matters eg the financial position of each society, the interest of the directors, any compensation or consideration proposed to be made, any changes in the terms governing outstanding loans, and details in relation to employees (ibid s.97).

The special resolution approving a transfer of engagements or undertaking to fulfil engagements must also approve any terms which include provisions (a) for compensation to be paid to a director or other officer for loss of office or diminution of emoluments, or (b) for part of the funds to be distributed among any of the members (ibid s.99(1)).

The Bank may confirm a transfer of engagements in which case it registers a copy of the instrument of transfer of engagements, and issues a *registration certificate* to the society taking the transfer; the property, rights and liabilities of the society transferring stand transferred to and vested in the society taking the transfer on such date as is specified in the certificate (ibid s.98(6)(a) and 96(5)). Where a society transfers all its engagements, the society stands dissolved on the date specified in the registration certificate (ibid s.96(7)).

The Bank may also refuse to confirm a transfer of engagements, eg where it considers that the transfer would not be in the public interest or that information relevant to the members' decision was not made available to those eligible to vote, or that some relevant requirement had not been fulfilled (ibid s.98(6)(b)). See STAMP DUTIES. See APPENDIX I.

travellers cheques. The issue of travellers cheques is a *financial service* (qv) which a building society may be empowered to provide: BS Act 1989 s.29(2)(q). See CHEQUE.

transfer of mortgage. See MORTGAGES, SALE OF.

transfer of share. See SHARE, TRANSFER OF.

trespass to land. A tort (qv) consisting of entering or remaining on land or premises in the possession of another without lawful justification. Trespass is actionable *per se* ie the plaintiff does not have to show damage to succeed. The owner of premises may re-enter his own property and expel a trespasser using reasonable force: Beattie v Mair (1882) 10 Lr Ir

208; however the use of *ejectment proceedings* is preferable. Defences to trespass include: consent (eg licence), legal authority, and necessity. See EJECTMENT; MESNE RATES.

trust. An equitable obligation binding a person (called the *trustee*) to deal with property over which he has control (called the *trust property*) for the benefit of persons (called *beneficiaries* or *cestuis que trust*) of whom he may himself be one, and any one of whom may enforce the obligation. The person creating the trust is called the *settlor* or *donor*. *Trusteeship* is a *financial service* (qv) which a building society may be empowered to provide: BS Act 1989 s.29(2)(m).

A trust is either a *private* trust, for the benefit of an individual or class but not for the benefit of the public at large; or a *public* or *charitable* trust for the benefit of the public at large, although it may confer a benefit on an individual or class.

A trust may be either an express, an implied, a resulting, or a constructive trust. In a will, an *executed* trust is one which is finally declared by the instrument creating it, where the executor may be said to be his own conveyancer. An *executory* trust is one created by a direction to make a settlement upon trusts which are indicated in, but are not finally declared by, the instrument containing the direction; some further act is required to give effect to it.

No special form of words are necessary to create a trust, but the words must be imperative, the subject-matter of the trust must be certain, and the objects or persons intended to benefit under the trust must be certain: Chambers v Fahy (1931) IR 17. See also Brown v Gregg (1945) IR 224.

It is usual in a building society mortgage of leasehold property to have a declaration by the borrower that if he becomes possessed of the *reversion* (qv), he will hold it in trust for the society, eg see APPENDIX 5 - TYPICAL MORTGAGE clause 6.

The usual way of vesting trust property in new trustees is by a *vesting declaration* in a deed appointing new trustees: Trustee Act 1893 s.12. In any case of difficulty the court will make a vesting order. See CONNECTED PERSON; TRUSTEE INVESTMENTS.

trust corporation. A corporation to which the High Court may grant *probate* or *administration* which (a) is appointed by the court or (b) is empowered by its constitution to undertake trust business (being established by Act or Charter or a Bank under the Central Bank Act 1942 or a company having an issued capital of at least £250,000 of which at least £100,000 has been paid up in cash) or (c) satisfies the President of the High Court that it undertakes the administration of any charitable ecclesiastical or public trust without remuneration: Succession Act 1965 s.30. See RSC O.79 rr.17-19; O.80 rr.21-23.

trust for sale. A trust created by the vesting of the legal estate of land in trustees on trust to sell the land and to hold the income until sale and the proceeds thereafter for the beneficiaries. Under the doctrine of conversion (qv), the rights of the beneficiaries are deemed to be rights in personalty. In a trust for sale, the trustees have an obligation to sell the land although they have a discretion to postpone the sale.

Land which is held on trust for

sale, where the proceeds are to be applied for any person for life or other limited period, is deemed to be *settled land;* the *tenant for life* in such case cannot exercise the statutory powers without the consent of the court: Settled Land Acts 1882 and 1890. See SETTLED LAND.

trustee, duty of. The primary duty of a trustee is to get in and preserve the property subject to the trust. He must administer the trust in accordance with the trust instrument. He must keep accounts and produce them to any beneficiary when required. He must pay over the trust property and income to the parties entitled. Unless the trust instrument directs the trustee to retain the trust in its present state, he must invest it in securities named by law: Trustee (Authorised Investments) Act 1958.

A trustee must not make a profit for himself; he is not allowed to put himself in a position where his interest and his duty conflict: Bray v Ford (1896) AC 44. However, the trust instrument may provide for remuneration of a trustee and the court has an inherent jurisdiction so to do. A trustee cannot purchase the trust property from himself and his co-trustees, unless there is an express power in the trust instrument or the court orders such a sale. Also a trustee cannot delegate his powers - the maxim *delegatus non potest delegare-* unless expressly authorised or delegation is usual in the ordinary course of the business; a trustee however may appoint a solicitor to be his agent to receive and give a discharge for any money receivable under the trust: Trustee Act 1893 s.17. See REMUNERATION OF TRUSTEE.

trustee, power of. A trustee has a wide range of powers, unless prohibited in the trust instrument eg power of sale, power to insure, to renew leaseholds, to give receipts, to compromise, to use income for a minor's maintenance: Trustee Act 1893 ss.13-14 and 18-21; Conveyancing Act 1911 ss.9-10 and 43; Succession Act 1965 s.58.

trustee, removal of. A trustee may be removed by a power in the trust instrument, or by the court, or by the provisions of the Trustee Act 1893 ss.10 and 25 where a trustee is unfit or incapable of acting or remains outside the jurisdiction for more than 12 months, or becomes a bankrupt (qv) or is guilty of a felony. The court places the welfare of the beneficiaries above all else. See Arnott v Arnott (1924) 58 ILTR 145. See BREACH OF TRUST.

trustee, retirement of. A trustee may retire in accordance with a provision in the trust instrument, or with the consent of the beneficiaries who are entitled to the whole beneficial interest, or when new trustees are lawfully appointed to replace him. He may also retire by *deed of retirement* or exceptionally, by payment of the trust money into court: Trustee Act 1893 ss.11 and 42.

trustee de son tort. [Trustee of his own wrongdoing]. A person who intermeddles in a trust without authority; he is held liable to account as a trustee. See In re Barney (1891) 2 Ch 265.

trustee investments. Investment of trust property which is permitted by law. These include securities of the government, of the ESB, ACC, Bord na Mona, and county councils, county borough corporations; debentures (qv) of any industrial or commercial company registered in the State, provided a dividend of not less than 5% has been paid on the ordinary shares in each of the five previous years; securities guaranteed by the Minister for Finance; loan stock of the Bank of Ireland and Allied Irish Banks; bank deposit accounts including the Post Office Savings Bank and the Trustee Savings Banks; real securities in the State: Trustee (Authorised Investments) Act 1958 s.1.

The Minister may vary the list of investments by order, which he has done on a number of occasions eg to include building societies (ibid s.2). A simpler method of amending the list of authorised trustee investments has recently been provided for: Central Bank Act 1989 s.138. Also, interest bearing deposits with the Central Bank have been made authorised investments for trustees (ibid s.137).

In relation to the power to invest in real securities in the State, this does not entitle the trustee to buy land, but merely empowers him to invest funds in mortgages of realty: see Trustee Act 1893 ss.3, 5, 8, 9. See also SROs or SIs 285 of 1967; 241 of 1969; 377 of 1974; 41 and 344 of 1977; and 407 of 1979. See also BS (Prescribed Investments) Regulations 1984 (SI No 186 of 1984) made under the BS Act 1976.

turbary, common of. The right of digging and taking away of turf as fuel from the land of another. See PROFIT A PRENDRE.

U

uberrimae fidei. [Of the utmost good faith]. A contract is said to be *uberrimae fidei* when the promisee is under an obligation to inform the promisor of all those facts and surrounding circumstances which may influence the promisor in deciding whether or not to enter the contract. All contracts of insurance fall into this class. In insurance contracts, the insured must also disclose those material facts which would affect the premium the insurer should impose, if he does accept the risk.

The consequences of non-disclosure is to allow the insurer to avoid the policy. Before renewing a policy of insurance, it is necessary for the insured to disclose material facts which could affect the renewal or the premium. Also a fraudulent claim by an insured may allow an insurer to avoid liability even though he was on risk when the loss occured.

See Furey v Eagle, Star British Dominions Insurance Co (1922) 56 ILTR 109; Irish National Assurance v O'Callaghan (1934) 68 ILTR 248; Griffin v Royal Liver Friendly Society (1942) Ir Jur Rep 29; Chariot Inns Ltd v Assicurazioni Generali SPA (1981) ILRM 173. See CONTRA PROFERENTEM; INSURANCE.

ultra vires. [Beyond the power]. An act in excess of the authority conferred by law and therefore invalid. A building society's powers are limited to those necessary for the achievement of its objects (qv) subject to compliance with any requirement that, for a power to be exercisable by the society, it must be *adopted* by the society: BS Act 1989 s.9(2)(a).

In company law it has been held that an ultra vires transaction cannot be rendered effective by all the company's members attempting to ratify it or by extending the objects clause with retrospective effect: Ashbury Railway Carriage Co v Riche (1875) LR 7 HL 653. However, ultra vires acts are effective in favour of a person relying on such acts, if he was not aware at the time that the company was acting beyond its powers: Companies Act 1963 s.8(1). A similar provision applies to ultra vires acts of a building society: BS Act 1989 s.12(1).

A member of a company or a debenture holder may on application to the court restrain a company from acting beyond its power: Companies Act 1963 s.8(2)). Under a similar provision in the BS Act 1989 s.12(2), the High Court may, on the application of a member, the Central Bank or any person having a material interest, restrain a society from doing any act or thing which it has no power to do.

A society is required to keep at least 50 per cent of its funding liability in the form of members' shareholding rather than through borrowing; however, if it exceeds the limit by borrowing money, the validity of the transactions effected in excess of the limit are not affected (ibid s.18(7)).

In insurance law, premiums paid to an insurance company on ultra vires policies are recoverable as money paid without consideration: Flood v Irish Provident Assur Co (1912) 2 Ch 597n. See ADOPTABLE POWERS; LOAN, PROHIBITED; POWERS OF A SOCIETY; RESOLUTION, PROPOSAL OF.

umpire. See ARBITRATION.

under lease. A sub-lease. See LEASE.

undischarged bankrupt. A bankrupt who has not obtained a discharge by way of a *certificate of conformity*, or after 1st January 1989, an order or certificate of *discharge:* Bankruptcy Act 1988 s.85. An undischarged bankrupt cannot own property, be a director of a company, be a member of the Oireachtas, a county councillor or a member of a local authority or be a solicitor or auctioneer. He is also disqualified from being appointed or acting as an officer, auditor, receiver or liquidator of a building society; see DISQUALIFICATION.

Under recent legislation, an insurance agent (qv) and insurance broker (qv) are disqualified from acting as such if adjudged bankrupt: Insurance Act 1989 s.55. See BANKRUPTCY.

unincorporated association. A body which has no legal existence separate from its members, who are individually liable for its debts without limit eg a partnership (qv). As regards the service on an unincorporated association of notices, directions or other documents required by the BS Act 1989, such service may be effected on any partner where it is a partnership, and where not, on any member of its governing body (ibid s.7(2)(b) and (c)).

unities, four. See JOINT TENANCY.

unnamed persons, insurance of. There is a general requirement in insurance law that each individual be named on a policy of insurance. In order to remove any obstacles that might have existed in relation to the issue of certain *group insurance* policies, the law was amended to provide that nothing in the Life Assurance Act 1774 s.2 (as applied by the Life Assurance [Ireland] Act 1866), shall invalidate a policy of insurance for the benefit of *unnamed persons* from time to time falling within a specified class or description, if the class or description is stated in the policy with sufficient particularity, to make it possible to establish the identity of all persons who, at any given time, are entitled to benefit under the policy: Insurance Act 1989 s.26.

unregistered rights. See BURDENS; INHIBITIONS.

unsecured loans. A building society is empowered to provide unsecured or partly secured loans, provided it has *adopted* the power so to do: BS Act 1989 s.23. For further details, see LOAN.

urban renewal. Statutory provision for the designation by the Minister for the Environment of *urban renewal areas* and for the remission of rates in such areas, is contained in the Urban Renewal Act 1986.

Tax incentives to promote the redevelopment of certain inner city *designated areas* is provided for: Finance Acts 1986 ss. 41-45, 1987 s.27. The qualifying period has been extended to 31 May 1991: Finance Act 1988 s.26. The tax incentives include capital allowances in respect of construction; deduction from rental income of construction expenditure and from the income of the individual owner occupier; and *double rent* deduction where occupied for the purpose of trade or profession.

V

vacancy. There are provisions in the BS Act 1989 governing the filling of vacancies in the office of director or the appointment of auditor, whether the vacancy is casual or otherwise. See AUDITOR, APPOINTMENT OF; DIRECTOR, APPOINTMENT OF; CO-OPTION.

valuable consideration. Money or money's worth. Where a declaration has been made by the High Court as to the personal liability of an officer (qv) of a building society in respect of the debts and other liabilities of the society, the declaration will not affect an assignee for valuable consideration (not including consideration by way of marriage) given in good faith and without notice of any of the matters on the ground of which the declaration has been made: BS Act 1989 s.112(3)(b). See HOLDER FOR VALUE.

valuation. The valuation of land is a *service relating to land* which a building society may be empowered to provide. It is also a *relevant service* which may render the person providing it, a *business associate* of the society, such as to require disclosure of the fees paid to that person. See BUSINESS ASSOCIATE; SERVICES RELATING TO LAND.

valuation of security. The written report on the value of the security for a loan to be secured by the mortgage of freehold or leasehold estate or interest, which must be furnished to the officer or employee of a building society who is making the assessment (qv) of the adequacy of the security for the loan: BS Act 1989 s.25(1).

The valuation must report on the value of the security and on any factors likely to affect its value. The report must be made by a person who is competent, and who must not have a financial interest (qv) in the disposition, or be in receipt of a commission (qv), and who must not be a person who makes assessments. See ASSESSMENT OF SECURITY; VALUATION REPORT. See also RETENTION OF MORTGAGED PROPERTY.

valuation report. The written report which must be available, dealing with the adequacy of the security to be taken by a building society in respect of a loan to be made by the society: Building

Society Act 1976 s.79. The report must be furnished to the member of the society at the same time as he is notified of the society's approval of the loan: Building Societies Act 1986 s.6(1)(b); SI No 27 of 1987, first schedule; SI No 339 of 1987, art.6.

Notwithstanding the repeal of the 1976 and 1986 Acts, this provision, that the valuation report must be furnished to the member, continues in force as if made by the Central Bank: BS Act 1989 s.6(2). However, see ASSESSMENT OF SECURITY.

In a recent UK case a surveyor, who prepared a valuation report for a building society (in the knowledge that the mortgage applicant, who had paid for the report and who herself had no relevant special skill, would probably rely on it) was found negligent and liable to the mortgage applicant: Smith v Bush (1987) 3 WLR 889. See APPENDIX 5 — TYPICAL MORTGAGE — ADDITIONAL PROVISIONS. See ASSESSOR'S REPORT; CERTIFICATE OF REASONABLE VALUE; HOUSING; RETENTION OF MORTGAGED PROPERTY.

value, certificate of reasonable. See CERTIFICATE OF REASONABLE VALUE.

vested. An estate is said to be vested when there is a present right to its ownership. See OWNERSHIP.

vesting. There is a restriction on the vesting of interests in land not situate in a county borough, borough, urban district or town where the person is not a *qualified person* unless the written consent of the Land Commission has been obtained: Land Act 1965 s.45.

vesting declaration. See TRUST.

video. See ADVERTISEMENT.

void agreement. An agreement which is destitute of legal effect. An agreement is void to the extent that it relieves (or may have the effect of relieving) a building society or any person from the obligation of ensuring that mortgaged property, sold in exercise of a power of sale, is sold at the best price reasonably obtainable: BS Act 1989 s.26(4).

voting. A member of a building society is entitled to vote on all resolutions (qv) of the society if for 6 months prior to the end of the previous financial year (qv) he held shares to the value of £100 or more, and continued to hold them on the *voting date*: BS Act 1989 s.69(1). In addition, persons who were borrowing members (qv) at the end of the last financial year and continue to be so on the voting date, are entitled to vote on a *conversion resolution* (qv).

A society may by its rules (qv) grant voting rights to members of any description (ibid s.69(2)). However, each member entitled to vote on a *special resolution* (qv) or conversion resolution, can have only one vote eg irrespective of size of shareholding or class of or dual membership (ibid s.69(3)).

Voting date in this context is the date of the meeting at which the resolution is moved, or where there is a postal ballot, the final date for receipt of completed ballot papers (ibid s.69(4)).

The persons entitled to vote in an election of directors of a society are those members of the society who are entitled to vote on an ordinary resolution, ie a resolution which is neither a *special* or *conversion* resolution (ibid s.50(3) and (17), and s.69). Such a person cannot be required to cast all or any of his votes (ibid s.50(4)). See JOINT BORROWER, REPRESENTATIVE; JOINT HOLDER, REPRESENTATIVE; POLL;

POSTAL BALLOT; SUPERVISOR OF ELECTION.

voting by post. See POSTAL BALLOT.

voting rights. The rules (qv) of a building society must provide for the voting rights of members: BS Act 1989, Second Schedule, Part II, para 5(q). Shares in a society must not be issued without voting rights (ibid s.18(4)). Under the repealed enactments (qv), it was held that a society could issue shares to which no voting rights attached or which had only qualified or no voting rights and that the voting rights which attached to some shares could be more weighty than others: Irish Civil Service Building Society v Registrar of Friendly Societies (1985) IR 167.

Under the 1989 Act, members have one vote irrespective of shareholding on *special* and *conversion* resolutions; on *ordinary* resolutions, the rules may provide for weighted voting. While unlimited share-weighted voting is provided for in the rules of two societies (Norwich Irish and Irish Life), the recent registration policy has been to limit the maximum number of votes of individual members to about five: Report of Registrar of Building Societies (1983) p.8.

Voting rights in a *successor company* (qv) to a building society, which are held by any one person or by persons acting in concert in excess of 15 per cent of the total voting rights , are not exercisable for a five year period from the conversion date (qv), unless the Central Bank directs otherwise (ibid s.102(3)-(4)). See SPECIAL RESOLUTION.

W

waiver. The principle of waiver is simply this: "If one party, by his conduct, leads another to believe that the strict rights arising under the contract will not be insisted on, intending that the other should act in that belief, and he does act on it, then the first party will not afterwards be allowed to insist on the strict legal rights when it would be inequitable for him to do so" Lord Denning in W J Allen Ltd v EI Nasr Co (1972) 2 QB 189, which judgment was relied upon in the dispute: Hudson v Irish Permanent Building Society (1982) — Report of Registrar of Building Societies (1981) p.29.

wall. See PARTY WALL.

warning notice. The notice which a planning authority (qv) has power to serve where it appears to them that land is being or is likely to be developed without permission or any unauthorised use is being made of land: LG(P&D) Act 1976 s.26. The warning notice may be served on the owner of the land and may also be given to any other person who, in their opinion, may be concerned with the matter to which the notice relates. It is an offence for a person knowingly to fail to comply with such a notice or to assist or permit the carrying out of a development affected by it.

It is usual to have a covenant (qv) in a building society mortgage whereby the borrower undertakes to give full particulars of such a warning notice to the society and to comply with it, eg see APPENDIX 5 — TYPICAL MORTGAGE clause 8(1).

warranty. Generally, a term in a contract which gives rise to a right to recover damages in the event that it is breached but which does not entitle the injured party to repudiate the contract. The grant of an *authorisation* (qv) by the Central Bank to a building society does not constitute a warranty as to the solvency of the society and the State or the Central Bank are not liable in respect of any losses incurred through the insolvency of the society; this also applies where an authorisation is deemed to have been granted: BS Act 1989 s.17(9).

way, right of. The right to pass over the lands of another. A right of way is either *public* or *private*. A public right of way is a highway (qv). A private right of way may arise by way of easement (qv) or by necessity eg the right of way presumed to be given by the grantor of land to a *close* surrounded by the grantor's lands.

If it is proposed in the draft *development plan* of a planning authority, to preserve a public right of way, notice must be given to the owner and occupier of the land over which the right of way exists; any person may appeal to the Circuit Court against such a proposal: LG(P&D) Act 1963 s.21(3).

A public right of way may be extinguished by an order of a local authority, made with the approval of the Minister for the Environment following a public local inquiry; LG(P&D) Act 1963 s.76. Also a public right of way on land owned by a local authority may be extinguished by a specified procedure: Local Government Act 1946 s.84(4). See EASEMENT.

wayleave. A right of way over or through land (eg for the carriage of goods, to carry gas in pipes; to carry wires on pylons, etc), created by express grant, by reservation or by statute. A sanitary authority is empowered to carry any sewer into, through, or under any lands whatsoever within their district after giving reasonable notice to the owner or occupier: Public Health (Ireland) Act 1878 s.18. Similar power is given in respect of the laying of pipes for the supply of water (ibid s.64). Compensation is payable for any damage sustained by the exercise of this power (ibid s.274).

well charging order. See MORTGAGE SUIT.

welsh mortgage. A mortgage whereby the mortgagor (qv) is under no obligation to repay the principal and whereby the mortgagee (qv) takes possession of the land and takes the rents and profits in lieu of interest or until payment of interest and principal; the mortgagee has no right to call in the principal whereas the mortgagor is entitled to redeem at any time on its payment. See Cassidy v Cassidy (1889) 24 LR Ir 577. See Statute of Limitations 1957 s.34.

wholesale funds. A building society is permitted to raise funds by borrowing on the wholesale money market. The traditional raising of funds by societies has been by way of *retail funds* in the form of shareholdings of members. Borrowings by way of deposits (including from wholesale funds) however, must not exceed those by way of shares, thereby maintaining the mutual basis of societies. See BORROWING.

winding up of society. The process whereby the end is put to the carrying on of the business of a building society. It is also called a *liquidation*. Subject to certain modifications, a society may be wound up under the Companies Acts as if the society were a company limited by shares: BS Act 1989 s.109.

A building society may be wound up by the High Court on the petition of the Central Bank or of any of the persons mentioned in the Companies Act 1963 s.215 eg creditors and contributories (ibid 1989 Act s.109(4)), where (a) the society resolves by *special resolution* (qv) to be wound up; (b) the number of members is reduced below 10 or the number of directors below 3; (c) *authorisation* (qv) has not been granted to a society more than a year after it was registered; (d) the society is unable to pay its debts; (e) the society's authorisation has been revoked; or (f) the Court is of opinion that it is just and equitable that the society be wound up (ibid s.109(3)).

Where a society fails to satisfy a judgment against it within 21 days, it will be deemed to be unable to pay its debts (ibid 1989 Act s.121).

The Central Bank may also petition the High Court to wind up a society where it appears to the Bank that it is expedient to do so, having considered the report of an inspector who has investigated the affairs of the society (ibid s.47(5).

The Bank may appoint a person who is thereby then entitled to attend any meeting of creditors of a society; he is also entitled to be a member of a *committee of inspection* and cannot be removed from office or be counted in computing any minimum or maximum number thereof (ibid s.109(11)-(12)).

Where a society is wound up, its assets are collected and realised, the resulting proceeds are applied in discharge of all its debts and liabilities, and any balance (surplus) which remains after paying the costs and expenses of winding up is distributed among the members according to their rights and interests. The winding up dates from the presentation of the petition and not from the date of the winding up order: 1963 Act s.220(2).

There is provision in the 1989 Act for the orderly termination of the business of a society, rather than having it wound up; see TERMINATION OF BUSINESS. See Report of Registrar of Building Societies 1984 p.10; Irish Savings Building Society (In Liquidation) & Ors v Plunkett & Ors (1987) ILRM 504. See DISTRIBUTION OF FUNDS; FALSE INFORMATION; INSPECTOR; INVESTIGATION; JUDGMENT CREDITOR; LIQUIDATOR; LOANS AND WINDING UP; NAME OF SOCIETY; OFFICER; SAVINGS PROTECTION SCHEME; WARRANTY; WITHDRAWAL. See APPENDIX I.

withdrawal. The rules of a building society must provide for the manner of determination of the terms on which shares are to be repaid: BS Act 1989, Second Schedule, Part II, para 5(c). The investing member retires from membership of the society by withdrawing the amount paid on his shares in the society and is thereby relieved from liability upon the shares withdrawn.

It has been held that a member who has given notice of withdrawal, but has not received his money, is still a member: Sibun v Pearce (1890) 44 Ch D 354. The rules of a society may provide that withdrawals may be paid in rotation according to priority of notice: Botton v City and Suburban Permanent Benefit Building Society (1895) 2 Ch 441. Also where members give notice of withdrawal in accordance with the rules and this notice has expired before the start of the society's winding up, then these members, in relation to all other members, will be entitled to any priority afforded by the rules: In re Middlesborough Permanent Building Society No 2 (1885) 53 LT 203.

In a winding up of a society, it has been held that since depositors were not members of the society, a depositor who had given notice of withdrawal, received no priority but ranked *pari passu* with the other creditors: In re Progressive Investment & Building Society Ltd (1886) 54 LT 45. See DEATH OF SHAREHOLDER.

withdrawal, unauthorised. In a particular dispute, it was held that a building society had by its conduct waived a condition in its rules (qv) requiring written notice of the theft of a member's pass book and was thereby liable to the member for an unauthorised withdrawal: Hudson v Irish Permanent Building Society (1982) — Report of the Registrar of Building Societies (1981) p.28. See BREACH OF DUTY.

withdrawal from jury. The procedure by which a judge withdraws an issue or a case from the jury eg when he decides that the plaintiff or the prosecution has failed to discharge the appropriate onus of proof. Where in any proceedings before a judge and jury for negligence, default, breach of duty or breach of trust against an officer or auditor of a building society, it appears to the judge that the defendant ought to be relieved in whole or in part from the liability, he may withdraw the case in whole or in part from the jury and direct judgment to be entered for the defendant on such terms as to costs or otherwise as the judge may think proper: BS Act 1989 s.115(3).

withholding information. It is an offence to withhold information from an inspector duly appointed to inspect or investigate a building society: BS Act 1989 ss.41 and 119(1)(a)(ii). It is also an offence to fail to provide information required by an auditor to a building society (ibid ss.90 and 119(3)(a)).

words, operative. See OPERATIVE WORDS.

words of limitation. The words in a conveyance (qv) or a will which have the effect of marking out the duration of the estate eg in a grant *to A and his heirs*, the words *and his heirs* are words of limitation and confer no estate on his heirs (Shelley's Case 1581) but create a *fee simple* in A. A fee simple may also be created by the words *to A in fee simple*: Conveyancing Act 1881 s.51.

A *fee tail* (qv) may be created by the words *to A and the heirs of his body* and a *life estate* (qv) by *to A for life* or by the use of expressions insufficient to create a fee simple or fee tail eg *to A* or *to A for ever*.

A devise of real estate in a will without words of limitation, is to be construed as passing the whole estate which the testator had power to dispose of, unless a contrary intention appears from the will: Succession Act 1965 s.94. See In re McIntyre, Crawford v Ruttledge (1970) HC. See WORDS OF PURCHASE; REMOTENESS; SHELLEY'S CASE, RULE IN.

words of purchase. The words in a conveyance (qv) or a will which denote the person who is to take an estate or interest in land eg in a grant *to A and his heirs*, the words *to A* are words of purchase and *and his heirs* are words of limitation. The words *heirs* when used as words of purchase are to be construed to mean those entitled under Part VI of the Succession Act 1965 (ibid s.15). See WORDS OF LIMITATION.

words of severence. See SEVERENCE, WORDS OF.

Y

year, executor's. See EXECUTOR'S YEAR.

year, financial. See FINANCIAL YEAR.

Z

zillmerizing. The method of modifying the *net premium reserve method* of valuing a long term insurance policy, by increasing the part of the future premiums for which credit is taken so as to allow for initial expenses: European Communities (Life Assurance) Regulations 1984 (SI No 57 of 1984), arts.2(1) and 17(2)(e)(ii).

zoning. Generally understood to mean the designation by a planning authority in its development plan of permitted uses for land eg for residential, commercial, or agricultural purposes. The actual term *zoning* is not referred to in the planning legislation.

Appendix I

OFFENCES UNDER THE BUILDING SOCIETIES ACT 1989

(The references in capital letters refer to entries in The Guide)

Section	Brief description of Offence	Maximum Fine/ Imprisonment
s.44(4)	Contravening s.44(1) ie disclosure of information concerning the business of any building society by the Governor, a director, officer or servant of the Central Bank. See CONFIDENTIALITY.	Summary: £1,000/12 months; Indictment: £25,000/5 years
s.51(8)	Soliciting (by an employee at the place of his employment or of a meeting of the society) support for a candidate for election as a director or inviting a member of the society to appoint as his proxy any particular person. See CANVASSING.	£300
s.55(4)	Failing to maintain a register of directors' service contracts. See CONTRACT OF SERVICE.	£1,000; Continuing offence £50 per day
s.119(1) (a)(i)	Obtaining an authorisation through false statements or any other irregular means. See AUTHORISATION.	Summary: £1,000/12 months; Indictment: £50,000/5 years; Continuing: Summary £100 per day; Indictment £5,000 per day

s.119(1)(a)(ii)	Contravening s.17 ie the provisions governing the authorisation to raise funds. See AUTHORISATION.	"
	Contravening s.18(3) ie in relation to the requirement that a society's aggregate liabilities by borrowing must not exceed its aggregate liabilities by the issue of shares. See BORROWING.	"
	Contravening s.25 ie the provisions governing the assessment of the security for loans. See ASSESSMENT OF SECURITY.	"
	Contravening s.41 ie the provisions governing the inspections of a society and the production of documents/information. See INSPECTION.	"
s.119(1)(a)(iii)	Committing by act or omission a breach of a condition duly imposed on an authorisation under s.17. See AUTHORISATION.	"
	Committing by act or omission a breach of a condition duly imposed on an approval to exercise a power under s.36. See ADOPTION OF POWERS.	"
s.119(1)(a)(iv)	Failing to comply with a direction under s.40 and the Fourth Schedule ie in relation to the suspension by a society of the raising of funds, making of payments or the acquisition or disposal of other assets or liabilities. See DIRECTION.	"
	Failing to comply with a direction under s.42 ie in relation to advertising. See ADVERTISEMENT.	"
	Failing to comply with a requirement under s.39 ie in relation to assets, liabilities and ratios. See LIQUID ASSETS.	"

s.119(3) (a)	Contravening a requirement of or under the 1989 Act or guilty of an offence for which no penalty is specifically provided	Summary £1,000/12 months; Indictment £10,000/3 years; Continuing offence — Summary: £50 per day Indictment: £1,000 per day
	eg — Failing to attend before an inspector appointed to investigate the affairs of a society (s.46(4)). See INSPECTOR.	,,
	— Entering into transaction or arrangement contravening the restrictions on loans to directors and connected persons (s.58(4) – (6)). See LOAN TO DIRECTOR.	,,
	— Acting as a director or auditor or permitting ones name to be put forward for election when disqualified (s.64(11) – (12)). See AUDITOR, QUALIFICATIONS OF; DISQUALIFICATION.	,,
	— Failing to secure compliance with the requirements governing accounting records, annual accounts, or systems of business controls (ss. 76(12) and 77(9)). See ACCOUNTING RECORDS: ANNUAL ACCOUNTS.	,,
	— As immediately above, where the society is being wound up and the court considers that the contravention has contributed to the society's inability to pay all of its debts, or has resulted in substantial uncertainty as to the assets and liabilities of the society or has substantially impeded the orderly winding up of the society (s.111(1)). See ACCOUNTING RECORDS.	,,
	— Failing to secure compliance with the requirement governing the keeping of title deeds (s.76(12)). See TITLE DEEDS.	,,

	— Failing to take all reasonable steps to comply with the requirements regarding directors' reports (s.78(4)). See DIRECTORS' REPORT.	"
	— Failing to comply with the requirements relating to (a) the balance sheet of a society (s.81(3)). See BALANCE SHEET. (b) the documents to be laid before the agm (s.82(6)). See ANNUAL GENERAL MEETING.	"
	— Making a false statement to an auditor or failing to provide information required by him (s.90). See MISLEADING STATEMENT.	"
	— Failing to comply with the requirements relating to an amalgamation with another society or the transfer of engagements (s.98(8)). See AMALGAMATION; TRANSFER OF ENGAGEMENTS.	"
s.120(1)	Furnishing of a document etc, false in a material particular, knowing it to be false, or recklessly providing it. See FALSE INFORMATION.	"
s.120(2)	As above, but where it contributed to a society being unable to pay its debts, or prevented or seriously impeded the orderly winding up of the society, or substantially facilitated the defrauding of creditors. See FALSE INFORMATION.	Indictment £50,000/7 years
s.120(3) & (4)	Destroying, mutilating or falsifying (or privy to) of any record or document of the society or making a false entry. See FALSIFICATION.	"
	Any such person who fraudulently parts with, alters or makes an omission in any such record or document (or privy to).	"
s.124(3)	Continuing an offence under a repealed enactment where that enactment provides a penalty for the continuation of the offence. See REPEALED ENACTMENTS.	Corresponding to the offence under the 1989 Act.

Appendix 2

REGULATIONS UNDER THE BUILDING SOCIETIES ACT 1989

(The references in capital letters refer to entries in The Guide)

The power to make Regulations is vested in the appropriate authority, namely the Ministers for the Environment, Justic and Finance, or the Central Bank of Ireland, by virtue of s.3 of the BS Act 1989. See REGULATIONS.

Code: * No Regulations made at the time of writing.
+ Regulations made by Central Bank.
("X") Regulations made by Minister for Justice.
("Y") Regulations made by Minister for Finance.
Other Regulations are made by the Minister for the Environment.

Section	SI No.	Description	Effective Date
s.1(2)	182 of 1989	BS Act 1989 (Commencement) Order 1989. Commencement date for all sections, except Part IX (Savings Protection), is 1st September 1989.	1st Sept 1989
s.4	*	Modification of 1989 Act to remove any difficulty arising in bringing a provision into force. (This power lapses after 3 years.) See REGULATIONS.	
s.5	*	Application to building societies of relevant changes in company and banking law. See REGULATIONS.	

s.6	27 of 1987; 339 of 1987	Building Society Regulations 1987 (as amended) continued in force as regards valuation reports, property insurance, legal charges, mortgage protection insurance, and redemption fees, except that the ban on redemption fees does not apply to fixed interest rate loans as from the commencement of s.6 of the 1989 Act. See INSURANCE: LEGAL COSTS, INVESTIGATION OF TITLE; MORTGAGE PROTECTION INSURANCE; REDEMPTION FEE; VALUATION REPORT.
s.11(2)(a)	*	+ Further provisions as regards the form and content of a memorandum of a society. See MEMORANDUM.
s.11(2)(b)	*	+ Prohibiting or restricting the charging of redemption fees. See REDEMPTION FEE.
	*	+ Making available to a member the report relating to the value of the security for the loan. See ASSESSMENT OF SECURITY; VALUATION REPORT.
	*	+ Removing or restricting the right of the society to effect insurance with an insurer directed by the society. See INSURANCE.
	*	+ Arranging by a society for the possession of mortgage protection insurance. See INSURANCE.
	*	+ Precluding or restricting a society from requiring a member to pay the society's costs of legal investigation of title. See LEGAL COSTS, INVESTIGATION OF TITLE.
s.17(10)	*	+ Prescription of another sum instead of the sum specified in the Act (£250,000), as the prescribed minimum in relation to qualifying capital. See QUALIFYING CAPITAL.
s.18(6)	*	Regulations in relation to the transfer, sale or assignment of mortgages held by a society. See MORTGAGES, SALE OF.

s.22(5)(a)	★	+ Charges or description of charges which would not materially affect the security of a mortgage of a house. See PRIOR MORTGAGE.
s.23(1)(d)	★	+ Substitution of another percentage for the maximum percentage (15%) of the purchase price specified in the Act for loans towards a deposit for the purchase of property. See LOAN.
s.31(1)	★	("X") Authorisation of societies to provide conveyancing services. See CONVEYANCING.
s.32(3)(a)(i)	★	("X") Regulations governing the provision by societies of auctioneering services. See AUCTIONEERING SERVICE.
s.32(3)(a)(ii)	★	Regulations governing the provision by societies of services relating to land. See SERVICES RELATING TO LAND.
s.50(6)	★	+ Substitution of another amount for the maximum amount specified in the Act (£500), which the rules of a society may impose as a condition of a person's eligibility to be nominated as a director. See DIRECTOR, NOMINATION OF.
s.50(9)	★	+ Substitution of other amounts instead of the amounts specified in the Act in respect of the maximum number of nominating members, the maximum period of membership, the maximum value of shares, and the maximum amount of the deposit, which the rules of a society may impose as a condition of a person's eligibility to be nominated as a director. See DIRECTOR, NOMINATION OF.
s.71(2)	★	+ Substitution of another amount instead of the amount specified in the Act (not less than £500) to qualify as a borrowing member. See BORROWING MEMBER.
s.77(8)	★	+ Further provision with respect to the annual accounts of a society. See ANNUAL ACCOUNTS.

s.91(5)	*	Devolution of arbitration function from the Central Bank to an adjudicator appointed under s.92 or under a voluntary "ombudsman" type arrangement established by societies. See DISPUTES.
s.92	*	Requirement for a society to establish or join in establishing a scheme for investigation of complaints against the society. See COMPLAINTS.
s.93(2)	*	Substitution of another amount for the amount of deposit specified in the Act (0.2 per cent of total liabilities) which is required to be maintained by a society with the Central Bank.
s.93(2) (b)	*	Prescription of other shares and deposits to be reckoned as part of total liabilities. See DEPOSIT WITH CENTRAL BANK.
s.94	*	Application to societies of the provisions of the Central Bank Act 1989 for the establishment of a savings protection scheme. See SAVINGS PROTECTION SCHEME.
s.94(2) (e)	*	Change of the rights and duties of a liquidator in the winding up of a society. See LIQUIDATOR.
s.108	*	("Y") Further provision in relation to the conversion of a building society into a company. See CONVERSION.

Appendix 3

LAW REPORTS

Abbrev.	Report	Period
AC	Appeal Cases	1891 – present
All ER	All England Law Reports	1936 – present
App Cas	Appeal Cases	1875 – 1890
Ball & B	Ball and Beatty, Chancery	1807 – 1814
B & C	Barnewall & Cresswell	1822 – 1830
Burr	Burrow	1756 – 1772
Ch D	Chancery Division	1875 – 1890
Ch	Chancery (UK)	1891 – present
Cl & Fin	Clark & Finnelly	1831 – 1846
Ex	Exchequer Cases	1865 – 1875
Fed Cas	Federal Cases (USA)	1789 – 1880
HC	High Court Ireland – unreported	–
HLC	House of Lords Cases	1847 – 1866
ICLR	Irish Common Law Reports	1849 – 1866
ILRM	Irish Law Reports Monthly	1979 – present
ILTR	Irish Law Times Reports	1867 – 1980
ILT & SJ	Irish Law Times and Solicitor's Journal	1980 – present
IR	Irish Reports	1838 – present
Ir Ch R	Irish Chancery Reports	1850 – 1856
IR CL	Irish Reports Common Law	1867 – 1877
Irish Digests	Maxwell	1894 – 1918
	Ryland	1919 – 1928
	Ryland	1929 – 1938
	Harrison	1939 – 1948
	Harrison	1949 – 1958
	Ryan	1959 – 1970
	De Blaghd	1971 – 1983
IR Eq R or Ir Eq	Irish Equity Reports	1838 – 1850
Ir Jur Rep	Irish Jurist Reports (New Series)	1935 – 1965 1966 – 1985
ITLR	Irish Times Law Report	1989 – present
KB (or QB)	King's or Queen's Bench	1841 – present
Ld Ray	Raymond	1694 – 1732
LJ CCA	Law Journal Newspaper County Court Appeals	1935 – present
LJ Ch	Law Journal Chancery	1831 – 1949
LJ KB(QB)	Law Journal Reports King's (Queen's) Bench	1831 – 1949

Lloyd's	Lloyd's List Law Reports	1951 – present
LRC	Law Reform Commission Reports	1981 – present
LR Eq	Law Reports, Exchequer Cases	1865 – 1875
LR HL	Law Reports, House of Lords	1865 – 1875
LR (Ir) or Lr Ir	Law Reports (Ireland)	1878 – 1893
LT	Law Times Reports	1859 – 1947
Mac & G	Macnaghten & Gorden	1849 – 1851
NI	Northern Ireland Law Reports	1925 – present
Peake	Peake	1790 – 1794
QBD	Queen's Bench Division	1875 – 1890
QB	Queen's Bench	1841 – present
Reg Rep	Reports of Chief Registrar of Friendly Societies (UK)	–
Russ	Russell	1823 – 1829
SC	Supreme Court Ireland – unreported	–
SLR	Scottish Law Reporter	1865 – 1925
TLR	Times Law Reports	1884 – 1952
Ves	Vesey	1789 – 1817
WLR	Weekly Law Reports	1953 – present

Appendix 4

BUILDING SOCIETY STATISTICS

Table 1

Growth of Building Societies 1922 — 1988.

Year	Societies number of	Share-holders number of	Assets £m	Liabilities £m	Reserves £m
1922	23	5,026	0.6	0.6	0.06
1930	19	5,262	0.7	0.7	0.09
1940	19	6,837	1.4	1.2	0.2
1950	16	15,713	9.5	9.0	0.6
1970	20+	28,017	17.8	16.7	1.1
1980	17	496,032	1251.5	1202.2	49.3
1981	17	582,702	1527.6	1461.8	65.8
1982	17	670,467	1878.0	1797.5	80.5
1983	15	794,577	2221.9	2119.7	102.2
1984	11	893,047	2574.2	2445.2	129.0
1988	10	n/a	3805.0	3551.1	253.9*

+ The number of societies peaked at 30 in 1975 prior to the enactment of the BS Act 1976.

* Reserves at end 1988 represented 6.7% of total assets.

n/a Not available.

Sources: Report of Registrar of Building Societies 1984;
Annual Reports of Societies 1988.

Appendix 4

Table 2

Assets of Building Societies 1984
(end of year)

Description	£m	% of Total
Mortgage Assets	1,965.3+	76.3
Investment (incl accrued interest)	362.8	14.1
Cash	177.0	6.9
Office Premises	64.0	2.5
Other Assets	5.0	0.2
TOTAL ASSETS	**2,574.2**	**100.0**
Liquid Assets*	464.6	19.2*

\+ This represented 130,880 mortgages with an average balance outstanding at end 1984 of £15,016.

* Liquid Assets were represented by cash on hand and in the bank (including the Central Bank deposit) plus the lower of market value or book value of securities, plus accrued interest, less loans and overdrafts and other liabilities (including taxation). The "Liquid Ratio" is the ratio of the liquid assets expressed as a percentage of shares, deposits and other liabilities, rather than as a percentage of total assets.

Source: Derived from Report of the Registrar of Building Societies 1984.

Table 3

Liabilities of Building Societies 1984
(end of year)

Description	£m	% of Total
Shareholders	2,289.1+	88.9
Depositors & Loans	102.0*	4.0
Other Liabilities	54.1	2.1
Reserves	129.0	5.0
TOTAL LIABILITIES	**2,574.2**	**100.0**

\+ This represented 893,047 shareholders, each with an average of £2,563 invested.

* Included in this were 42,094 depositors, each with an average of £1,978 invested.

Source: Derived from Report of the Registrar of Building Societies 1984.

Appendix 4

Table 4

Building Societies operating in the State in 1927
(Total 20)

Permanent Societies	Year Incorporated
Irish Civil Service Permanent	1874
Workingman's Benefit	1875
Irish Industrial Benefit	1878
City and County Permanent	1877
Dublin Mercantile Permanent	1878
O'Connell Benefit	1879
Irish Permanent Benefit	1884
Guinness Permanent	1901
Ireland Benefit	1915
Cork Permanent	1888
Munster Permanent	1889
Terminating Societies	
Dublin Model	1889
Second Commercial Travellers Terminating	1892
Second Model	1892
Second Victoria Mutual (Terminating)	1893
Second Co-operative Benefit	1894
Cork Mutual Benefit Terminating	1893
Second Cork Mutual Benefit Terminating	1893
First Limerick 782nd Starr Bowkett	1886
First Dundalk Model	1892

Source: Report of Registrar of Friendly Societies 1927

Appendix 4

Table 5

Building Societies operating in the State in 1977
(Total 25)

		Year Incorporated
Irish Permanent Building Society	(a)	1884
Educational		1935
First National	(b)	1875
Irish Civil Service	(c)	1874
Irish Nationwide	(d)	1878
Norwich Irish		1974
Midland & Western		1956
Irish Mutual	(e)	1970
Postal Service Permanent	(f)	1966
O'Connell Benefit	(g)	1879
Guinness Permanent	(h)	1901
Irish Savings	(i)	1973
Metropolitan		1939
Garda	(j)	1974
Munster & Leinster	(k)	
Ireland Benefit	(h)	1915
Four Provinces	(l)	
Dublin Model	(m)	1889
Ballygall	(n)	
City and Provincial	(l)	
Independent	(n)	
West of Ireland	(n)	
National Provincial	(n)	
Dublin Savings	(n)	
Progressive	(n)	

Irish Life Building Society was registered in 1979.

Notes:

(a) Incorporated as The Irish Temperance Permanent Benefit Building Society in 1884; changed its name to the Irish Permanent Benefit Building Society in 1888 and to the Irish Permanent Building Society in 1940.

(b) Established as the Workingman's Benefit Building Society in 1861, incorporated in 1875, and changed its name to First National Building Society in 1960.

(c) Established as the Irish Civil Service Permanent Building Society in 1864 and incorporated in 1874; the "Permanent" was officially dropped from its name in 1969, and its name changed to the ICS Building Society in 1986.

(d) Established in 1873 and incorporated in 1878 as the Irish Industrial Benefit Building Society; changed its name to Irish Industrial Building Society in 1969 and to Irish Nationwide Building Society in 1975.

(e) Changed name from Allied Irish Building Society in 1976.
(f) Transferred its engagements to First National Building Society in 1985.
(g) Transferred its engagements to Irish Civil Service Building Society in 1983.
(h) Transferred its engagements to First National Building Society in 1984.
(i) Application for winding up granted by court in 1984.
(j) Transferred its engagements to Irish Nationwide Building Society in 1983.
(k) Transferred its engagements to Irish Permanent Building Society in 1978.
(l) Registration cancelled in 1978.
(m) Registration cancelled in 1984.
(n) Registration cancelled in 1977.

Sources: Annual Reports of Registrar of Building Societies 1977 — 1984; Information from individual societies.

Table 6

Building Societies operating in the State in 1989
(Total 10)

	Year of Incorporation	At 31 December 1988 Assets £m	Reserves £m
Irish Permanent	1884	1374.9	90.2
First National	1875	811.0	46.3
Educational	1935	766.3	55.4
Irish Nationwide	1878	306.7	42.1
ICS	1874	301.4	10.7
Irish Life	1979	86.4	2.7
Irish Mutual	1970	73.9	2.3
Norwich Irish	1974	53.0	2.8
Midland & Western	1956	24.4	1.2
Metropolitan	1939	6.8	0.2
	TOTAL	**3805.0**	**253.9**

(figures are rounded to nearest single decimal)

Source: 1988 Annual Reports of individual Societies.

Appendix 5

TYPICAL BUILDING SOCIETY MORTGAGE

(in use in May 1989, prior to enactment of the BS Act 1989)

Note: — words in italics have an entry in The Guide.
— words in capital letters in square brackets refer to an entry in The Guide which could be usefully consulted eg [Note: See LEASEHOLD, MORTGAGE OF].
— in some building society standard mortgage instruments there are clauses which do not reflect the changes introduced by the BS Act 1986 (and continued by the BS Act 1989) eg in relation to the abolition of *redemption* fees and the statutory access to valuation reports. Some building societies have indicated that their standard forms of mortgage are currently being updated and revised.

LAND REGISTRY

COUNTY .... FOLIO.....................................

THIS INDENTURE made the ....day of .... One Thousand Nine Hundred and .... BETWEEN ....(hereinafter called "the *Borrower*") of the one part and .... Building Society whose *Chief Office* is at ....in the City of .... , a *building society* duly *incorporated* under the Building Societies Act 1976 (hereinafter called "the Society") of the other part.
[Note: In future, mortgages will refer to the Building Societies Act 1989].

ADVANCE

WITNESSETH in *consideration* of the sum of .... Pounds (hereinafter called "the *Loan*") this day advanced by the Society to the *Borrower* who is a *member* of the Society and is entitled as such to receive an advance out of the funds of the Society (the receipt whereof the *Borrower* hereby acknowledges) as follows:-

DEFINITIONS

1. Herein where the context so admits:-

(a) "The *Borrower*" includes the heirs *executors* and *administrators* of the *Borrower* and the person or persons deriving *title* under him to the *hereditaments* described in the Schedule hereto. [Note: "The Borrower" is described as "The *Mortgagor*" in some *mortgage* instruments].

(b) "The Society" includes its assigns and its successors.

(c) "The *Rules*" means the *Rules* of the Society in force from time to time including such as may be adopted or amended after the date of this *mortgage*.

(d) "The Mortgaged Property" means the *freehold* and *leasehold land* described in the Schedule hereto with any buildings now erected or in the course of erection or hereafter to be erected thereon and every part thereof.

(e) "The appropriate rate" means .... per centum per annum or such increased or reduced rate of *interest* as may from time to time be applicable under the terms hereof.

(f) "Month" means a calendar month.

(g) "Year" means year from the First day of January to the Thirty-first day of December.

(h) "Person" includes a corporation the singular includes the plural and vice versa and the masculine includes the feminine, common and neuter genders.

[Note: In an *Endowment* type *mortgage* there is sometimes inserted:
(i) "The Policy" means the Policy of Assurance issued by the
.... as follows:-

POLICY NO	DATE SUM	ASSURED	LIFE ASSURED
....	....	....	.............................]

OBLIGATIONS

2. Obligations undertaken in these presents by more than a single person are *joint and several* obligations.

COVENANT FOR PAYMENT

3. The *Borrower* hereby covenants with the Society:-

(a) To pay to the Society monthly instalments of £................................. each the first instalment to be paid on the .... day of the month next ensuing the day of these presents and subsequent instalments on the .... day in every succeeding month thereafter until the whole of the *Loan* and all other principal sums which shall be advanced to the *Borrower* on the security hereof with *interest* at the appropriate rate and all other moneys hereby covenanted to be paid by the *Borrower* shall have been fully paid and satisfied and to pay any *premium* or premiums on any *Mortgage Protection* or other *life policy* effected by the *Borrower* and required by the Society.

[Note: In an *Endowment* type policy, the above provision will typically be:

(a) To re-pay the *Loan* to the Society on the 31st day of December next.

So long as any principal money or moneys remain owing to the Society to pay *interest* thereon at the appropriate rate by monthly instalments of £..
each the first instalment to be paid on the ....
day of the month next ensuing the day of these presents and subsequent instalments on the ....
day in every succeeding month for so long as the moneys secured by these presents shall remain due and owing to the Society.]

PROVIDED ALWAYS:-

(i) That (without prejudice to the provisions of Clause 10 hereof) the *Borrower* may at any time *redeem* this *mortgage* on the conditions set out in the *Rules* save that for the purpose of this mortgage the expression "before the expiration of the term specified in the mortgage" shall mean before the payment of all instalments hereby covenanted to be paid by the *Borrower* in accordance with the foregoing *covenant* in that behalf. [Note: See REDEMPTION; REDEMPTION FEE].

(ii) That where part only of an intended advance or further advance has been made the *Borrower* shall not be charged *interest* exceeding that attributable to the sum or sums actually advanced but in the meantime (until all liability of the *Borrower* hereunder is discharged) the monthly instalments payable by the *Borrower* shall be of the same amount as if the whole intended advance or further advance had been made.

(b) Upon the expiration of one month's *notice* in writing to that effect given by the Society to the *Borrower*:-

(i) to pay to the Society all principal money then outstanding hereunder together with *interest* at the appropriate rate from the date hereof (so far as outstanding) and all fines subscriptions and other moneys due from the *Borrower* to the Society under this *mortgage* or the *Rules* or otherwise and in default.

(ii) to pay to the Society *interest* at the appropriate rate upon the total of the sums hereinbefore in this paragraph covenanted to be paid from the date of the expiration of the said *notice* until the whole of such sums shall have been paid and satisfied.

(c) To pay to the Society such further sums as by the *Rules* or the provision of this *mortgage* shall from time to time become due from the *Borrower* to the Society.

(d) That in keeping the account of the *Borrower* with the Society the Society shall be entitled in any year to charge *interest* at the appropriate rate on the amount of the total indebtedness of the *Borrower* to the Society on the first day of January in the same year and also *interest* at the appropriate rate on the full amount of any money advanced to or becoming owing by the *Borrower* during the year as from the date on which it was advanced or became owing AND the *Borrower* will pay *interest* accordingly AND no part of any payment made by the *Borrower* shall be treated as a repayment of principal money until all *interest* due or accrued has been paid. [Note: See COMPOUND INTEREST].

(e) That if upon realisation of the Mortgaged Property by the Society the net proceeds shall prove insufficient to pay the sum or sums in or towards which they are applicable hereunder then the deficiency shall forthwith become due and payable by the *Borrower* to the Society with *interest* thereon at the appropriate rate (as well before as after any judgment) until payment.

[Note: In an *Endowment* type mortgage there will typically be added —

(f) To pay all premiums on the Policy immediately they fall due.

(g) To pay to the Society on demand all premiums on the Policy paid by the Society pursuant to the power of the Society in that behalf hereinafter contained.

(h) To pay to the Society on demand all sums paid by the Society for the *insurance* of the buildings on the Mortgaged Property pursuant to the power of the Society in that behalf hereinafter contained.]

VARIATION OF INTEREST RATE

4. The Society may from time to time by *notice* given to the *Borrower* in writing increase or reduce the appropriate rate and in regard thereto the following provisions shall apply and have effect:-

(a) The appropriate rate shall not be increased above the rate at which at the time when such *notice* of increase is given *interest* is charged on new advances which the *Board of Directors* of the Society considers to be advances of the same type for *mortgage* purposes as the advance hereby secured and in this respect the decision of the Board of Directors shall be final and conclusively binding on the *Borrower*.

(b) Any increase or reduction in the appropriate rate shall take effect from such date as the *notice* of increase or reduction shall specify but not being earlier in the case of an increase than seven days after the date on which such notice is served.

(c) By any *notice* of increase or reduction the Society may fix an increased or reduced rate of monthly instalments to become payable on account of the whole or any part of the increase or reduction. [Note: See INTEREST]

[Note: Some mortgage instruments specify that notice may be given to the *Borrower* by publication of an advertisement in a National daily newspaper].

CONVEYANCE, SUB-DEMISE, CHARGE

5. AND THIS INDENTURE FURTHER WITNESSETH as follows:-

(a) For the *consideration* aforesaid the *Borrower* as *beneficial owner* doth hereby grant convey assign transfer and demise UNTO the Society ALL THAT AND THOSE the Mortgaged Property TO HOLD the same as to so much thereof as is of *freehold* tenure UNTO the Society and its assigns and as to so much thereof as is of *leasehold* tenure UNTO the Society for the residue or residues of the term or respective terms of years for which the *Borrower* now holds the same as stated in the Schedule hereto (less the last 10 days of each such term) SUBJECT to the proviso for *redemption* hereafter contained. [Note: See HABENDUM; LEASEHOLD, MORTGAGE OF]

(b) The *Borrower* as *beneficial owner* and as registered owner or the person entitled to become registered as owner hereby *charges* so much of the mortgaged property the ownership whereof is registered in the Land Registry or is required to be so registered pursuant to the Statutes in that behalf with the payment to the Society of all moneys payable by the *Borrower* to the Society by virtue of these presents and the *Rules*. [Note: See LAND REGISTRATION]

[Note: In an *Endowment* type mortgage, there will typically be added:

"For the *consideration* aforesaid the *Borrower* doth hereby assign unto the Society ALL THAT the Policy and all moneys to become payable thereunder TO HOLD the same unto the Society SUBJECT to the proviso that when the said amount of £.. and all other sums due to the Society under the *mortgage* shall be discharged the Society will re-assign the said Policy to the *Borrower* at the expense of the *Borrower*].

PROVIDED ALWAYS, that if the *Borrower* shall duly and punctually pay to the Society according to the *Rules* and the *covenants* on his part herein contained the *Loan* and all other sums of money fines and fees payable by him to the Society according to provisions of these presents and the *Rules* the Society shall vacate this security by a receipt or *reconveyance* according to the provisions of the Statute in that behalf and the *Rules*. [Note: See REDEMPTION].

(c) The *Borrower* so far as he has power to do so as *beneficial owner* doth hereby assign UNTO the Society (but subject to *redemption*) the benefit of:-

(i) any *covenant* agreement or undertaking for road-making or for the payment of road charges or other private street improvement or drainage expenses in respect of the Mortgaged Property or any *indemnity* against payment of such charges or expenses.

(ii) any other *covenant* agreement undertaking *charge* right remedy or *indemnity* in relation to the Mortgaged Property or any part thereof or any *rent* payable thereout or charge thereon.

(iii) all rights of the *Borrower* to be paid or receive compensation under any Statute by reason of any *compulsory acquisition* requisitioning or other exercise of compulsory powers in relation to the Mortgaged Property or any refusal withdrawal or modification of *planning permission* or approval relative thereto or any control or limitation imposed upon or affecting the use of the Mortgaged Property or any part thereof and so that the production of these presents to the Authority or person liable to pay such compensation shall be a sufficient authority to it or him to pay all such moneys to the Society.

(d) Save in any case to which paragraph (c) of this Clause applies the *Borrower* appoints the Society irrevocably (but subject to *redemption*) to be the *attorney* of the *Borrower* in his name and on his behalf:-

(i) To claim assess agree recover and receive any such compensation.

(ii) To exercise any such right or to give any such *notice* or counter-notice concerning the Mortgaged Property as by or under any Statute the *Borrower* may be entitled to exercise or give against or to any local or other competent or appropriate authority. [Note: See POWER OF ATTORNEY]

DECLARATION OF TRUST OF THE NOMINAL REVERSION

6. The *Borrower* hereby declares that he the *Borrower* shall henceforth stand possessed of the *reversion* or respective reversions hereby reserved of the term or several terms of years for which the Mortgaged Property or any part or parts thereof is or are held by the *Borrower* in *trust* for the Society subject to such *equity of redemption* (if any) as may for the time being be subsisting therein by virtue of these presents and to dispose thereof as it shall direct AND hereby authorises the Society to appoint a new *trustee* or new trustees of the said reversion or respective reversions and in particular at any time to appoint such new trustee or new trustees in the place of the *Borrower* or any trustee or trustees appointed under this power as if he or they were incapable of acting in the *trusts* thereof hereby declared AND the *Borrower* hereby irrevocably appoints the *Secretary* for the time being of the Society the *attorney* of him the *Borrower* in his name and on his behalf at any time to assign the same *reversion* or respective reversions to the Society or its assigns as the Society shall think fit and subject to such *equity of redemption* (if any) as may for the timebeing be subsisting as aforesaid and to execute and do all instruments and acts necessary or proper for that purpose. [Note: See LEASEHOLD, MORTGAGE OF; POWER OF ATTORNEY]

POWERS OF THE SOCIETY

7. it is hereby agreed and declared as follows:-

Entry

(a) At any time during the continuance of this security the Society may without any further consent from or *notice* to the *Borrower* or any other person:-

(i) enter into possession of the Mortgaged Property or any part thereof.

(ii) put and keep every building comprised in this security in good and tenantable repair and condition without becoming liable as a *mortgagee in possession*. [Note: See however MORTGAGEE, RIGHTS OF]

[Note: Where a society advances money in respect of a Public House, it is usual to have a provision included which entitles the Society to enter into possession of the Mortgaged Property in the event that the holder of the Publican's Licence is convicted of an offence under the Intoxicating Liquor Acts and the conviction is endorsed in the licence].

Sale or Receiver

(b) The Society may at any time or times after the date when the first monthly instalment payable has become due (on which date the moneys hereby secured shall be deemed to become due within the meaning of and for all purposes of the Conveyancing Acts, 1881 to 1911 and any enactment amending extending or replacing the same) without further consent from or *notice* to the *Borrower* or any other person exercise the powers of sale and of appointing a *receiver* conferred on mortgagees by the Conveyancing Acts, 1881 to 1911 and the Registration of Title Act, 1964 and the provisions of the said Acts except so far as the same are hereby varied or extended and except the provisions contained in Section 20 of the Conveyancing Act, 1881 restricting the exercise of the powers of sale and all the provisions of the said Acts with reference to sales effected thereunder shall respectively apply to the power of sale hereby conferred and to any sale thereunder and to any appointment of a *receiver* as if such powers were respectively the statutory powers in that behalf. [Note: See MORTGAGEE, RIGHTS OF; RECEIVER OF MORTGAGED PROPERTY]

(c) PROVIDED NEVERTHELESS that the Society shall not exercise its powers of entry into possession or its powers of sale and of appointing a *receiver* or any of the said powers unless and until:-

Default

(i) Default shall have been made by the *Borrower* for one month in the payment of some instalment or other moneys payable by the *Borrower* under this *mortgage* or under the *Rules*, or

(ii) default shall have been made by the *Borrower* in making payment pursuant to sub-paragraph (i) of paragraph (b) of Clause 3 hereof, or

Breach of Covenant

(iii) there shall have been a breach by the *Borrower* of some *covenant* on his part herein contained or of some provision in the *Rules* or of some *covenant* by Statute or otherwise herein implied and on the part of the *Borrower* to be performed or observed (other than a *covenant* for payment of money), or

Bankruptcy

(iv) the *Borrower* (being an individual) shall have become *bankrupt* or have entered into a composition or arrangement with his creditors or (being a company) shall have gone into liquidation whether compulsory or voluntary, or

Security Depreciated

(v) any building on the Mortgaged Property shall be pulled down, removed or injured so as materially to depreciate the value of this security, or

Dealing with the Equity

(vi) the *Borrower* shall have charged, conveyed, assigned, assured let or parted with the possession of the Mortgaged Property or any part thereof without the written consent of the Society.

AND without prejudice to paragraph (b) of this Clause and the provisions of Sections 21 and 22 of the Conveyancing Act, 1881 and Section 5 of the Conveyancing Act, 1911 so far as the same are for the protection and safety of purchasers it is hereby agreed that upon any sale purporting to be made in pursuance of the aforesaid power of sale the purchaser or purchasers shall not be bound to see or enquire whether any of the cases mentioned in paragraph (c) of this Clause has happened or whether any default has been made by the *Borrower* in the payment of any of the moneys hereby secured or whether any money remains owing on this security or as to the necessity or expediency of the conditions subject to which any sale is made or otherwise as to the regularity of any such sale or be affected by express *notice* or any irregularity whatsoever therein and notwithstanding any such irregularity every such sale shall so far as regards the safety and protection of the purchaser or purchasers be deemed to be within the aforesaid power in that behalf and be valid and effectual accordingly and the remedy of the *Borrower* in respect of any breach of the said power of sale or any irregularity in any such sale shall be in damages against the Society only.

Principal Money to become Due

(d) And in case at any time the right of the Society to enter into possession shall become enforceable or the powers of the Society to sell and to appoint a *receiver* shall become exercisable or the Mortgaged Property or any part thereof shall be *compulsorily purchased* or acquired or requisitioned then and in any such case (independently of and without prejudice to the provisions of paragraph (b) of Clause 3 of this *mortgage*) the whole of the principal money then remaining unpaid hereunder shall (if not already due) forthwith become due and payable from or by the *Borrower* to the Society and together with any instalments and other moneys then in arrear or owing shall be recoverable by the Society with *interest* (as well after as before any judgment) at the appropriate rate by action against the *Borrower* or by enforcement of any of the rights powers and remedies of the Society whether under these presents by Statute or otherwise in that behalf. [Note: See MORTGAGEE, RIGHTS OF]

Receiver

(e) If a *receiver* is appointed pursuant to the power in that behalf hereinbefore contained he shall be entitled to such commission or remuneration not exceeding Ten Pounds per cent of the gross receipts as the *Board of Directors* of the Society shall consider reasonable.

Withdrawal of Possession or Receivership

(f) The Society may at any time after entering into possession or appointment of a *receiver* of the Mortgaged Property or any part thereof relinquish such possession or remove such receiver on giving *notice* to the *Borrower*.

FURTHER COVENANTS

8. The *Borrower* hereby *covenants* with the Society as follows:-

Observe Rules

(a) To observe and be bound by the *Rules* and that the *Rules* (so far as applicable) shall be incorporated in this *mortgage* save that in case of any difference or discrepancy between the provisions of the *Rules* and the provisions of this mortgage the provisions of this mortgage shall prevail.

Observe Restrictive Covenants and Covenants in Lease (if any) and Pay Outgoings

(b) To observe and perform the restrictive *covenants* (if any) affecting the Mortgaged Property and the covenants and provisions binding upon the tenant under the *Lease* or Leases (if any) under which the Mortgaged Property or any part thereof is held and duly and punctually to pay all *rates* taxes rents *rentcharges* and outgoings and impositions payable in respect of the Mortgaged Property and to keep the Society indemnified against the same.

Complete Unfinished Buildings

(c) To the satisfaction of the surveyor of the Society:-

(i) Without delay and in a proper and workmanlike manner to complete and finish any buildings now in the course of erection on the Mortgaged Property and that if the *Borrower* makes default in so doing it shall be lawful for the Society and their agents, workmen, surveyors with all necessary machinery and equipment to enter upon the Mortgaged Property and so complete the said buildings.

(ii) To execute within three months from the date hereof the repairs (if any) already prescribed by the Society to be carried out on the Mortgaged Property.

Repairs

(d) To keep the Mortgaged Property in good and tenantable repair to the satisfaction of the Society and to permit the Society's agents with or without workmen and others in the daytime to enter on the Mortgaged Property and examine the conditions thereof and forthwith to repair and make good all defects and wants of repair of which *notice* in writing shall be given to the *Borrower* by the Society and in case of default to permit the Society's agents and others as aforesaid to enter on the Mortgaged Property and effect such repairs as the Society may consider necessary.

Insurance

(e) That the Society may without being obliged to do so at the expense of the *Borrower* insure and keep insured any buildings on the Mortgaged Property against loss or damage by fire and against such other risks as the Society may from time to time think expedient and in any case for such amount and in such manner as the Society may from time to time think fit. [Note: See INSURANCE]

(f) That the *Borrower* shall not except at the request and with the consent in writing of the Society effect or keep on foot any *insurance* in respect of the Mortgaged Property or any part thereof where the Society effects and keeps on foot such insurance.

(g) That the Society shall have full power to settle and adjust with the insurers all questions with respect to the amount of the moneys payable under the policy and with respect to the liability of the insurers.

(h) That any moneys received on any *insurance* of the premises whether effected by the Society or the *Borrower* (without prejudice to any obligation to the contrary imposed by law or special contract) shall be applied at the option of the Society either in or towards making good the loss or damages in respect of which the moneys are received or in or towards the discharge of the moneys hereby secured and the *Borrower* shall hold any moneys received by him upon *trust* for the Society.

[Note: Where a society advances money in respect of a Public House, it is usual to have a *covenant* whereby the *Borrower* undertakes to keep the Publican's Licence insured against loss or forfeiture in the joint names of the *Borrower* and the Society in a specified sum].

Expenses

(i) All that money paid by the Society in completing any unfinished buildings on the Mortgaged Property or in repairing or insuring the Mortgaged Property or in making any payment for outgoings in relation to the Mortgaged Property or for the protection or improvement of this security for the costs or expenses incurred by the Society incidental thereto (which costs and expenses the Society shall be entitled to recover on the basis of *indemnity*) shall be repaid within fourteen days after the date on which the same was paid by the Society with *interest* at the appropriate rate, from the date of payment and until repayment the said money with *interest* as aforesaid shall be a *charge* on the Mortgaged Property.

Not to Prejudice Insurance

(j) That nothing shall be done on the Mortgaged Property which may prejudicially affect any *insurance* thereof or which may increase the *premium* payable for any such insurance.

Alteration or Change of User

(k) Not without the written consent of the Society to make any structural alteration to the Mortgaged Property or carry out any operation or institute or continue any use of the Mortgaged Property for which permission is required under any enactment relating to planning and development. [Note: See PLANNING PERMISSION]

Bye Laws etc

(l) To comply with all bye laws and with all enactments and regulations relating to planning and development which may from time to time affect the Mortgaged Property and within seven days of the receipt by the *Borrower* of any notice order or proposal made given or issued by any competent authority to give full particulars thereof to the Society and also without delay to take all reasonable or necessary steps to comply with such notice or order. In the case of any permission consent or licence or other document affecting this security such document shall be handed over to the Society to be kept with the Deeds and documents of *title* affecting the Mortgaged Property. [Note: See BUILDING BYE-LAWS]

The Rules

(m) The Society shall have all powers and rights in respect of the Mortgaged Property that are from time to time mentioned in that behalf in the *Rules*.

Improvements Loans and Grants

(n) Not without the consent in writing of the Society to apply for any grants or loans under the Housing Acts 1966 - 1979 or any amendment or re-enactment thereof or any enactment replacing the same or any Act referred to in sub-section 5 of Section 121 of the Housing Act 1966. [Note: See HOUSING]

[Note: Some mortgage instruments may require the *Borrower* to apply for all grants supplementary to any Housing Grant already notified to the Society and if and when same are received to repay same to the Society in reduction of the amount of the *Loan*].

LETTING BY THE BORROWER

9. The powers of leasing and agreeing to *lease* and of accepting *surrenders* of leases conferred on a *mortgagor* in possession by the Conveyancing Acts 1881 to 1911 shall not apply to this *mortgage* and the *Borrower* will not grant or agree to grant any lease or tenancy of the Mortgaged Property or any part thereof without the consent in writing of the Society. [Note: See MORTGAGOR, RIGHTS OF]

[Note: A mortgage may provide that where the consent of the Society is given to leasing by the *Borrower*, a higher rate of *interest* on the outstanding advance becomes payable by the *Borrower*].

CONSOLIDATION

10. (a) Section 17 of the Conveyancing Act, 1881 shall not apply to this *mortgage*.

(b) This *mortgage* shall be a security not only for all moneys hereby covenanted to be paid but also for all moneys which may now be or may hereafter from time to time become owing by the *Borrower* to the Society on any account whatever and no property held by the Society as security for moneys advanced or to be advanced to the *Borrower* by the Society shall (unless the Society otherwise decides) be released or discharged until the whole of the moneys owing by the *Borrower* to the Society shall have been paid to the Society. [Note: See CONSOLIDATION]

TRANSFER

11. (a) The Society may at any time after its power of sale has become exercisable transfer the benefit of this *mortgage* to any person. [Note: See MORTGAGES, SALE OF]

(b) On any such transfer the whole of the moneys then owing to the Society in respect of this *mortgage* shall become principal money immediately payable to the transferee and shall thenceforth bear *interest* at the appropriate rate prevailing at the time of the transfer and payable from the date of the transfer by successive six monthly payments the first of such payments to be made at the end of six months from the date of such transfer.

(c) The transferee and the persons deriving *title* under him shall have all the powers conferred on mortgagees by the Conveyancing Acts 1881 to 1911 in the like manner as if the transfer had been an original *mortgage* by deed to the transferee for the principal moneys which under the provisions hereof are on such transfer to be payable to the transferee and for the *interest* to become due thereon.

(d) After the execution of any transfer references in this *mortgage* to the *Rules* shall cease to have effect and references to the appropriate rate shall be read as references to the appropriate rate prevailing at the time of the transfer.

(e) Every statement of fact made in good faith and contained in such transfer shall as against the *Borrower* be conclusive and binding.

LANDLORD AND TENANT ACTS 1967 TO 1980

12. The *Borrower* hereby irrevocably appoints the *Secretary* for the time being of the Society his *attorney* and in his name and on his behalf to do all or any of the following acts and things that is to say:-

(a) To serve any notice of intention to claim relief under the Landlord and Tenant (Amendment) Act 1980.

(b) To commence institute and prosecute such proceedings and applications in the appropriate Court as may be necessary for the purpose of obtaining a New Tenancy under Part II of the Landlord and Tenant (Amendment) Act 1980 in the Mortgaged Property.

(c) To commence institute and prosecute such proceedings and applications in the appropriate Court as may be necessary for the purpose of obtaining a *Reversionary Lease* of the Mortgaged Property under Part III of the Landlord and Tenant (Amendment) Act 1980.

(d) To discontinue or compromise any such proceedings and applications and to appeal against any judgments in any Court in any such proceedings or applications.

AND IT IS HEREBY AGREED AND DECLARED that all moneys expenses costs and expenses incurred by the Society in any such proceedings or applications shall be a *charge* on the Mortgaged Property with *interest* thereon at the appropriate rate from the date of payment and the *Borrower* hereby *covenants* with the Society to pay the said moneys expenses costs and expenses with *interest* thereon at the appropriate rate.

(e) And the *Borrower* hereby *covenants* with the Society that should the *Borrower* at any time enlarge his *interest* in the Mortgaged Property into a *fee simple* he shall forthwith lodge the documents of *title* to the fee simple with the Society. [Note: See GROUND RENT]

FURNITURE

13. (a) If at the time of entering into possession or receipt of the rents and profits of the Mortgaged Property by the Society or by any *receiver* appointed by the Society the Mortgaged Property or any part thereof shall be let furnished under a tenancy which is or becomes binding on the Society then and in any and every such case the Society or such receiver shall be entitled to receive and apply the whole of the *rent* reserved by such tenancy as if it were rent of the Mortgaged Property and neither the Society nor any such receiver shall be required or bound to make any apportionment of such rent in respect of any furniture or *chattels* of the *Borrower* comprised in such tenancy. And the *Borrower* hereby irrevocably appoints each of them *Secretary* for the time being of the Society and any such receiver the *attorney* of him the *Borrower* to demand and recover from all tenants of him the *Borrower* under any such letting as aforesaid all rents and sums of money payable under such tenancy from time to time and give receipts therefor and to sign and give notices to any such tenant to quit or to abate a nuisance or to remedy a breach of any *covenants* agreements or conditions of such tenancy and to commence institute and prosecute all such actions and proceedings in the appropriate Court as may be necessary for recovering possession of the Mortgaged Property or such part or parts thereof as may be comprised in any such tenancy together with such furniture and *chattels* as aforesaid to discontinue or compromise any such action or proceedings and to appeal against any judgment or decision of any Court in any such action or proceedings.

(b) If upon entry by the Society into possession of the Mortgaged Property or any part thereof the Mortgaged Property shall contain any furniture or *chattels* of the *Borrower* which the *Borrower* shall refuse or fail to remove within twenty eight days of his being required by *notice* in writing by the Society so to do then and in every such case the Society shall thereupon become and be the *agent* of the *Borrower* with full authority at his expense to remove store preserve sell and otherwise dispose of such furniture and *chattels* as last aforesaid in such manner in all respects as the Society shall think fit PROVIDED that the Society shall not sell such furniture or chattels hereunder until after the expiration of two months from the date upon which the *Borrower* was required by the Society to remove them from the Mortgaged Property as aforesaid.

(c) The provisions of paragraphs (a) and (b) of this Clause shall not be construed or operate to confer on the Society any right in *equity* to any furniture or *chattels* of the *Borrower* or any *charge* or security thereon or otherwise so as to constitute this *mortgage* a bill of sale.

CONCESSIONS

14. The Society may from time to time in writing at its absolute discretion authorise the *Borrower* to pay or repay any money by other instalments than those hereinbefore provided for either by increased or reduced instalments or may remit any instalment or give further time for the payment of any moneys hereby secured or generally make such other arrangements as to the mode and time of payment of any money (whether in the nature of principal *interest* or otherwise) as it may think fit PROVIDED that no such arrangement shall affect the power of sale or other powers hereby or by Statute conferred on the Society or render the Society liable in damages or otherwise for the exercise of any such power in any case where if the arrangement had not been made no such liability would have arisen.

NOTICE

15. Any *notice* required or authorized by these presents to be served by the Society on the *Borrower* shall be sufficiently served if sent by ordinary pre-paid post in a letter addressed to the *Borrower* at the Mortgaged Property and such notice shall be deemed to have been served on the *Borrower* at the time at which the letter would in the ordinary course of post be delivered at the Mortgaged Property.

[Note: Some mortgage instruments specify that the address to which notice may be served include the address of the *Borrower* registered in the books of the Society, or where the *Borrower* is a limited liability company, the registered office for the time being of such company].

REGISTERED LAND AND LAND THE REGISTRATION WHEREOF IS COMPULSORY

16. The *Borrower* hereby assents to the registration of the *charge* hereby created as a *burden* on the property/*leasehold* interest described in the Folio of the register of freeholders/leaseholders County .... and to the registration of the Society as the owner of this charge. [Note: See LAND REGISTRATION]

LAND ACT 1965 CERTIFICATE

17. The Society hereby certifies that an appropriate consent has been given under Section 45 of the Land Act, 1965, and that the conditions attached to such consent have been complied with. [Note: See VESTING]

IN WITNESS WHEREOF the *Borrower* has hereunto set his hand and *seal* and the Society has caused its common seal to be hereunto affixed the day and the year first above written. [Note: See TESTIMONIUM].

SCHEDULE

DESCRIPTION OF PROPERTY

HELD IN FEE SIMPLE

PARTICULARS OF FEE FARM GRANT

PARTICULARS OF LEASE

DATE

PARTIES

TERM

RENT

SIGNED, SEALED AND DELIVERED
by the *Borrower* in the presence of:

PRESENT when the Common *Seal* of the
.... Building Society was affixed hereto:

....

ENDORSEMENT UNDER Family Home Protection Act, 1976

I, ...HEREBY CONFIRM, as follows:

1. I am the lawful spouse of the within-named *Borrower*.

2. I am aware that by virtue of Section 3 of the Family Home Protection Act 1976, the premises comprised in the within *mortgage* cannot be mortgaged or charged without my consent in writing.

3. I hereby consent to the within *mortgage*.

[Note: See FAMILY HOME]

SIGNED by the said

immediately prior to the execution by *Borrower* of the within *mortgage* in the presence of:

GUARANTEE

THIS INDENTURE made the ....day of .... One Thousand nine hundred and ....BETWEEN ....
....
.... of ....
....
(hereinafter called the "Guarantor") of the one part AND the within-named ....
BUILDING SOCIETY (hereinafter called "the Society") of the other part WITNESSETH in *consideration* of the advance made by the Society

to the within named .... (hereinafter called "the *Borrower*") as follows:-

1. The Guarantor hereby *covenants* with the Society that the *Borrower* will duly and punctually observe and perform all the *covenants* and obligations of the *Borrower* contained in the within written Indenture and that if and so far and so often as the *Borrower* shall fail or omit so to do the Guarantor will observe and perform such covenants and obligations PROVIDED nevertheless that the Guarantor shall not be liable to the Society in respect of any further advance or *interest* thereon unless such further advance be made with the consent or at the request of the Guarantor.

2. Without prejudice to any right of the Guarantor against the *Borrower* as principal debtor the Guarantor shall under the *covenant* by the Guarantor hereinbefore contained be deemed to be a principal debtor to the Society and not merely a surety. Accordingly the Guarantor shall not be discharged nor shall his liability be affected by any giving of time for payment of any money or by any agreement not to call in moneys secured by the said Indenture before a specified time or by any other arrangement between the Society and the *Borrower* or by any omission on the part of the Society to enforce any *covenant* or obligation enforceable against the *Borrower* or by any other act thing or omission or means whereby the liability of the Guarantor would not have been discharged or affected if the Guarantor had been a principal debtor.

3. Save as in Clause 1 provided the Guarantor shall be liable for the whole indebtedness of the *Borrower* to the Society and until such indebtedness has been fully discharged the Guarantor shall not be entitled to participate in any security held or money received by the Society in respect of any such security or money.

4. Obligations undertaken in these presents by more than a single person are *joint and several* obligations.

IN WITNESS whereof the Guarantor has hereunto set his hand and the Society has caused its common *seal* to be hereunto affixed the day and year first herein written. [Note: See TESTIMONIUM].

SIGNED, SEALED AND DELIVERED by
the Guarantor in the presence of:

[Note: See GUARANTEE; STATUTE OF FRAUDS (IRELAND)].

RECEIPT

The .... BUILDING SOCIETY hereby acknowledges to have received all moneys intended to be secured by the within written Deed. In witness whereof the *seal* of the Society is hereto affixed this .... day of .... One Thousand Nine Hundred and .... by Order of the *Board of Directors* in the presence of

[Note: See REDEMPTION]

Present Director ....

Secretary ....

ADDITIONAL PROVISIONS IN SOME MORTGAGES

WARRANTIES

Some mortgage instruments may contain provisions which seek to exclude any liability for a surveyor's report or for the *title* of the Mortgaged Property eg

"The valuer has been retained by and on behalf of the Society for the purposes of preparing a Valuation of the Mortgaged Property for and on behalf of the Society so as to enable the Society to fulfil its obligations under the Building Societies Act and the *Rules*, and for no other purpose, and the Report of the Valuer shall be the sole property of the Society, and neither the Society nor the Valuer shall be deemed to be or be taken to be making any warranty or representation as to the value of the Mortgaged Property, or any part thereof, or as to the structural soundness or condition or state of repair or otherwise of the Mortgaged Property in accepting the Mortgaged Property as security for the loan or in making any advance to the *Borrower* of the Security of the Mortgaged Property. The Society may, in its sole discretion, furnish a copy of the Report to the *Borrower*, but neither the Society nor the Valuer shall be deemed to be or be taken to be making any warranty or representation in relation to the Mortgaged Property in furnishing such Report, or by reason of any statement contained therein". [Note: However, see VALUATION REPORT for the statutory requirement that a society furnish the valuation report to the *Borrower*].

"The Society shall not be deemed to be making any warranty or representations as to the *title* to the Mortgaged Property in accepting the Mortgaged Property and the *title* of the *Borrower* thereto as security for the *Loan*".

CERTIFICATION

A mortgage may also include a requirement that the *Borrower* CERTIFY that

"(a) he is over the age of 18 years

(b) he has not entered into any agreement to marry which has been terminated within a period of three years prior to the execution of the *mortgage*". [Note: See MATRIMONIAL PROPERTY]

ENDOWMENT MORTGAGE

In some societies, an *Endowment* Mortgage is executed as a variation to the standard annuity repayment mortgage; the Supplemental Deed usually includes the following provisions:

1. A requirement that the *Borrower* repay the moneys advanced on the 31st December next or at any time thereafter on demand, together with *interest* thereon at the appropriate rate; however, the Society agrees not to demand repayment prior to the due date if the *Borrower* duly and punctually pays the monthly instalments of *interest* on the moneys advanced.

2. A requirement that the *Borrower* pay the premiums on an endowment assurance policy.

3. An entitlement by the Society, while under no obligation to do so, to pay the premiums in the event of default by the *Borrower* and to require payment by the *Borrower* to the Society of such premiums.

4. An assignment by the *Borrower* to the Society of the *endowment* insurance policy and all payments thereunder subject to the re-assignment back to the *Borrower* on repayment of all advances outstanding.

Sources: Standard Mortgage instruments from individual societies.

Appendix 6

BIBLIOGRAPHY

Notes:

\+ In preparation

* Regular updating service

Publications are Irish unless otherwise indicated

Author	Title and Edition
AGENCY	
Bowstead	Bowstead on Agency (1985 UK)
ARBITRATION	
Kilty B J	Arbitration in Ireland (1989 +)
Bernstein R	Handbook of Arbitration Practice (1987 UK)
Russell	The Law of Arbitration (1982 UK)
BANKING (See also Negotiable Instruments)	
Central Bank of Ireland	Exchange Control Manual (1979*)
Paget	Law of Banking (1982 UK)
BILLS OF EXCHANGE (See Negotiable Instruments)	
BUILDING	
Government Publications	Proposed Building Regulations (1983)
Lyden J & MacGrath M	Irish Building and Engineering Case Law (1989)
BUILDING SOCIETIES	
Aspect Magazine	Building Society Privatisation (April 1989)
Business & Finance	The Building Societies Phantom Profits (4th May 1989)

Government Publications	Report of the Registrar of Friendly Societies (1927-76)
	Report of the Registrar of Building Societies (1977-84)
	Report of Enquiry into the Policies of Building Societies in regard to Insurance related to Mortgaged Properties and Valuation Reports on Properties (1985)
	Discussion Document on Legislative and Regulatory Arrangements in relation to Building Societies (1986)
Cleary E J	Building Societies in Ireland (1974)
	National Prices Commission Paper No 14
Kenneally M	Concentration and Regulation in Irish Mortgage Market (1982); Journal of Irish Business and Administration Research, Vol 4, No 1.
Barnes P	Building Societies: The Myth of Mutuality (1984 UK)
Building Societies Commission	Application by the Abbey National Building Society for confirmation of the proposed transfer of its business to Abbey National plc (June 1989 UK)
Building Societies Association	The Future Constitution and Powers of Building Societies (1983 UK)
HMSO	Building Societies: A New Framework (1984 UK) Cmnd 9316
Ovey E & Waters M	Building Societies Act 1986 (1987 UK)
Thornton C E I & McBrien JP	Building Society Law - Cases and Materials - (1970 UK)
Wurtzburg & Mills	Building Society Law (1976 UK)

CHARITIES (See Trusts)

COMPANY LAW

Forde M	Company Law in Ireland (1985)
Keane Judge R	Company Law in the Republic of Ireland (1985)
Ussher P	Company Law in Ireland (1986)
Palmer	Palmer's Company Law (1987 UK)

CONSUMER LAW

Grogan V, King T, Donelan E J	Sale of Goods and Supply of Services (1983)
Linehan D	Irish Consumer Law (1980)

CONVEYANCING

Linehan D M	Irish Land and Conveyancing Law (1989)
Wylie J C W	Irish Conveyancing Law (1983)

DEFAMATION

McDonald M	Irish Law of Defamation (1987)
Duncan & Neill	Defamation (1983 UK)
Gatley	Gatley on Libel and Slander (1981 UK)

ENVIRONMENT

Cabot D & Haigh N	EEC Environment Legislation (An Foras Forbartha) (1987) - A Handbook for Local Authorities
Keane Judge R	The Law of Local Government in the Republic of Ireland (1982)
O'Sullivan P A & Shepherd K	Source Book on Planning Law in Ireland (1987)
Nowlan K I	A Guide to the Planning Acts (1978) A Guide to Planning Legislation in the Republic of Ireland (1988)
Walsh E M & Keane R	Planning Development Law (1984)

EQUITY (See Trusts)

EUROPEAN LAW

McMahon B M E & Murphy F	European Community Law in Ireland (1989)

FAMILY LAW

O'Connor P A	Key Issues in Irish Family Law (1988)
Shatter A J	Family Law in the Republic of Ireland (1986)
Wylie J C W	Irish Land Law (1986). A Casebook on Irish Land Law (1984)

INSURANCE

Ellis H	Insurance Brokers - Their Role and Regulation in the Republic of Ireland (1987)
MacGillivray	Insurance Law (1988 UK)

LAND (See also Conveyancing; Family Law)

Linehan D M	Irish Land and Conveyancing Law (1989)
Wylie J C W	Irish Land Law (1986). A Casebook on Irish Land Law (1984)

LANDLORD & TENANT

de Blacam M	The Control of Private Rented Dwellings (1984)
Deale K E L	The Law of Landlord and Tenant in the Republic of Ireland (1968)
Wylie J C W	Irish Land Law (1986). A Casebook on Irish Land Law (1984)

LAND REGISTRATION

Fitzgerald J B	Land Registry Practice (1989)

Linehan D M	Irish Land and Conveyancing Law (1989)
McAllister D L	Registration of Title (1973)
Wylie J C W	Irish Land Law (1986). A Casebook on Irish Land Law (1984)

LEGISLATION

Humphreys R F	Index to Irish Statutory Instruments (1988)
Sweet & Maxwell	Irish Current Law Statutes Annotated (1984*)

MEETINGS

Shaw Sir S & Smith E D	Law of Meetings (1979 UK)

MORTGAGES

Linehan D M	Irish Land and Conveyancing Law (1989)
Madden D H	Deeds, Conveyances and Judgment Mortgages (1901)
Scanlon J W	Practice and Procedure in Administration and Mortgage Suits in Ireland (1963)
Wylie J C W	Irish Conveyancing Law (1983)
Wylie J C W	Irish Land Law (1986). A Casebook on Irish Land Law (1984)
Fisher & Lightwood	Law of Mortgage (1988 UK)

NEGOTIABLE INSTRUMENTS

Byles	Bills of Exchange (1983 UK)
Richardson D	Negotiable Instruments (1983 UK)

PLANNING (see Environment)

PRACTICE

Bean D	Injunctions (1984 UK)
Brady J C & Kerr T	The Limitation of Actions in the Republic of Ireland (1984)
Keane Judge R	Equity and the Laws of Trusts in the Republic of Ireland (1988) - re injunctions

PROBATE (See Succession)

SALE OF GOODS (See Consumer Law)

SUCCESSION

McGuire W J	The Succession Act 1965; A Commentary (Second Edition by Robert A Pearce) (1983)
Maxwell T H	Miller's Probate Practice (1900)
Mongey E G	Probate Practice in a Nutshell (1980)
Theobald	Theobald on Wills (1982 UK)

SUPPLY OF SERVICES (See Consumer Law)

SURETY	
Rowlatt, Marks & Moss	Law of Principal and Surety (1982 UK)
TAXATION	
Appleby T & Roche J	Capital Gains Tax (1988)
Bale N & Condon J	Capital Acquisitions Tax (1986)
Cremins D	Value Added Tax (1983); Supplement (1986) New Edition (1988)
Government Publications	Law of Value-Added Tax (1987*)
Judge N E	Irish Income Tax (1987*)
McAteer W & Reddin G	Income Tax (1987)
Moore P & Brennan F	Corporation Tax (1987) Supplement (1988)
O'Connor M & Carroll P S	The Law on Stamp Duties (1988)
O'Reilly M F & Carroll B A	Carrolls' Tax Planning in Ireland (1986)
Williams A G	Principles of Corporation Tax in the Republic of Ireland (1981)
TORTS	
McMahon B M E & Binchy W	Irish Law of Torts (1982) Casebook on the Irish Law of Torts (1983)
Salmond & Heuston	The Law of Torts (1987 UK)
TRUSTS	
Delaney V T H	The Law relating to Charities in Ireland (1962)
Keane Judge R	Equity and the Laws of Trusts in the Republic of Ireland (1988)
Kiely T O'Neill	The Principles of Equity as applied in Ireland (1936)
Wylie J C W	A Casebook on Equity and Trusts in Ireland (1985)
Snell	Snell's Principles of Equity (1982 UK)

WINDING UP (See Company Law)

NOTES: